IMAGES
of America

Summer Camps around Asheville and Hendersonville

On the Cover: According to a 1969 brochure, camp taught boys "how to feather an arrow as the Indians did," "pike dive and not end up in a belly flop," sail a boat, whittle a "whim dittle," "walk softly through the pines and watch the timid deer drinking at dusk," and "pack a forty pound load over the trail and love every minute of it," amongst other skills. (Courtesy of Falling Creek Camp.)

IMAGES
of America

Summer Camps around Asheville and Hendersonville

Melanie English

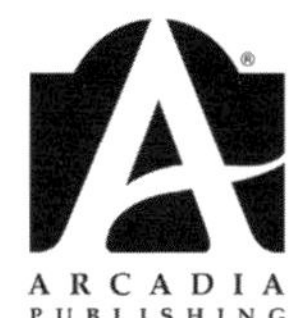

ISBN 978-1-4671-1609-1

Published by Arcadia Publishing
Charleston, South Carolina

Printed in the United States of America

Library of Congress Control Number: 2015952324

For all general information, please contact Arcadia Publishing:
Telephone 843-853-2070
Fax 843-853-0044
E-mail sales@arcadiapublishing.com
For customer service and orders:
Toll-Free 1-888-313-2665

Visit us on the Internet at www.arcadiapublishing.com

To all of the campers past, present, and future of western North Carolina.

Contents

ACKNOWLEDGMENTS

I am grateful to the area summer camps who permitted me to research their extensive archives, including, in alphabetical order, Blue Star Camp, Camp Crestridge, the Daniel Boone Council of Boy Scouts of America, Eagle's Nest Camp, Falling Creek Camp, Girl Scouts Carolinas Peaks to Piedmont, Camp Green Cove, Camp Greystone, Camp Henry, Camp Highlander, Camp Hollymont, Camp Illahee, Camp Kanuga, Keystone Camp, Camp Merri-Mac, Camp Merrie-Woode, Camp Mondamin, Camp Pinnacle, Camp Ridgecrest, Rockbrook Camp, Camp Rockmont, and Camp Ton-a-Wandah. Special thanks to the D.H. Ramsey Library Special Collections at University of North Carolina Asheville, the Henderson County Genealogical and Historical Society, the North Carolina Room at Pack Memorial Public Library, the Swannanoa Valley Museum, and Wilson Library at the University of North Carolina for aiding in my research. Unless otherwise noted, all images are from the collection of the author.

INTRODUCTION

The first summer camps originated in the late 19th century as the United States became more industrialized, urban, and socially and culturally heterogeneous. Organized summer camps, like vacation resorts and national parks, offered respite from the perils of modernity through nature. These man-made natural environments fulfilled the Arcadia myth while retaining modern sensibilities.

Between 1890 and 1920, the notion of childhood as separate from adulthood was firmly established as child labor laws and compulsory education safeguarded the sanctity of youth. Spaces outside the home—distinct from schools and catering exclusively to the needs of children—arose, such as playgrounds, children's libraries, and children's hospitals. As social reformers advocated the social value of play, some Progressive Era educators recommended a 12-month school year and, along with parents, worried that summer vacations were detrimental to the intellectual, moral, and physical development of youth. Further, crowded cities deprived children of the wide-open spaces necessary for play, while substandard sanitation threatened children's health. As the population shifted from rural to urban, youth organizations emerged to counter the problems of modern childhood. Ernest Thompson Seton's Woodcraft Indians, founded in 1902 to mold good citizens in the great outdoors, influenced youth organizations like the Boys Scouts and Camp Fire Girls, both formed in 1910. Young Men's and Young Women's Christian Associations (YMCA and YWCA) also initiated youth development programs.

As an amalgamation of these ideas, residential summer camps arose to nurture the moral character, physical health, social development, and spiritual growth of children. Camps fortified the notion of childhood as a protected and yet playful stage of development requiring adult supervision and age-appropriate opportunities for recreation and socialization. The pace of modern technology left new generations deficient in the skills of their pioneer forbearers. Amidst the rapid changes in contemporary life, camps taught youngsters age-old skills like canoeing and cooking over campfires. As man-made natural environments, camps reconciled the savage freedoms of the wilderness with highly structured programs aimed at inculcating American values. At first these camps were aimed specifically at young boys, but by the early 20th century, camps for girls gently challenged the cultural constraints of girlhood. By the mid-20th century, going to sleepaway camp was a childhood rite of passage, deeply ingrained in the American cultural experience.

The first residential summer camps cropped up in New England, the Adirondacks, and around the Great Lakes. Like these regions, the fresh mountain air of the southern Appalachians of western North Carolina had long attracted tourists and health seekers. Lured by the rugged natural majesty of the Blue Ridge and Great Smoky Mountains and the cool temperatures of the highlands, summer visitors founded resorts and religious assemblies around the towns of Asheville, Hendersonville, Brevard, Black Mountain, and Lake Lure, North Carolina. Organized camps for the children were natural offshoots of these summer colonies, as educators envisaged the natural playground of the "Land of the Sky" and established the first overnight camps in the second decade of the 20th century.

The earliest summer camps in western North Carolina were organized to supplement the school year. Regional tourism booster Sanford H. Cohen promoted the area to educational institutions throughout the South. As early as 1914, the Southern Railway ran special passenger trains to accommodate over 500 boys attending Camp Cherokee in Bryson City, Camp Jackson in Sylva, Camp Sapphire and Camp French Broad in Brevard, and Camp Laurel Park in Hendersonville. The militarism and rugged masculinity of these early boys' camps endeavored to counteract the feminization of the domestic sphere through strenuous hikes, competitive sports, calisthenics, and rough-and-tumble games.

The nascent camping industry in western North Carolina grew exponentially following World War I. Henderson County's accessibility, many lakes, and scenic vistas had long secured its reputation as a summer haven for Deep South visitors. After Laurel Park Summer School and Camp for Boys' founding in 1910, Camp Minnehaha for girls opened in Bat Cave in 1912. Nearby Camp Chimrock opened in 1917, ideally located in Chimney Rock, removed from what some called the "demoralizing influences of the city." Like the Hendersonville area, the "Land of the Waterfalls" around Transylvania County and the Sapphire Valley has long enchanted summer tourists. Some of the earliest boys' camps were located around Brevard. Camp French Broad opened in 1913, followed by Camp Sapphire in 1914. The area also spawned a number of girls' camps. Keystone Camp welcomed its first campers in 1916, and Camp Merrie-Woode, near Sapphire, commenced summer sessions in 1919. Today, Keystone is the oldest privately owned camp still in operation in the Southeast. Youth organizations like the Boy Scouts, Girls Scouts, and the YMCA and its counterpart the YWCA recognized the value of summer camps for shaping young leaders and also founded camps in the area.

The prevalence of girls' camps around western North Carolina signaled changing cultural perceptions about the "weaker sex." College-educated "New Women" deployed traditional maternal skills in the male-dominated profession of education and camping to instruct adolescent girls in both feminine gentility and physicality in the outdoors. Such women founded Camp Minnehaha, Keystone Camp, and Camp Merrie-Woode with pluck and intrepidity. Camps like the now closed Camp Dixie for Girls, once known as "the queen of camps," were pivotal in a schoolgirl's development. One Camp Dixie girl fondly recalled, "No one can ever know how much my stay at camp has meant to me. I realize more and more what a wonderful time I had and I shall remember those weeks as the happiest I have ever spent." Other girls' camps nearly forgotten in cultural memory include Chunns Cove Camp in Asheville, Camp Cherryfield and Connestee Cove Camp in Brevard, Camp Elizabeth in Hendersonville, Rhododendron Camp in Laurel Park, and Lake Eden Camp in Black Mountain. Many boys' camps of yore like Camp Sequoyah in Weaverville, Camp Transylvania in Brevard, and Camp Osceola in Hendersonville also once dotted the landscape. Today, many existing camps continue to endorse the ideas of separate socialization, although some coeducational camps exist. Still, many of these operate concurrent "brother" and "sister" programs.

As the Roaring Twenties unfolded and the regional tourist industry boomed, more camps appeared throughout the region. A number of camps were concentrated in the Green River area of Henderson County and around the Pisgah National Forest in Brevard. Many of these early camps continue to operate today—some by the same families. For the Bell family, who founded Camp Mondamin, Camp Arrowhead, and Camp Green Cove around the newly created Lake Summit between the 1920s and 1940s, camping is a family business. Descendants of Camp Greystone's founder continue to operate the camp today. Campers, too, return to the same camp year after year and later send their own children. A 2011 study conducted by North Carolina State University found that over 40 percent of parents of current campers were either former campers or camp staffers themselves. In the shadows of Pisgah Forest, Camp Illahee and Camp Rockbrook both opened in 1921 and Eagle's Nest Camp was founded in 1922. As word spread of the recreational amenities of the area's mountains and lakes, many religiously affiliated camps sprung up around the numerous conference and retreat centers near Asheville and Hendersonville starting in the late 1920s, such as Camp Kanuga in Hendersonville and Camp Ridgecrest in Ridgecrest.

Following World War I, summer camps of western North Carolina, like many camps around the country, de-emphasized militarism and instead nostalgically evoked the American frontier. Some of the earliest camp directors drew inspiration from the rustic lodges of the "Great Camps" of the Adirondack region of upstate New York. Utilizing native construction materials, camp landscapes featured primitive log cabins, woodcraft shops, and lodges to complement their natural settings. While initially many lodges once housed dining halls and assembly halls, gradually these activities were separated into distinct freestanding buildings as camp program ideas evolved. Despite the homespun and utilitarian aesthetic of camp architecture, camps placed a premium on health and sanitation and were wired with electricity and hot running water. Modern kitchens were carefully separated from more rustic mess hall–style dining halls. Today, a number of area camps are listed in the National Register of Historic Places.

While interwar era camp architecture nostalgically recalled pioneers, other camp names and rituals overtly referenced Native American culture. Both Camp Mondamin and Camp Minnehaha were inspired by Henry Wadsworth Longfellow's 1855 epic poem "The Song of Hiawatha." Many other camps employed Native American names, such as Chickasaw, Illahee, Junaluska, Mishemokwa, Osceola, Powhatan, Sequoyah, and Ton-a-wandah. Although western North Carolina is home to the Eastern Band of the Cherokee, the notion of the vanishing Indian and the cultural currency of Wild West shows led to the commodification of Plains Indians' feathered headdresses and teepees at local camps. A number of camps employed Native American rituals, such as Camp Rockmont and Camp Falling Creek. Camp Ton-a-wandah and Camp Merri-Mac organized campers into tribes. Today, many former campers still consider themselves Cherokees, Mohawks, and Navaho. Council rings are another important enduring camp ritual. Seton's *The Book of Woodcraft* linked the sacred council ring campfire with premodern authenticity and fellowship. Such rituals liberated children from routines, away from families and schools. Native American iconography reinforced the camp's separation from the outside world, as temporal child-centered spaces. Western North Carolina camps, like the camps of the North and Great Lakes, helped codify the cultural landscape and rituals of American childhood.

The Great Depression only slowed the camp movement temporarily, and the decades following World War II saw a revitalized growth and emergence of new camps as organized camping took hold of the nation's cultural imagination. After 1945, the American Camping Association officially promoted interracial, interfaith, interethnic, and interclass tolerance, and although the color line persisted, area camps became more inclusive. By the millennium, the region's summer camps were a multi-million-dollar industry, augmenting vital tourist revenue. For over a century, thousands of youngsters have camped in the recreational areas of western North Carolina, securing the region's international reputation as a summer camp destination. While the packing list of what to bring to camp has changed over the years, and campers are no longer instructed to pack white middy blouses and wool swimsuits, many of the traditions established in local summer camps endure. Campers today participate in the same council rings and sing the familiar camp songs recalled nostalgically by generations of those who came before them.

One

The Land of Waterfalls

Summer Camps around Brevard

Tucked in the Blue Ridge Mountains and adjacent to Pisgah National Forest, Gorges State Park, and DuPont State Forest, Transylvania County, with over 250 cascading waterfalls, has historically attracted outdoor enthusiasts and tourists. Known as "Land of the Waterfalls," Transylvania County was an ideal setting for organized summer camps, and by the 1920s, boasted 14 camps. Many of the first camps in western North Carolina were organized around the county seat of Brevard. Camp French Broad for Boys commenced operation in 1913, Camp Sapphire for Boys opened in 1914, and Camp Transylvania began operating in 1920. Camp Transylvania is now the site of the acclaimed Brevard Music Center. Still operating today, Camp Carolina welcomed its first boys in 1924.

As gender norms eased during the era of women's suffrage, many of the region's first camps for girls were founded around Brevard and continue operations. Keystone Camp was established in 1916, and Camp Merrie-Woode, in nearby Sapphire, opened in 1919, followed by Rockbrook Camp and Camp Illahee in 1921. Other girls' camps were short-lived, such as Camp Ivy Hill, open from 1921 to 1923, and Camp Toxaway for Girls, established in 1922 and forced to close during the Great Depression. Camp Cherryfield for girls opened in 1926 but also failed during the Depression; in 1963, the camp reopened as Camp Kahdalea. Other camps have endured changes in ownership and name. Connestee Cove Camp for Girls operated from 1923 to 1942 and since 1943 has been the coed Camp Gwynn Valley.

Much of the camp architecture around Brevard reflects the influence of the rustic Adirondack style, evocative of the "Great Camps" of upstate New York, characterized by the use of natural materials such as split logs, bark shingles, twigs, and stone, which integrate harmoniously with the environment. Camp Merrie-Woode, listed in the National Register of Historic Places, is the most intact representation of the historic style in western North Carolina. Pragmatic and aesthetic, the camp architecture of the region takes into account each property's natural features while designing a built environment for child-centered recreation. The Brevard area's outdoor heritage and historic camp architecture have helped establish western North Carolina's preeminence as the center of organized camping in the South.

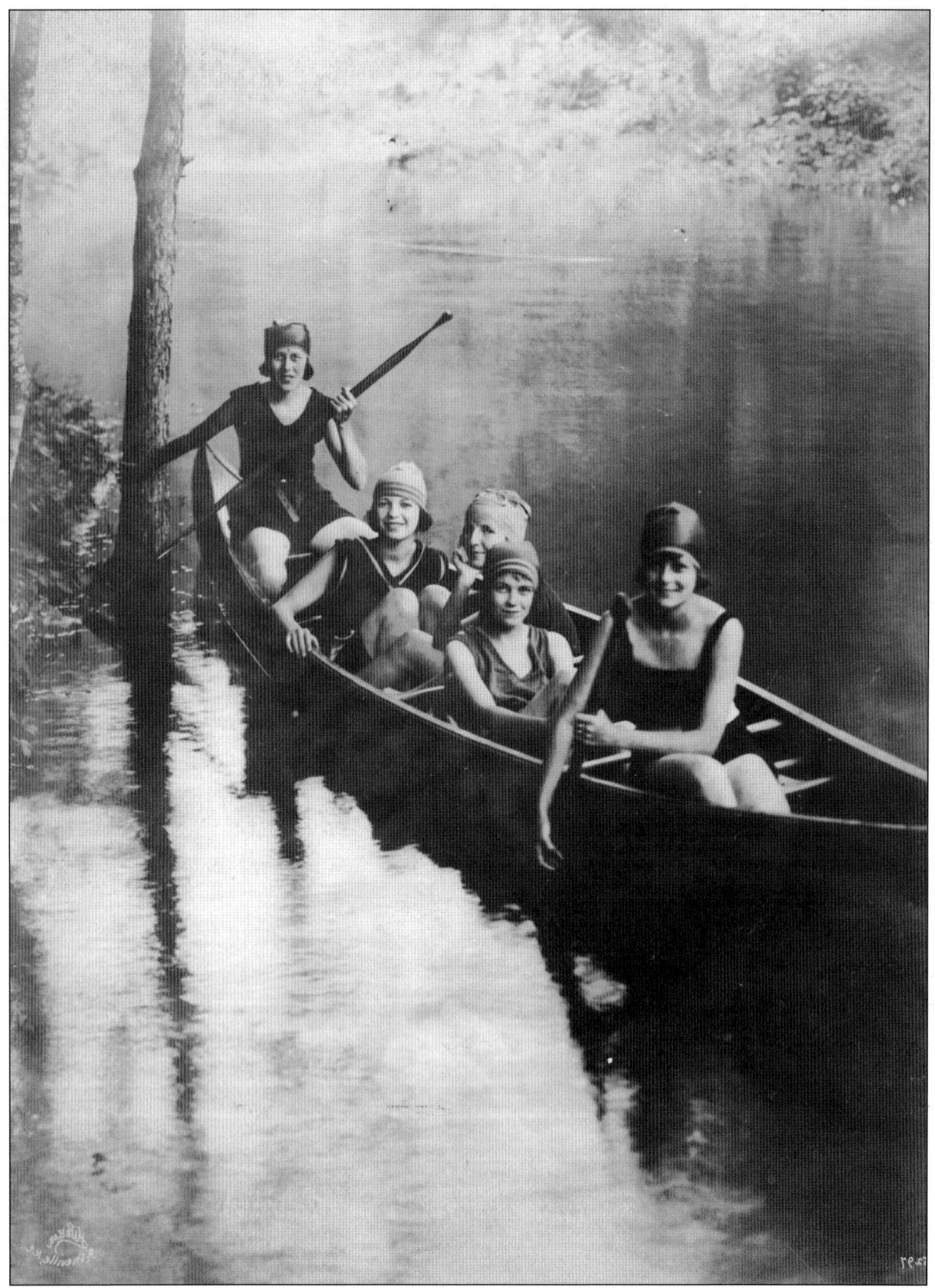

Founded in 1916 by Fannie Webb Holt and Florence Ellis, two self-described "young girls with no experience and no capital but with lots of ideals and lots of determination," Keystone Camp is the oldest privately owned girls camp in the Southeast still in existence. (Courtesy of Keystone Camp.)

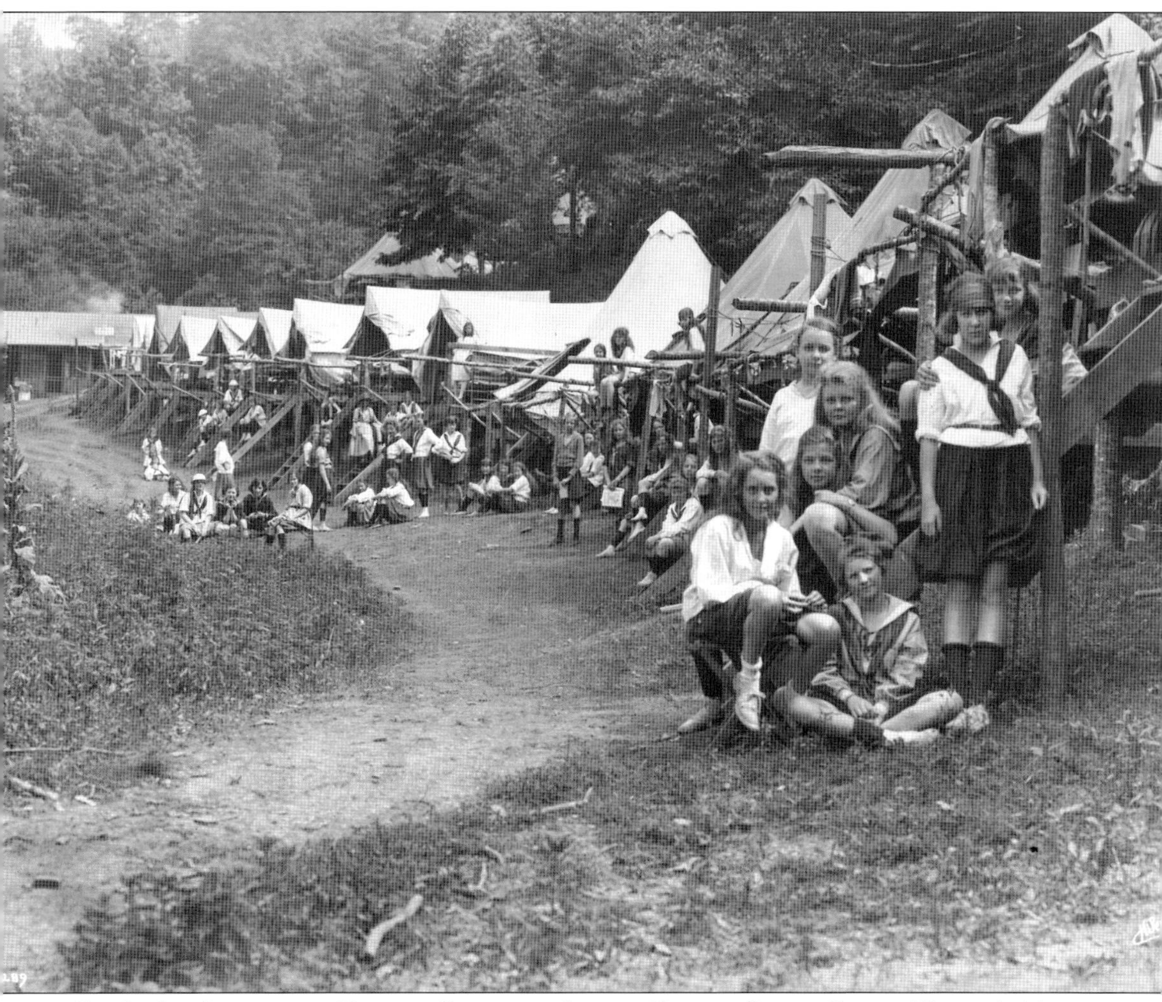

For the first few summers, Keystone Camp rented sites in Fairview, Bryson City, and Brevard. After a 1919 typhoid fever outbreak, the camp moved to its present location outside the Brevard city limits. Campers and counselors shared cotton tents until construction commenced on cabins in the early 1920s. While tents were the norm at early camps, cabins lessened the spread of illness. (Courtesy of Keystone Camp.)

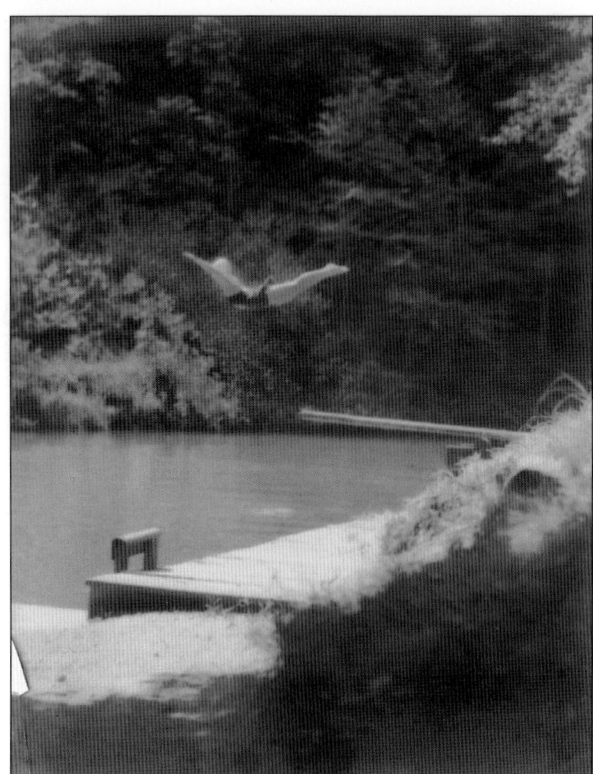

Operated by a single family, Keystone passes on camp traditions across generations. After Keystone cofounder Florence Ellis's death in 1926, Fannie Holt continued to operate the camp until 1942, when Ellis's niece Catherine Ellis Ives took over as director until 1961. Her son William Maner Ives directed the camp from 1961 to 1984, after which his daughter Page Ives Lemel assumed the directorship. (Courtesy of Keystone Camp.)

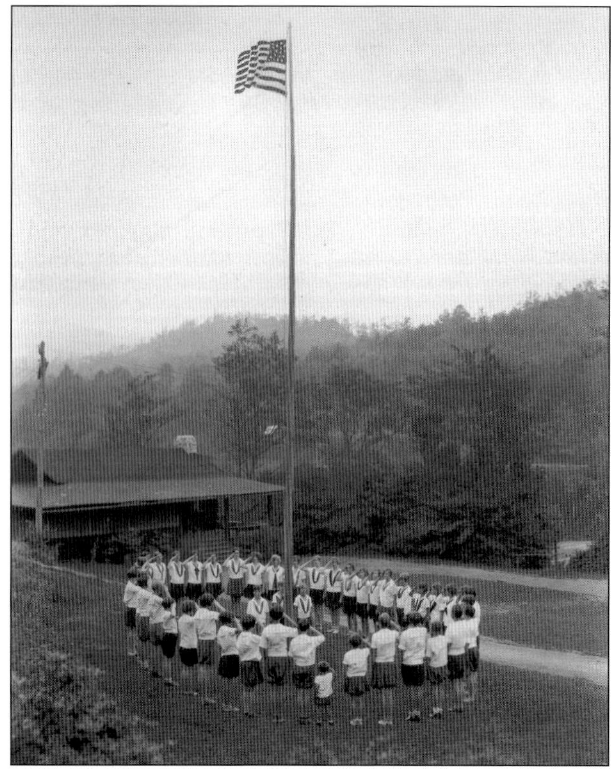

Fairview was the first permanent cabin built in 1923, named both for the camp's first location and the pleasant view from its porch. The second cabin, Peachtree, got its name after a girl's family brought her a basket of peaches when visiting, since candy was not permitted. The camper refused to share, the peaches rotted, and she threw them outside. Eventually, a peach tree sprouted beside the cabin. (Courtesy of Keystone Camp.)

Nestled in the Blue Ridge Mountains, Keystone Camp provides a nurturing environment for girls to develop lifelong skills through programs in horsemanship, tennis, land and water sports, gymnastics, arts and crafts, and rock climbing and hiking in nearby Pisgah National Forest. (Courtesy of Keystone Camp.)

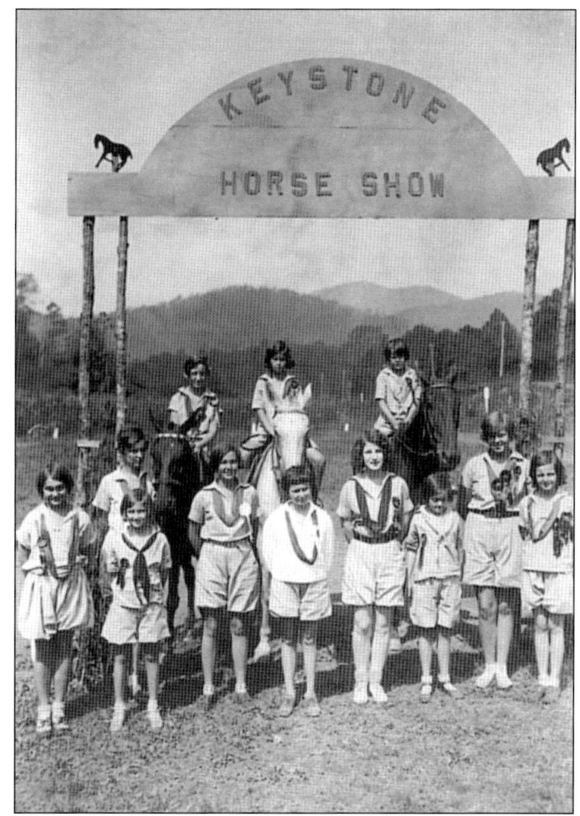

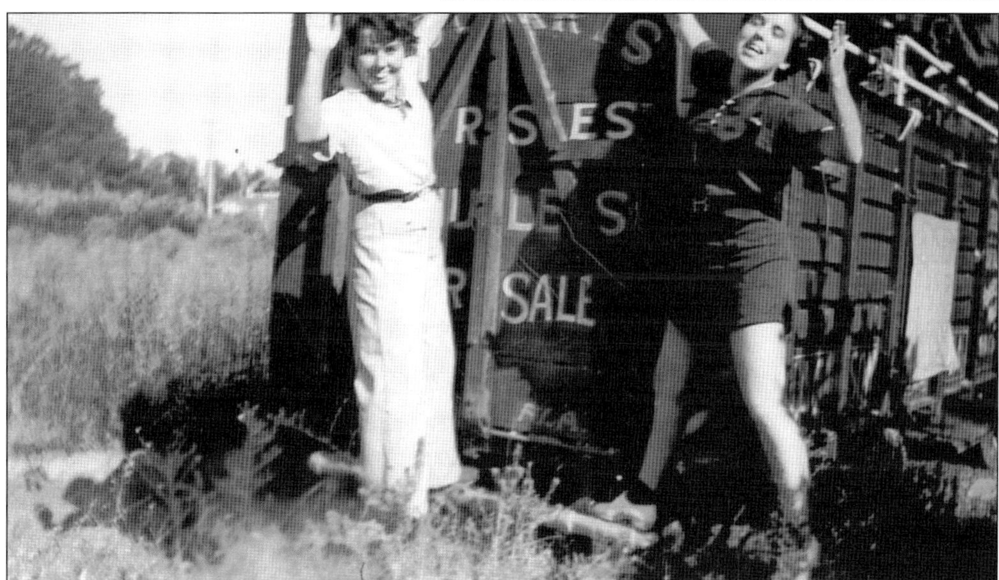

Passenger trains carried campers to western North Carolina in the early 20th century. During Keystone Camp's first year, the flood of 1916 washed the bridge out, delaying the train for several days. The campers finally took a wagon to their destination. As the number of area summer camps increased, special train lines were set up to run to the camps, until World War II. (Courtesy of Keystone Camp.)

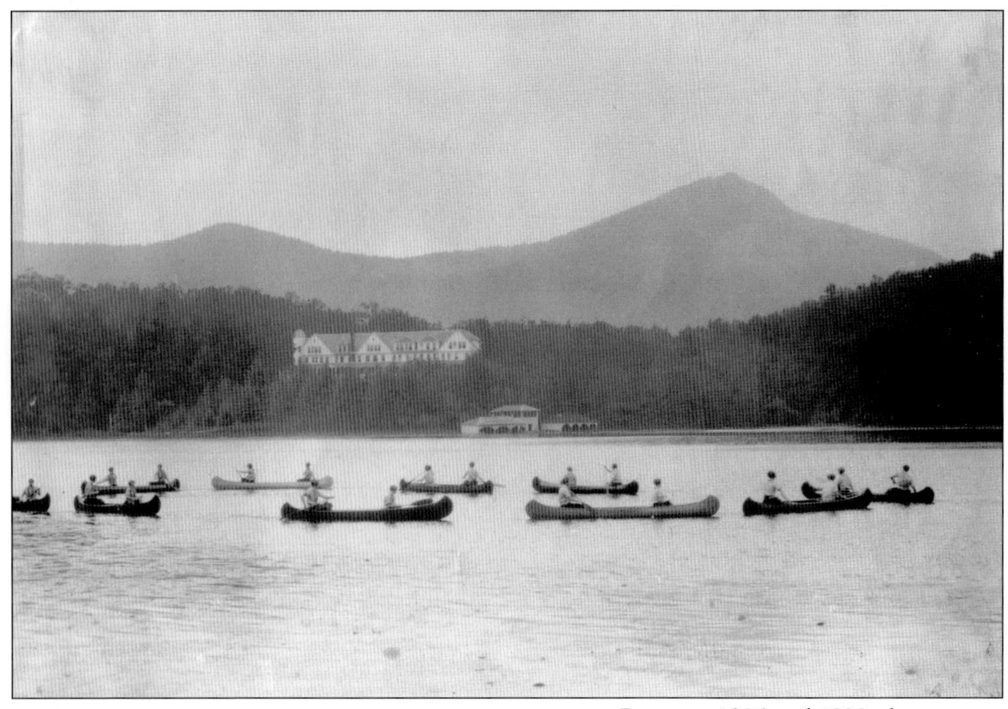

Between 1896 and 1898, the Toxaway Company built Lake Fairfield and the Fairfield Inn in the Sapphire Valley. Oil magnate Edward Jennings purchased the property in 1911, and in 1919, he gave Marjorie Harrison 40 acres on the north shoreline of the lake to open Camp Fairfield Lake for the daughters of the inn's guests. Fire destroyed the inn, pictured above, in 1986. (Courtesy of Camp Merrie-Woode.)

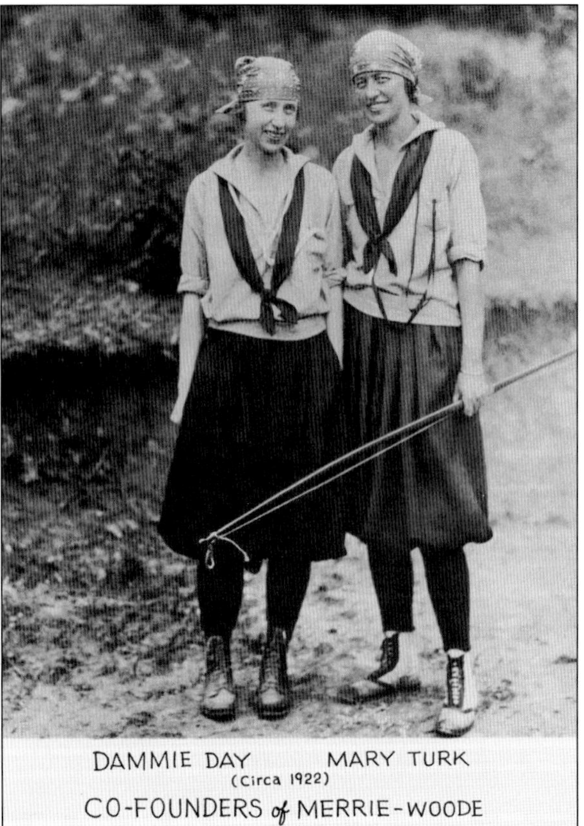
DAMMIE DAY (Circa 1922) MARY TURK
CO-FOUNDERS of MERRIE-WOODE

Marjorie Harrison met Mary Turk while teaching high school in Tazewell, Virginia, and invited her to help run Camp Fairfield Lake. In 1920, Turk became an instructor for New York City's YWCA. The organization's secretary Dammie Day accompanied Turk to Lake Fairfield that summer and purchased the camp the next year. Turk served as head counselor until 1929. Day remained the director until 1952. (Courtesy of Camp Merrie-Woode.)

In 1919, as European leaders signed the Treaty of Versailles ending World War I, Merrie-Woode welcomed a small group of girls for its first summer. With cooler temperatures and unspoiled wilderness, the mountains of western North Carolina were a popular vacation destination. A thriving tourist industry catered to urbanites from across the Southeast. Camp taught girls the simple lessons of the natural world. (Courtesy of Camp Merrie-Woode.)

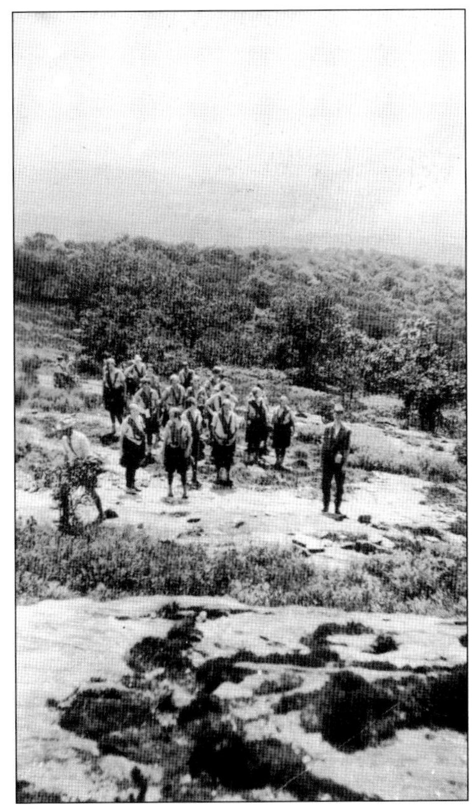

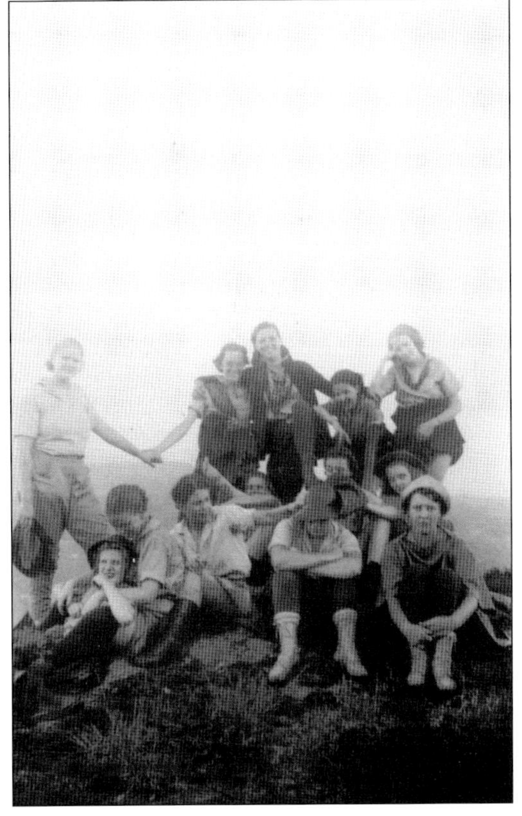

Women earned the right to vote in 1920. Merrie-Woode's founders embodied the Jazz Age's "New Woman." Merrie-Woode is a democratic community where everyone is valued equally—from the cook to the youngest camper to a favorite horse. At camp, human relationships thrive under the aegis of mutual understanding and appreciation. The girls clad in bloomers in this 1924 photograph bond at the top of Thorn Mountain. (Courtesy of Camp Merrie-Woode.)

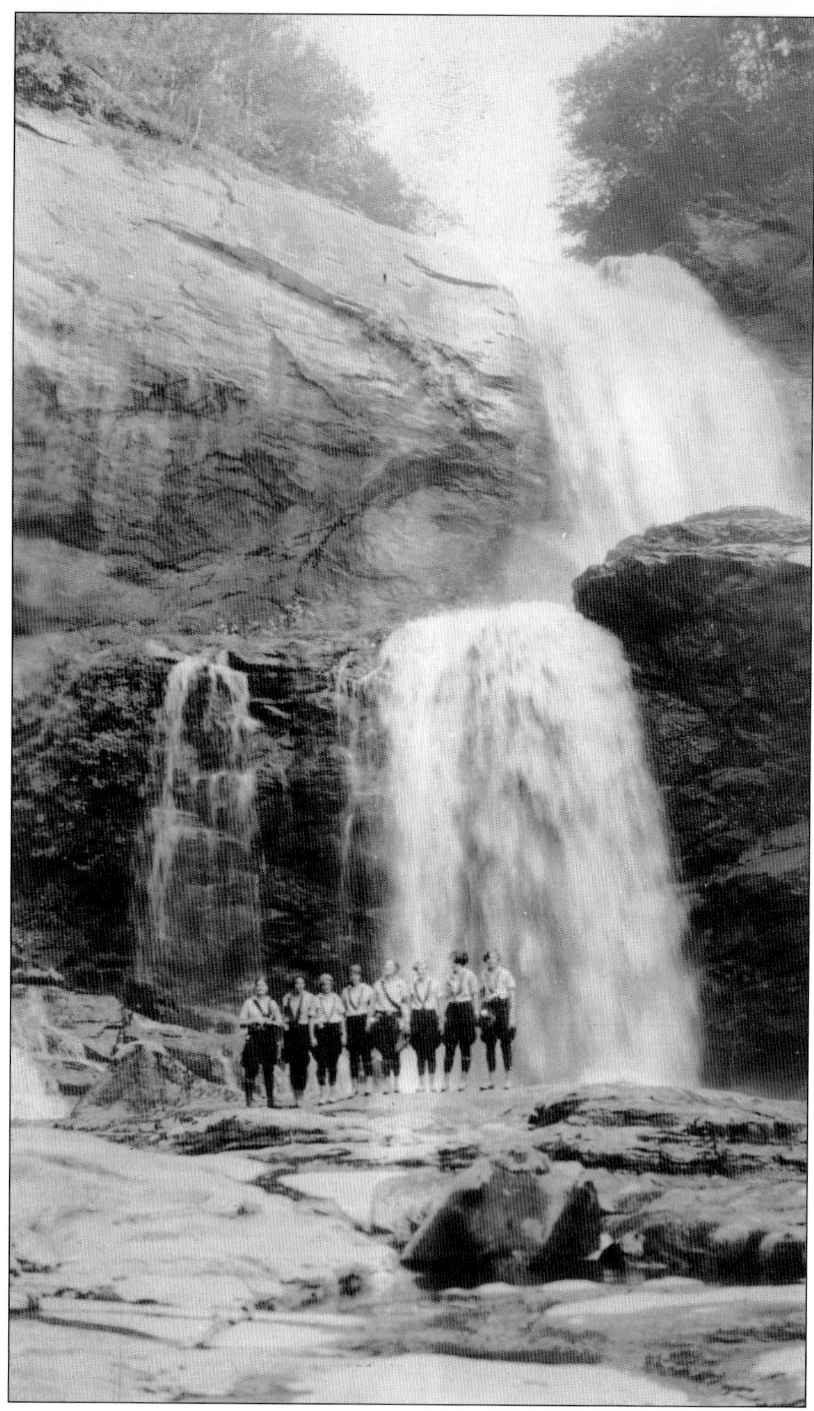

Western North Carolina features hundreds of waterfalls. This 1927 photograph shows a group of campers at the base of Fairfield Falls clad in the traditional camp uniform of middie blouses, green ties, and dark green shorts. During the interwar period, Merrie-Woode, like other girls' residential camps, exposed young women to nature to counter the effects of changing cultural norms and industrialization. (Courtesy of Camp Merrie-Woode.)

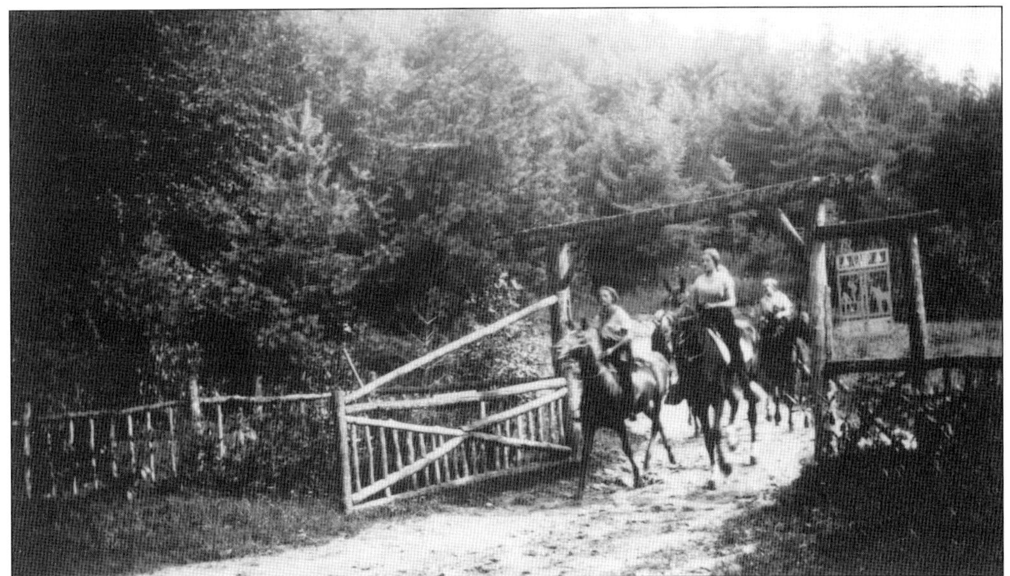

Horseback riding, shown in this 1934 photograph, is one of the many activities offered at Merrie-Woode. Many girls have passed through this gate over the years. The camp, which still bears the same logo designed by Princeton student Melville C. Branch in the 1930s, "is a composite thing made up of all those who through the years have loved it and given it their best," in the words of founder Dammie Day in 1919. (Courtesy of Camp Merrie-Woode.)

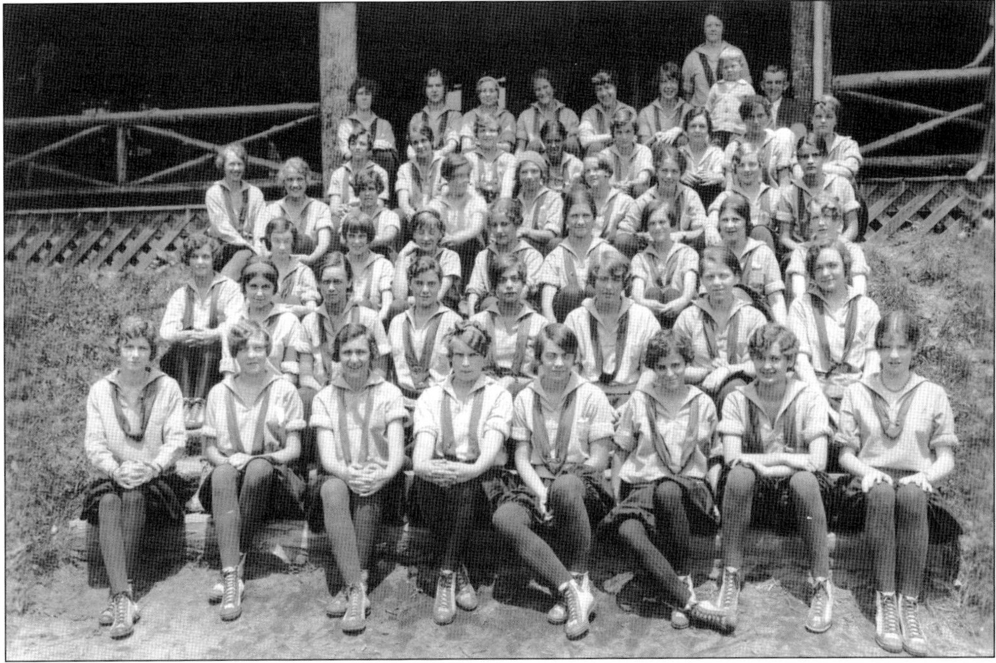

Inspired by her British ancestry rather than Indian iconography like other camps, Dammie Day changed the camp's name to Merrie-Woode in 1921 and incorporated Arthurian legends into camp traditions and architecture. This photograph shows campers in front of the Castle, built in 1935. The Adirondack-style lodge hosted plays, classical music recitals, and poetry readings, as well as more informal camp assemblies and morning devotionals. (Courtesy of Camp Merrie-Woode.)

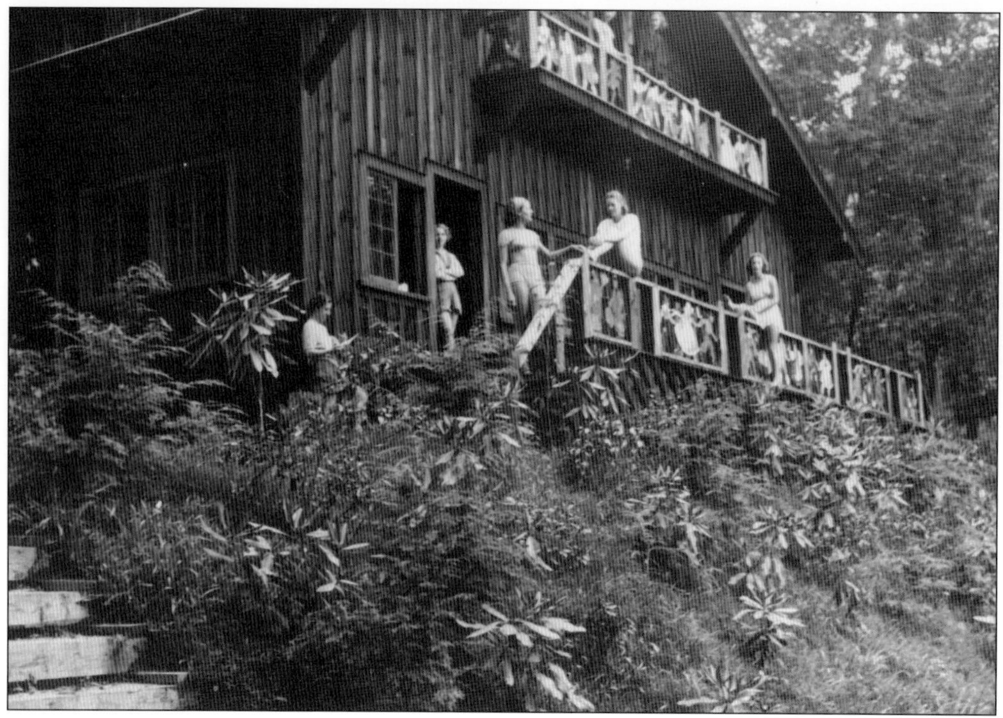

Named for the mischievous creature akin to a tiger, jaguar, or badger that grew out of camp lore in the early 20th century, the Swiss chalet–style Tajar building, constructed around 1940, features whimsical painted figures along the porch's balustrade. This photograph also shows the native rhododendron prevalent on the property. The building hosts sewing and knitting classes and houses the camp library. Tajar tales are commonly told around campfires. (Courtesy of Camp Merrie-Woode.)

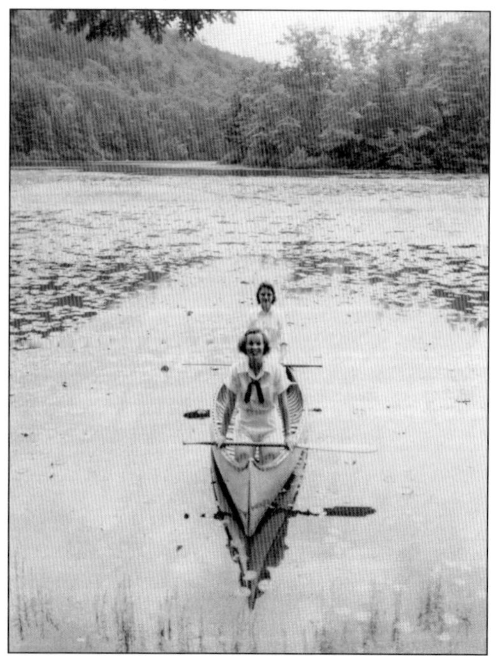

Activities at Merrie-Woode have historically included sports such as archery, tennis, canoeing, sailing, swimming, riding, badminton, and riflery, and woodcraft skills like camping, fire-building, and cooking. The camp also encourages arts and crafts and performing arts with offerings in weaving, carving, lapidary, photography, music, and dramatics. (Courtesy of Camp Merrie-Woode.)

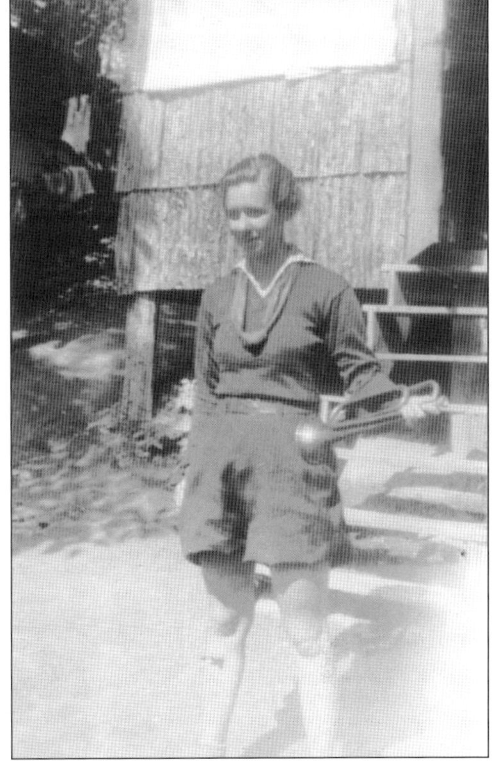

Anne Otter Downs created Merrie-Woode's Captain's Program in 1938 to develop campers' waterfront skills. Hailing from Kentucky, Downs attended a Vermont camp where she attained the highest rank in the canoeing program. In 1936, at age 19, she became a counselor at Merrie-Woode. She took over the boating program in 1938 and instituted ranks based on skills. (Courtesy of Camp Merrie-Woode.)

Campers strove toward achieving the highest rank, "Captain." The first summer, six campers rose to the rank of captain and received a coveted white hat during a campfire ceremony. Downs left the camp in 1942, but the Captain's Program endures. (Courtesy of Camp Merrie-Woode.)

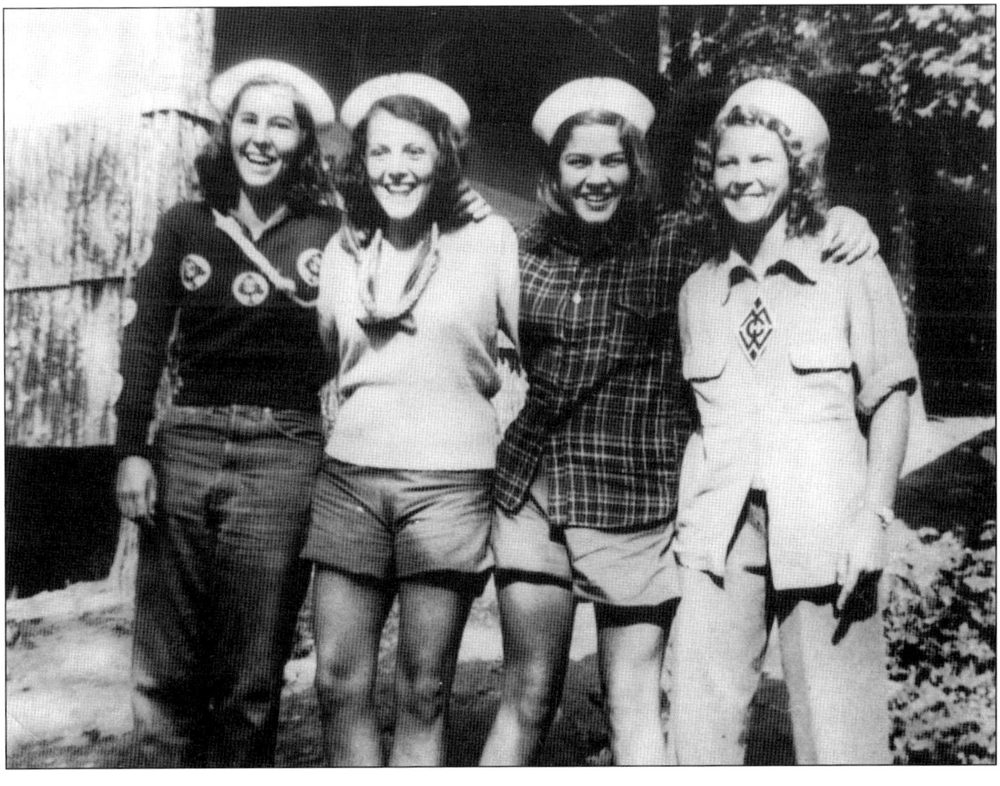

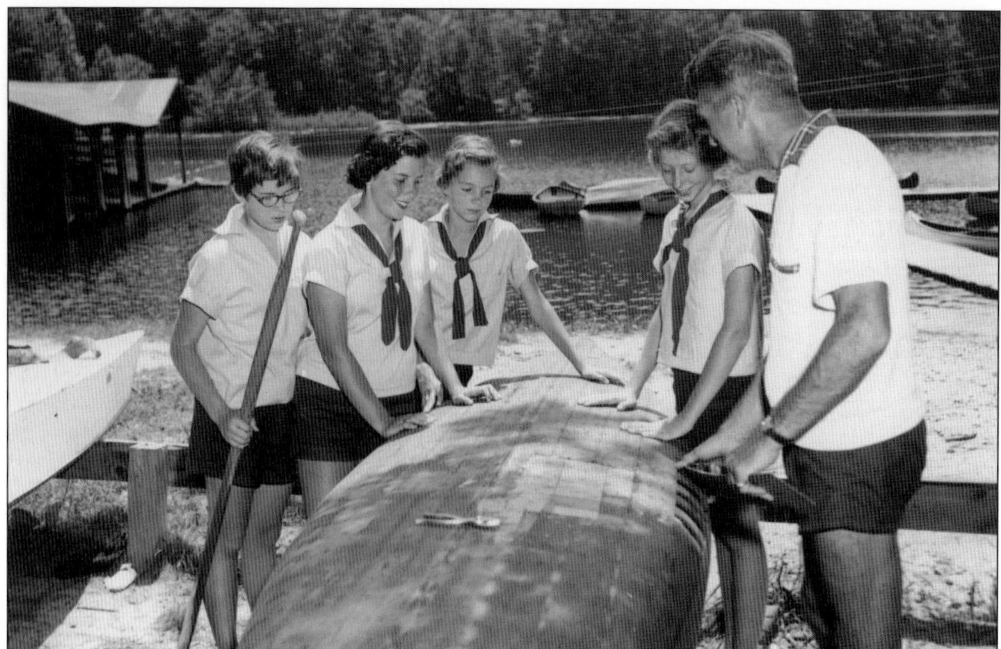
With rapids ranging from Class I to Class III in difficulty, western North Carolina's rivers are perfect for whitewater boating and instruction at a wide variety of skill levels. Campers take river trips on the Nantahala, French Broad, Green, and Chattooga Rivers. (Courtesy of Camp Merrie-Woode.)

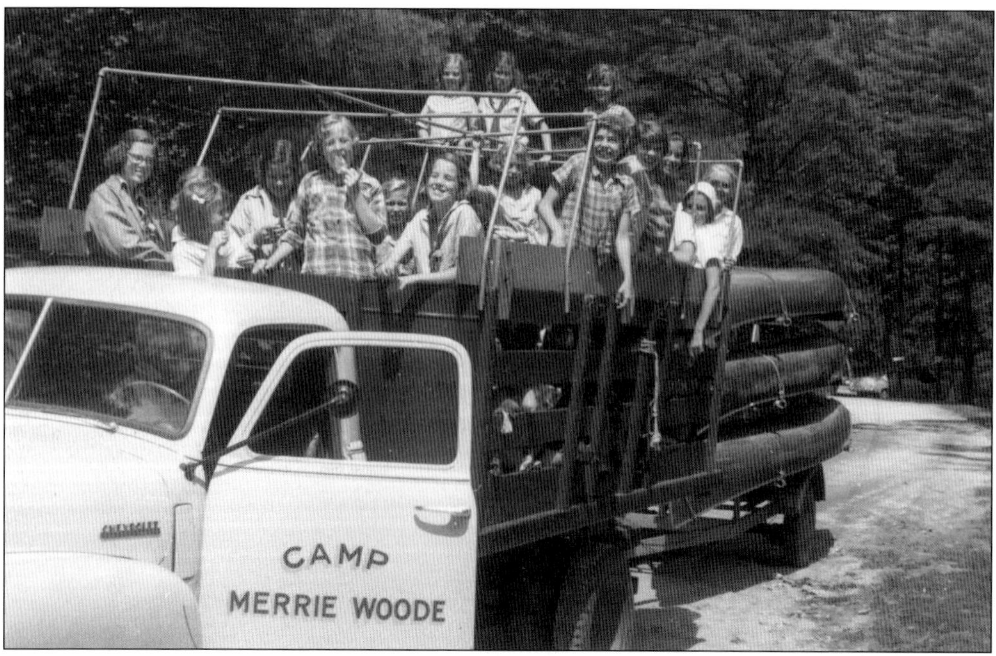

After Dammie Day retired, Fritz and Augusta Orr purchased the camp in 1952. Following his father's passing in 1968, Fritz Orr Jr. and his wife, Dottie, operated the camp until 1978. The Orrs were instrumental in developing the camp's canoeing and wilderness program. (Courtesy of Camp Merrie-Woode.)

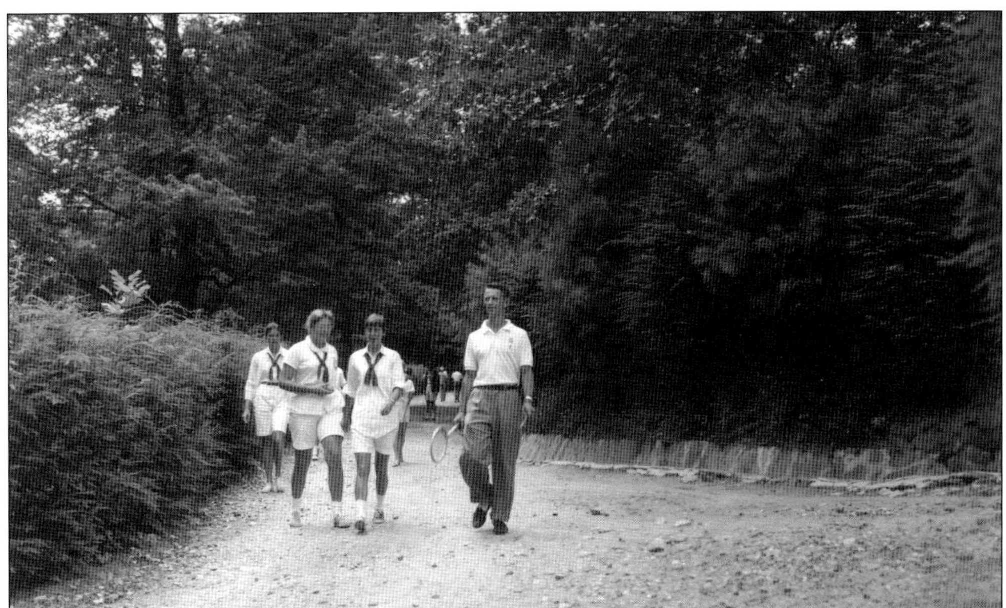

Hugh Caldwell was a professor of philosophy at The University of the South, also known as Sewanee, and a member of the Merrie-Woode staff beginning in 1952, serving as head of the whitewater paddling program. When the camp was listed for sale in 1978, Caldwell led alumnae to form the nonprofit Merrie-Woode Foundation in 1979 to purchase the camp, and he served as the director until 1985. (Courtesy of Camp Merrie-Woode.)

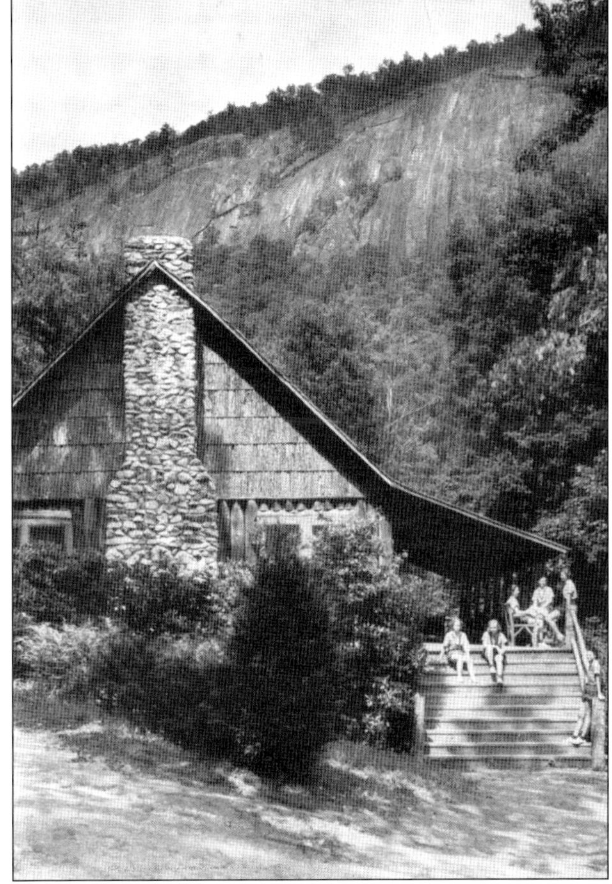

Balds are sparsely forested summits distinctive to the southern Appalachians. The granite-faced Bald Rock Mountain, nicknamed "Old Bald," shown here is a prominent feature of Merrie-Woode, rising over the rustic Adirondack-style dining hall, built in 1920. (Courtesy of Camp Merrie-Woode.)

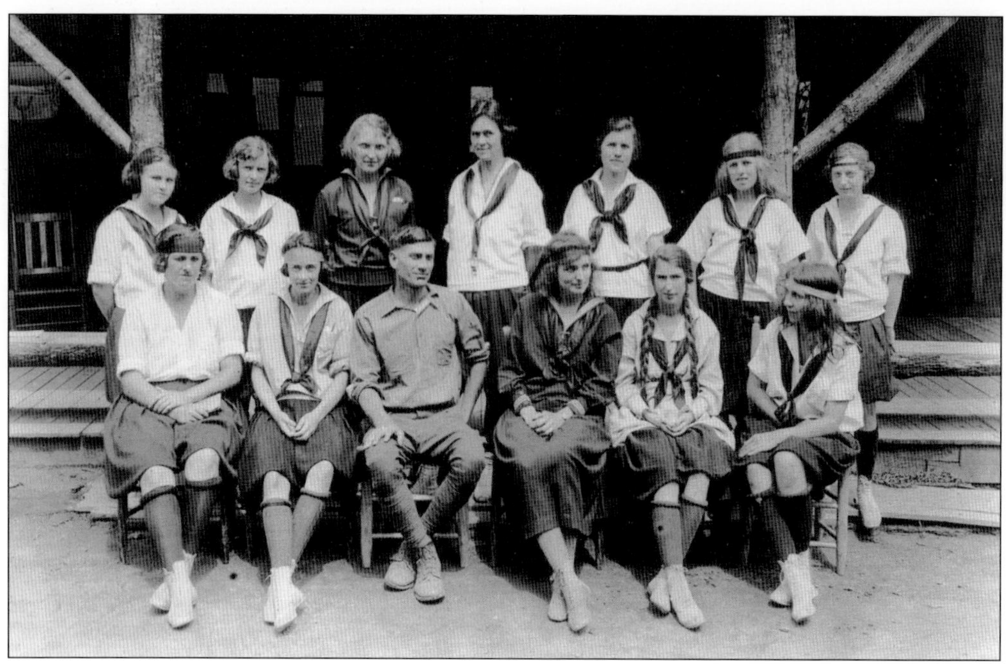

Mississippi educator Hinton McLeod and his wife, Frances, a North Carolina native, pictured here, established Camp Illahee in 1921 and served as the directors until 1936. An outdoor enthusiast, McLeod had been a counselor at the nearby Camp Sapphire for boys and sought to create a similar camp for girls. (Courtesy of Camp Illahee.)

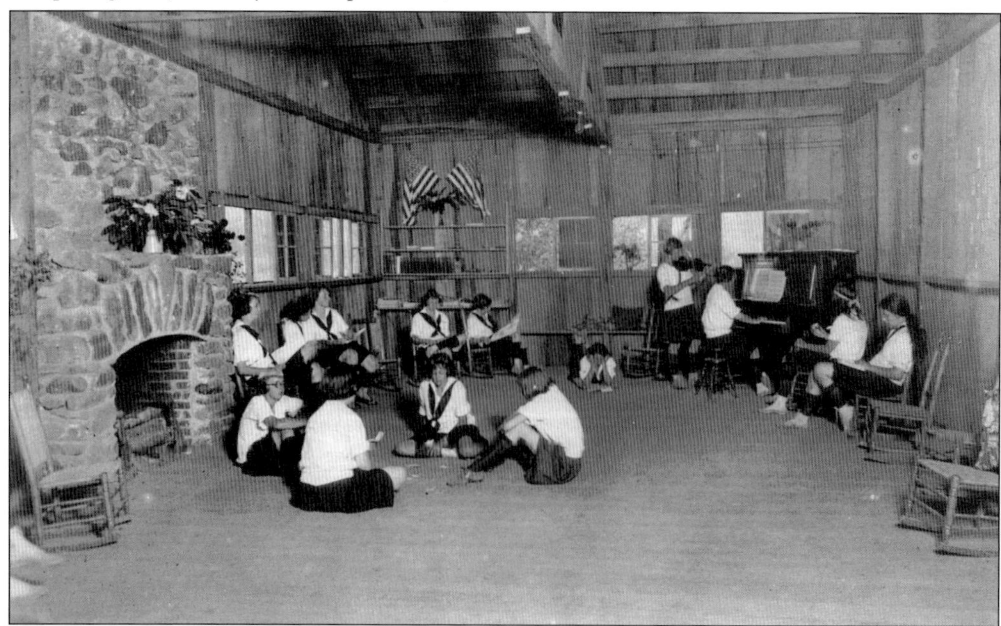

The McLeods leased 30 acres near Brevard, North Carolina, from J.H. Tinsley in 1920. Under the terms of the lease, the McLeods served as directors and Tinsley readied the property for the first summer. He erected one main building to serve as the lodge and dining hall from local materials hauled in by draft horses. The structure featured a rock fireplace, fieldstone porch, and a working kitchen. (Courtesy of Camp Illahee.)

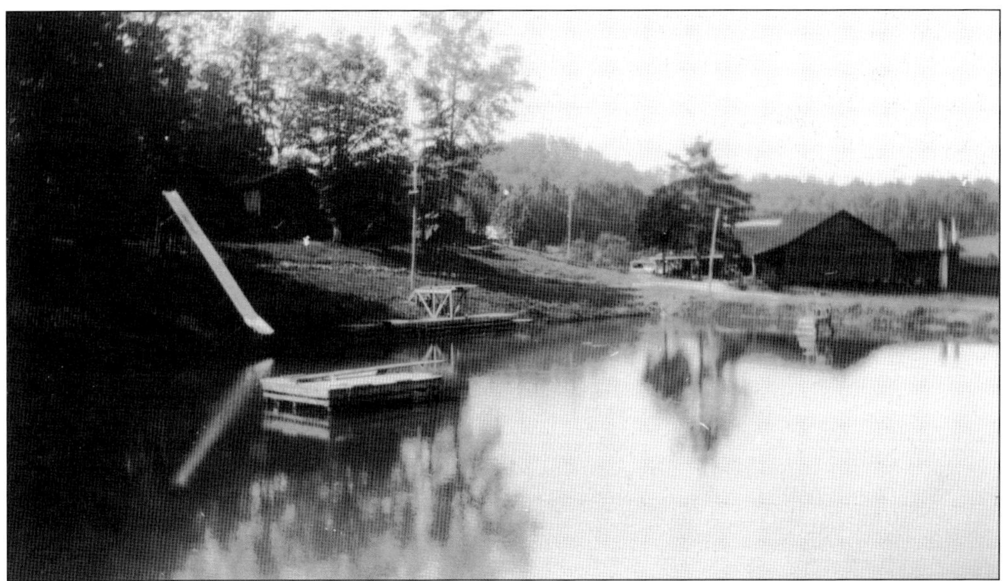

In the contract, Tinsley also agreed to build a dam for a swimming lake. The lake was 12 feet deep at its center and was fed by two mountain springs to maintain its water levels. Meanwhile, the McLeods scrambled to install electricity, grade athletic fields, construct four clay tennis courts, plant a garden, and erect a horse barn in preparation for the first campers. (Courtesy of Camp Illahee.)

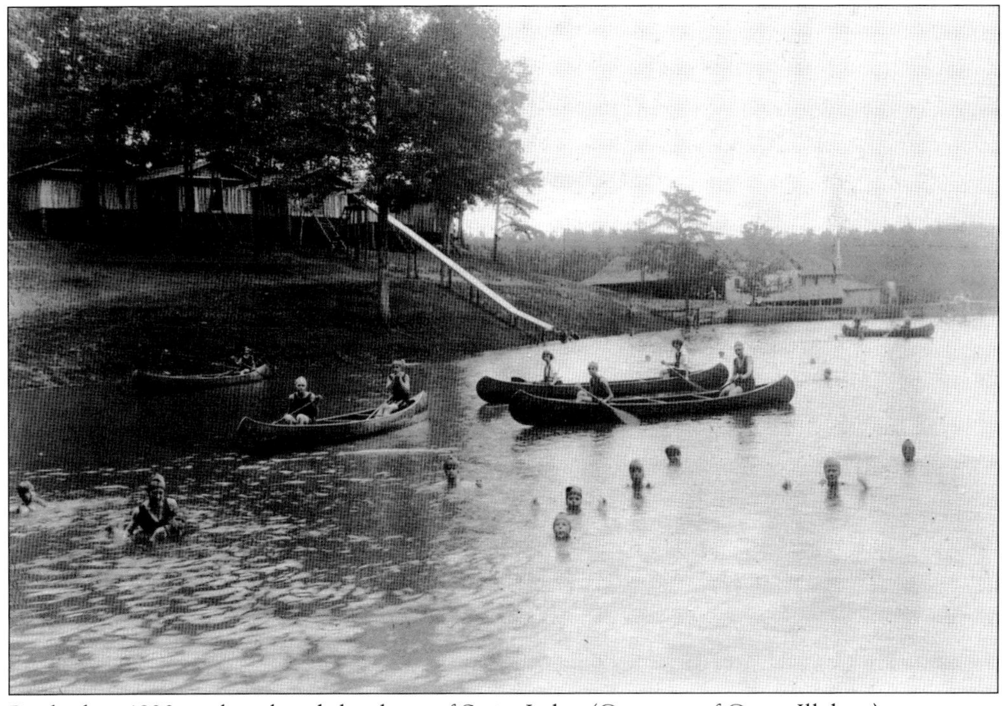

By the late 1920s, cabins lined the shore of Swim Lake. (Courtesy of Camp Illahee.)

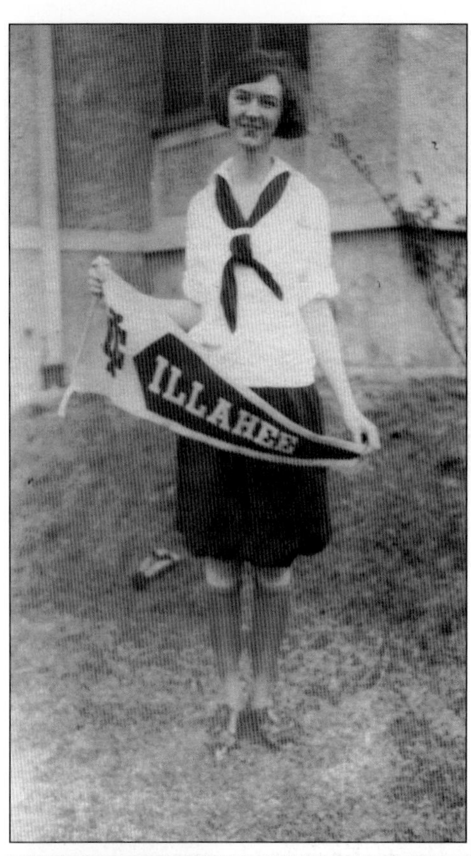

Camp Illahee's name is a Cherokee word meaning "heavenly world." It is not known whether Tinsley or the McLeods selected the name. (Courtesy of Camp Illahee.)

On June 27, 1921, the camp truck, later affectionately named "Henry" by the campers, drove the first 11 girls from the train station in Hendersonville to Illahee with their steamer trunks packed for the eight-week session. The McLeods and four counselors met them at the camp. (Courtesy of Camp Illahee.)

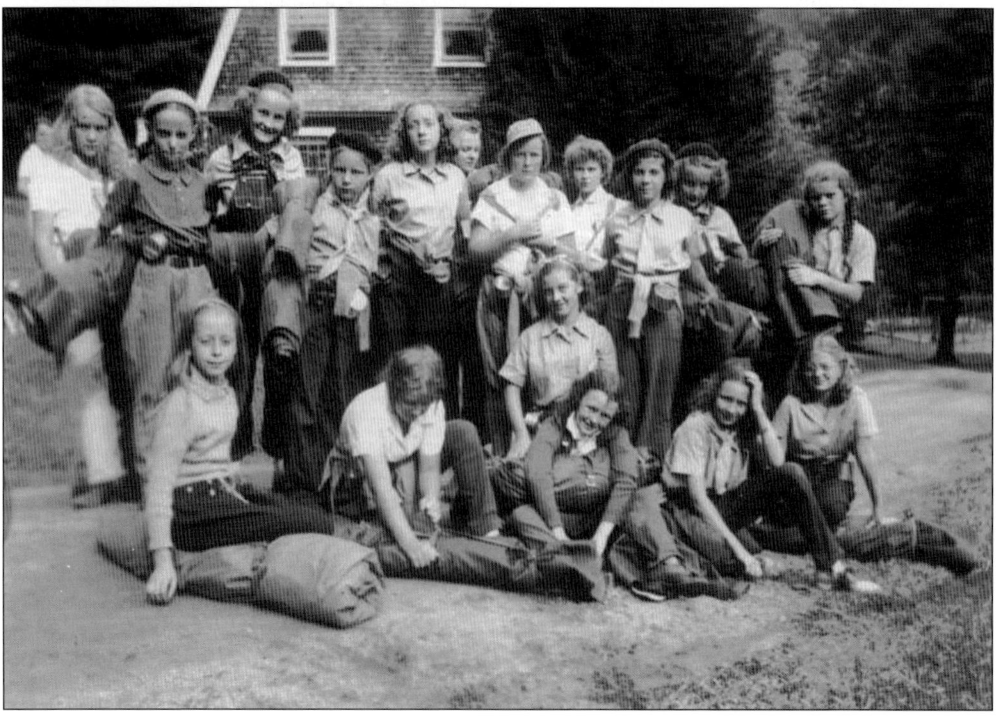

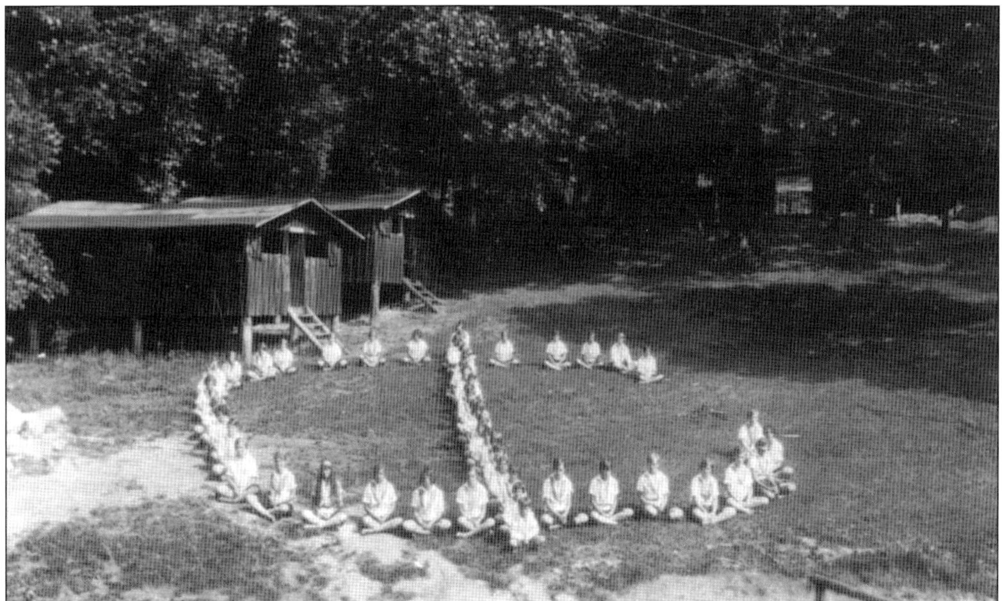

McLeod endeavored "to furnish a place suitable for invigorating and delightful recreation" where "under the leadership of expert athletic directors, and in the companionship of a splendid force of Christian women, a girl may safely enjoy all the pleasures of ideal camp life, and receive the physical benefit and the unconscious moral and spiritual uplift which inevitably result from a close communion with nature." (Courtesy of Camp Illahee.)

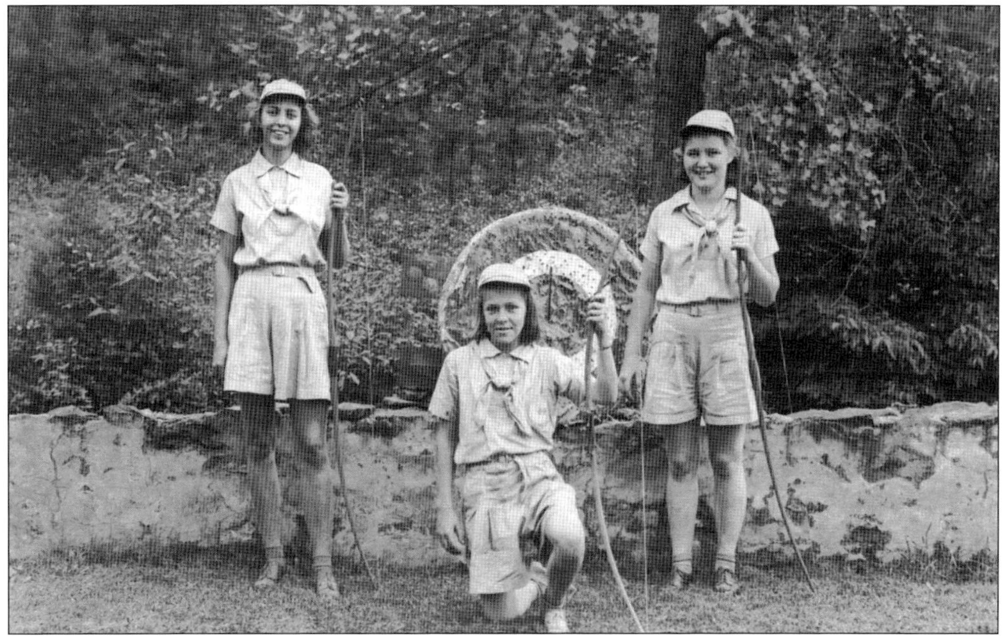

McLeod believed that campers should experience fully the "invigorating properties of the natural world." Each morning, campers were awakened by a shrill whistle and expected to be lakeside at a quarter till seven for an invigorating dip in the ice-cold lake. Though a camper might shiver the first morning, by the next she dove right in, proving that she had the qualities of an Illahee girl. (Courtesy of Camp Illahee.)

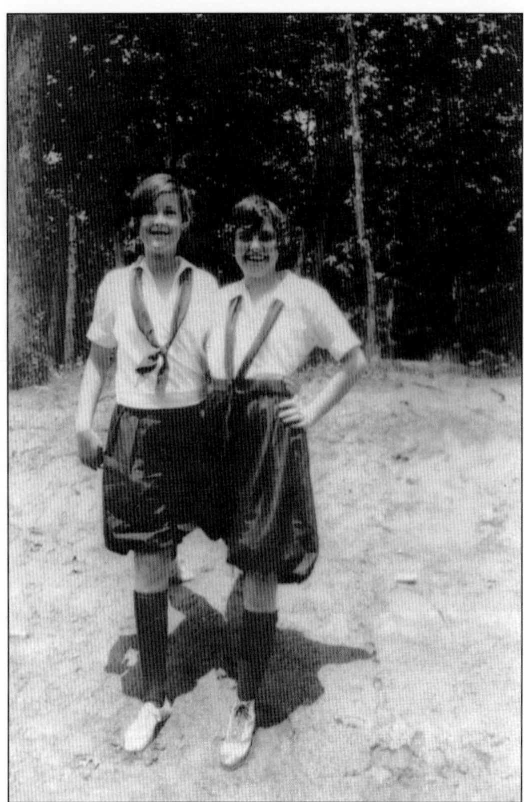

Sleepaway camps imparted a taste of freedom, lasting friendships, and fond memories. Camp Illahee was particularly beloved. One early camper wrote in the camp log, "No one can tell how our hearts ached to leave that dear place, but we made a vow then and there to be back next year if at all possible." (Courtesy of Camp Illahee.)

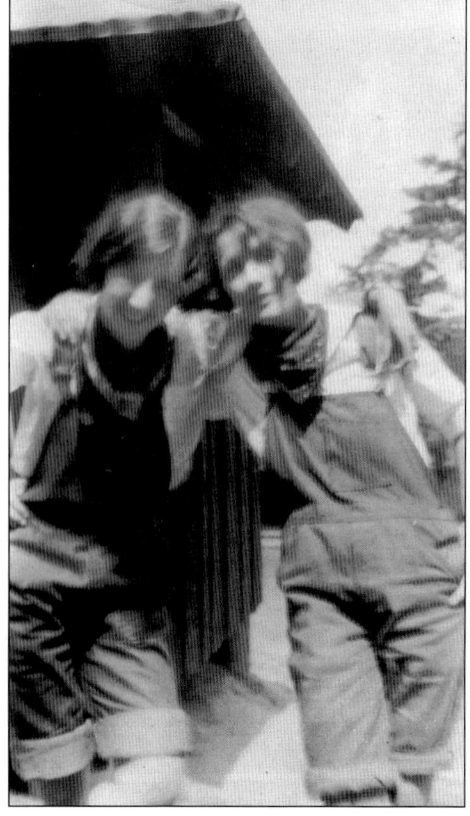

Away from the pressures of school, Illahee campers have fun while learning lifelong skills and making new friends, along with developing the values of courage, loyalty, unselfishness, honesty, and good sportsmanship. (Courtesy of Camp Illahee.)

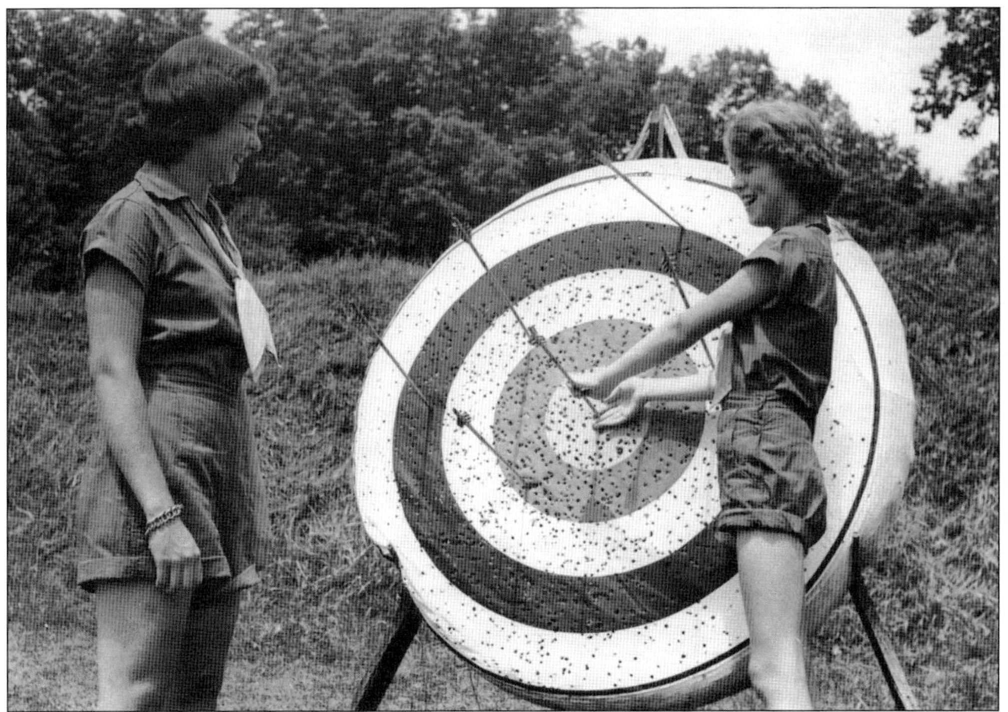

Daily activities in Camp Illahee's first years included dance lessons, basketry, weaving, archery, signing, tennis, canoeing, and swimming. Horseback riding was also a favorite pastime. In fact, horses were so beloved that when *National Velvet* opened in 1945, a total of 157 uniformed campers marched into Brevard to watch it at Co-Ed Theater. Girls also enjoyed hiking in the "Land of the Waterfalls." (Courtesy of Camp Illahee.)

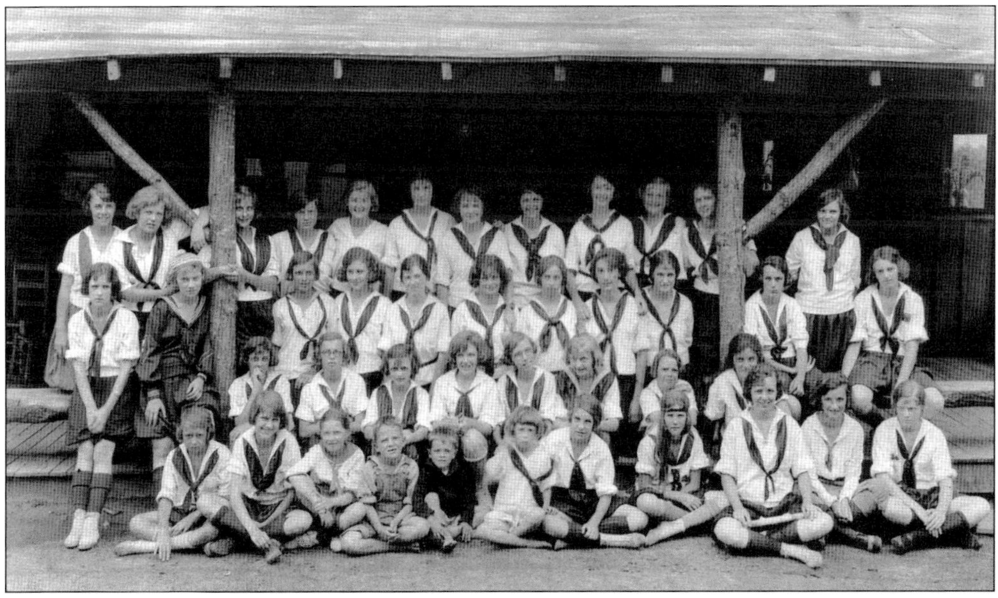

Camp Illahee's enrollment grew each year, and by 1927, there were 58 campers and 21 counselors. The cost of the eight-week session was $250. The camp brochure reasoned that money spent in a summer camp "is not an expense but a well paying investment." (Courtesy of Camp Illahee.)

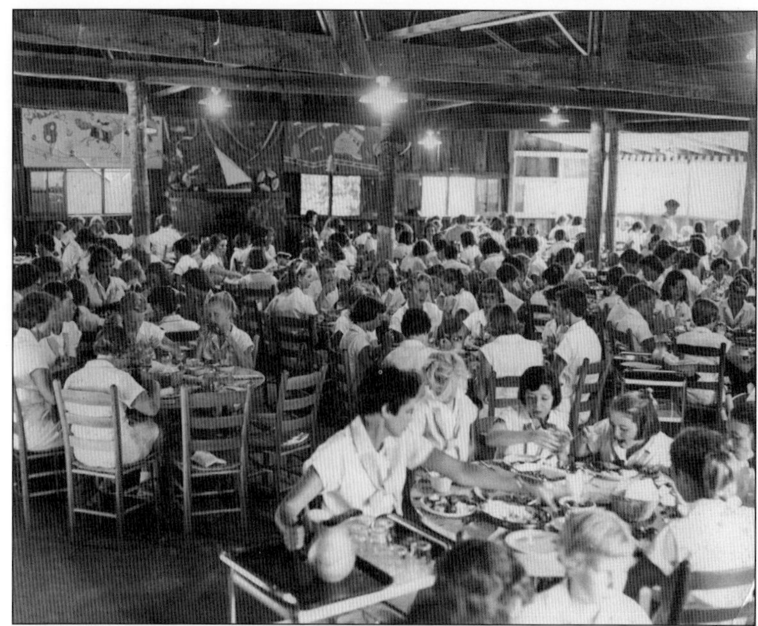

The camp's brochure stated, "Campers share worthwhile friendships, health-giving sunlight, knowledge of the open, unfailing energy, the goodness of sound sleep, and the delight of wholesome food. These are essentially the kingdom of youth." (Courtesy of Camp Illahee.)

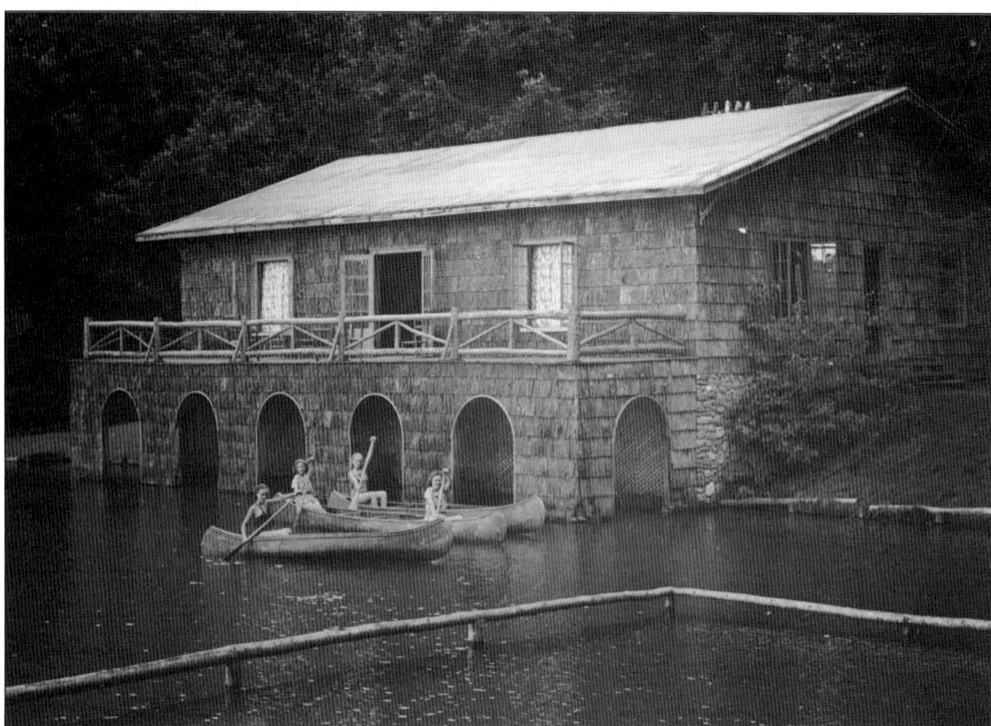

Increased enrollment necessitated new facilities. In 1924, the McLeods built a new lodge for added activity and gathering space. The entire lodge was sided with chestnut bark, giving it a rustic appearance. Situated opposite the dam, the porch extended over the lake for girls to canoe under. The new structure was designated McLeod Lodge in honor of the founders in 1977. (Courtesy of Camp Illahee.)

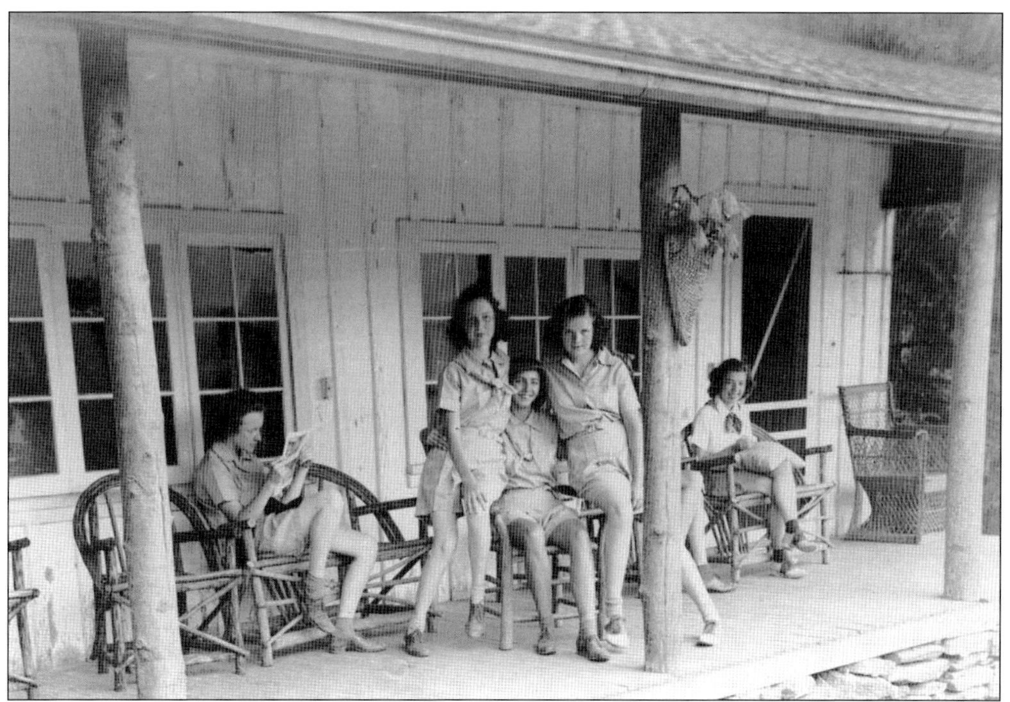

Camp Illahee struggled as the Great Depression set in. By 1934, the camp was slated for auction. With no bidders, the camp was returned to the McLeods, but Hinton McLeod passed away the following year. His wife attempted to keep the camp going but was either forced to sell, or it was repossessed in 1937. (Courtesy of Camp Illahee.)

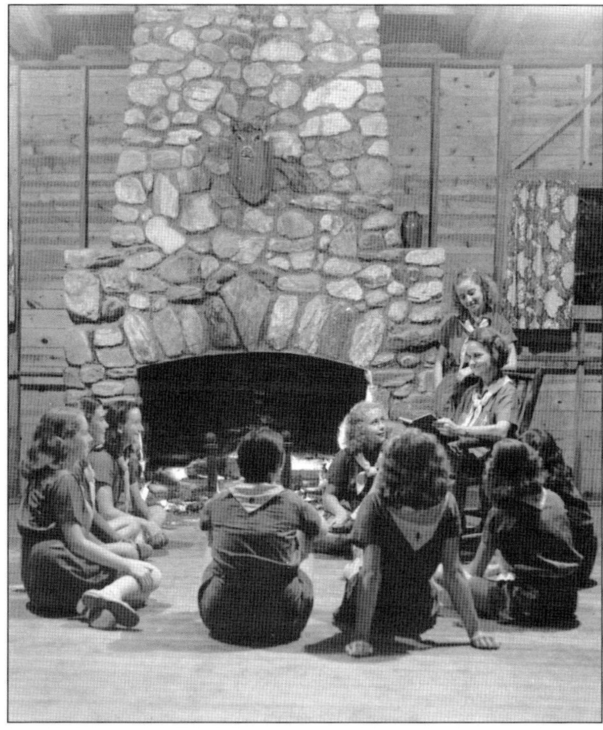

Massachusetts native Kathryn "Robin" Francis Curtis served on the national staff of the Girl Scouts and tried her hand at directing a girls' camp at Chunns Cove Camp in Asheville in 1938 and knew instantly that she had found her life's calling. A real estate agent convinced her to lease Camp Illahee, and the camp reopened in 1939 with 75 campers, including many from Chunns Cove. (Courtesy of Camp Illahee.)

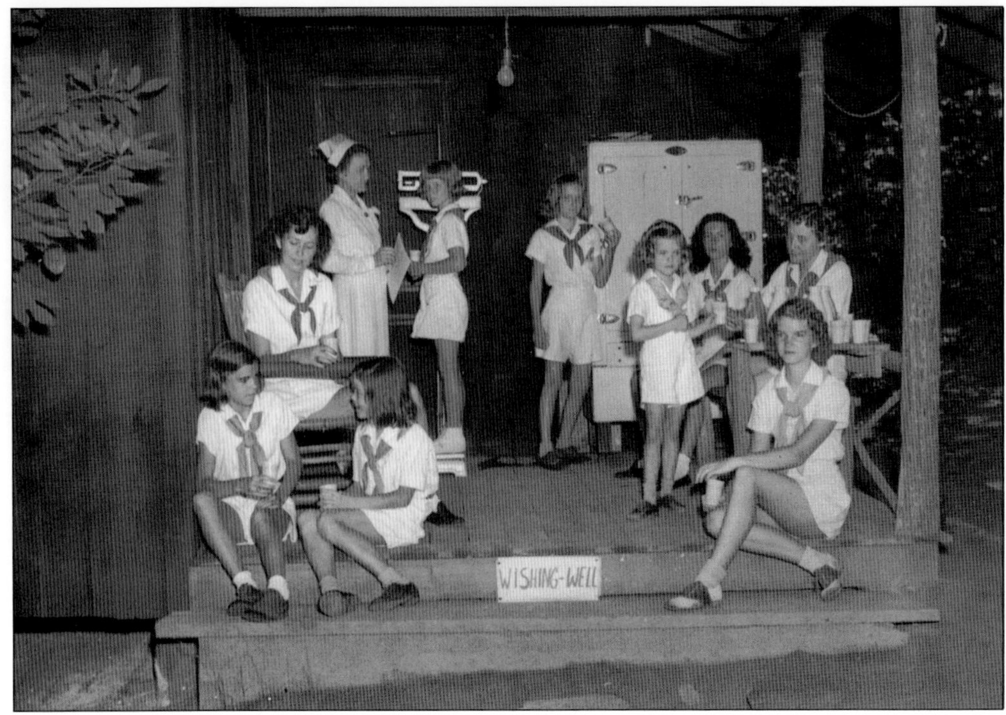

In the 1940s, Camp Illahee consisted of the lodge, the dining hall, the office, Heigh Ho and Hillbrook cabins, a barn, a riding ring, Swim Lake, a campfire circle, athletic fields for badminton and softball, a putting green, two tennis courts, a croquet ground, an archery field, a cook's cabin, a crafts hut called the Hobby House, and a nurse's cabin known as the Wishing Well. (Courtesy of Camp Illahee.)

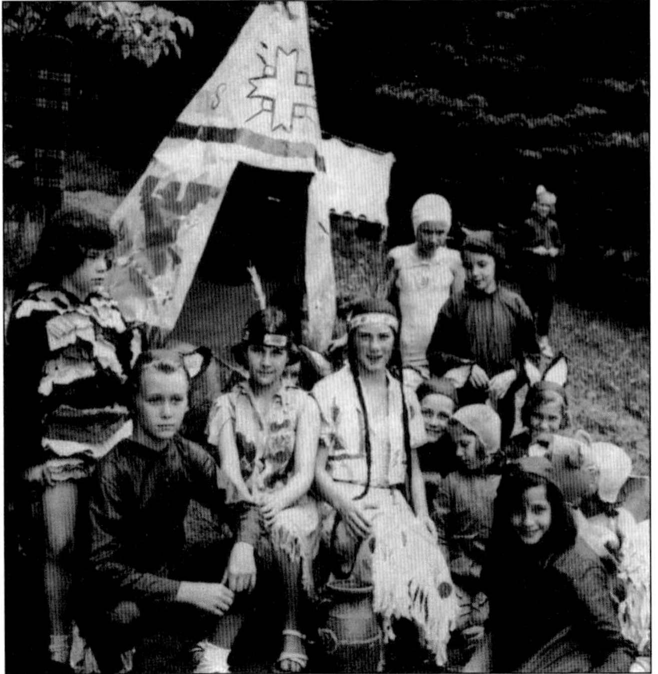

The evening program was always much anticipated. Each cabin had a chance to entertain the camp with plays, dances, group singing, dance recitals, taffy pulls, or even games like kick the can. Dances with nearby Camp Sapphire and Keystone Camp brought jubilant excitement as girls fretted about what to wear. (Courtesy of Camp Illahee.)

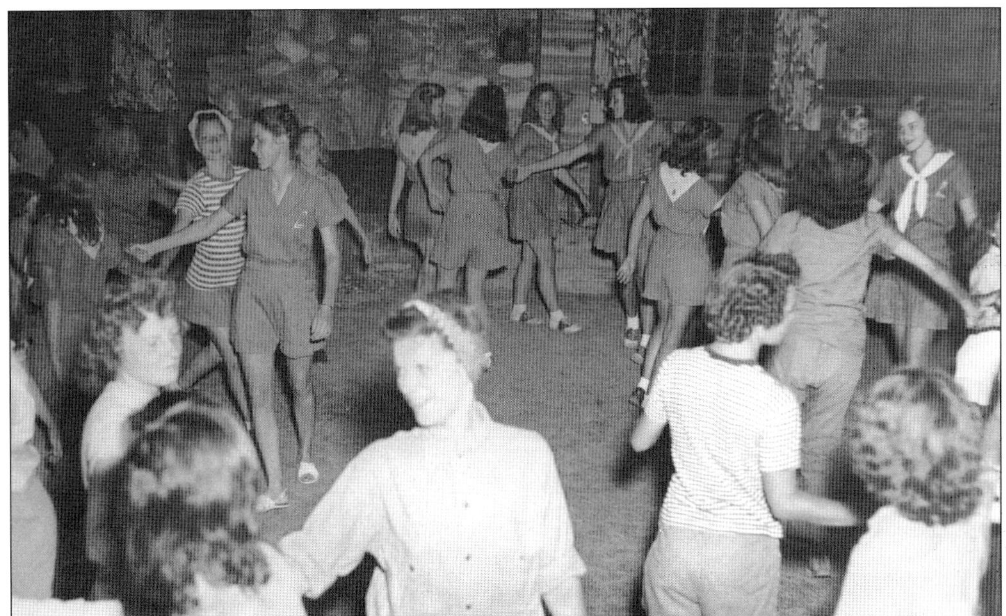

Square dances were a popular Saturday evening pastime in the 1940s and 1950s. Since there were no boys to dance with, half the campers donned blue jeans as the "boys," and the other half wore skirts as "girls." On occasion, boys from Camp Carolina were invited to the dances, and the girls devoted much of the day to trying to look their best. (Courtesy of Camp Illahee.)

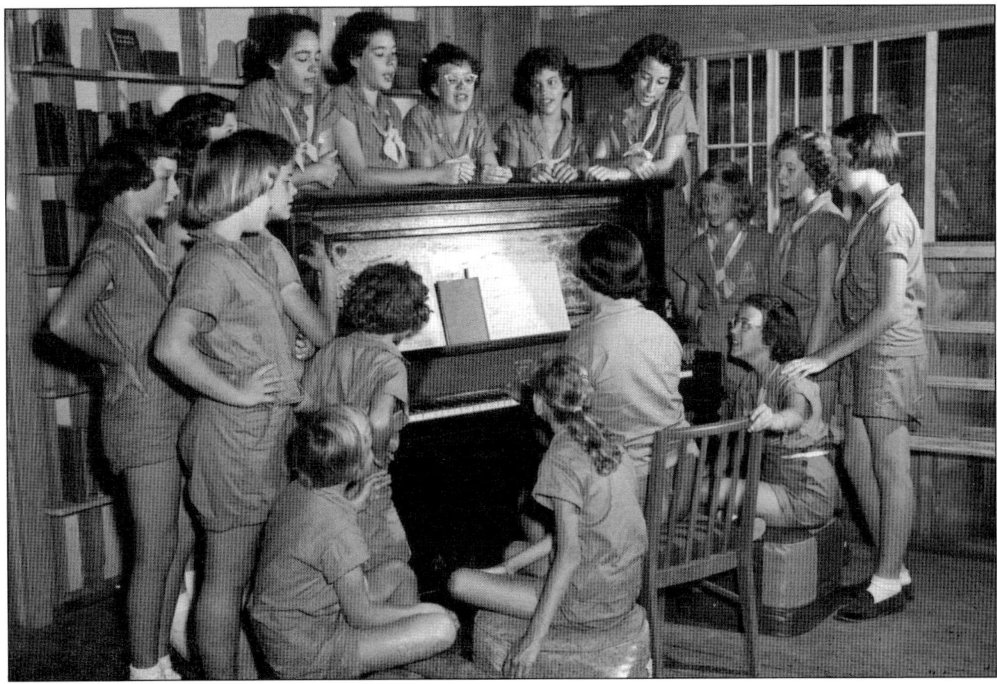

One hundred campers signed up for the glee club in 1952. The girls sang classical music with boys from Camp Mondamin along with the camp orchestra during the annual water pageant. When rock and roll invaded camp, glee club members frequently performed Elvis Presley impersonations between camp songs. (Courtesy of Camp Illahee.)

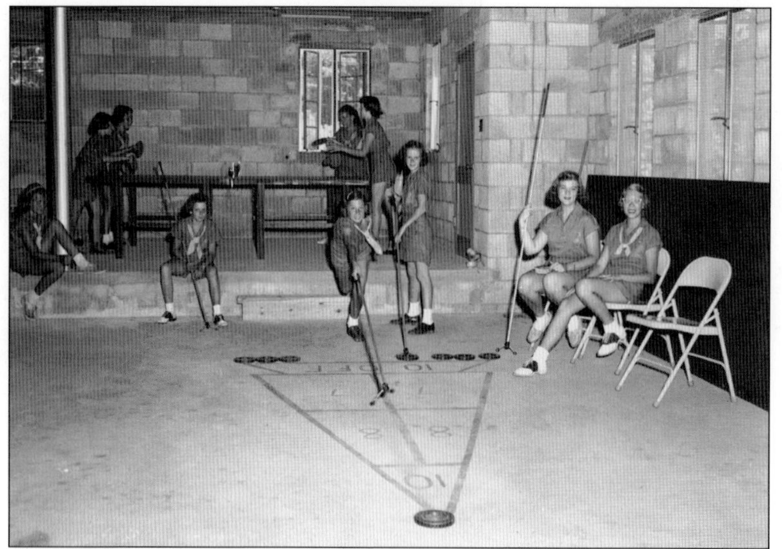

Shuffleboard was a popular pastime at Camp Illahee in the 1950s. (Courtesy of Camp Illahee.)

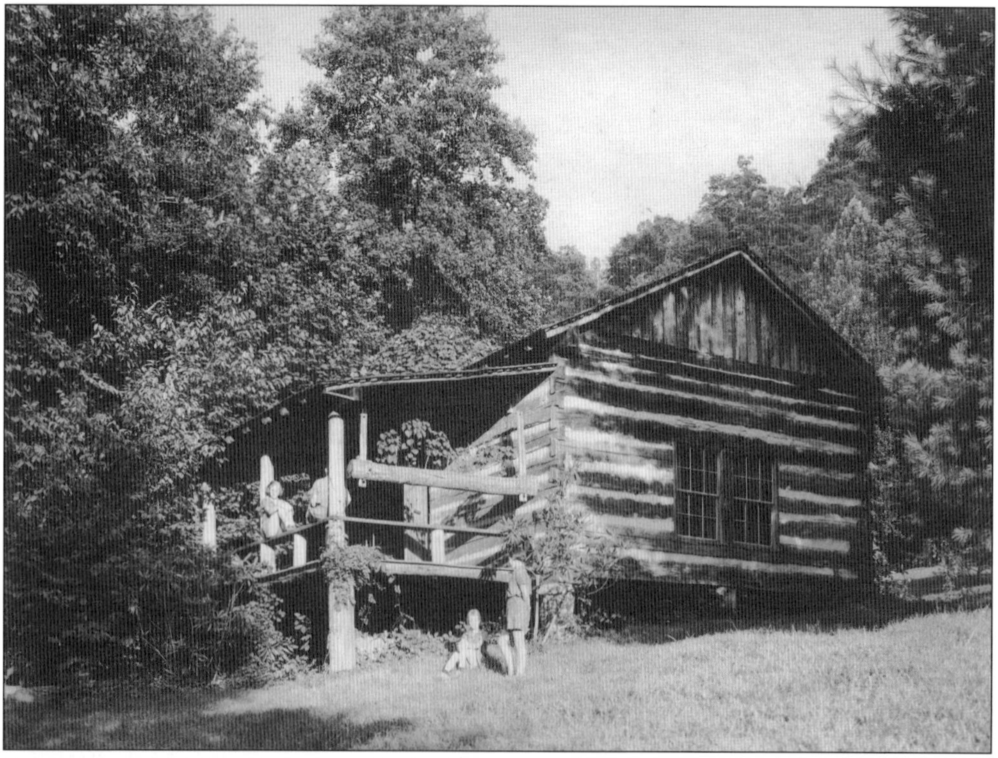

Rockbrook Camp's founder Nancy Clarke Carrier was the great-granddaughter of showman P.T. Barnum. The circus wintered in Columbia, South Carolina. In 1888, Barnum bequeathed her parents $100,000 to purchase the nearby Goodwill Plantation, located in Eastover, South Carolina, where Carrier was born. In 1895, the family purchased 800 acres in Brevard where Carrier founded Rockbrook Camp in 1921. She brought two hand-hewn chestnut log cabins from the plantation to the camp. (Courtesy of Rockbrook Camp.)

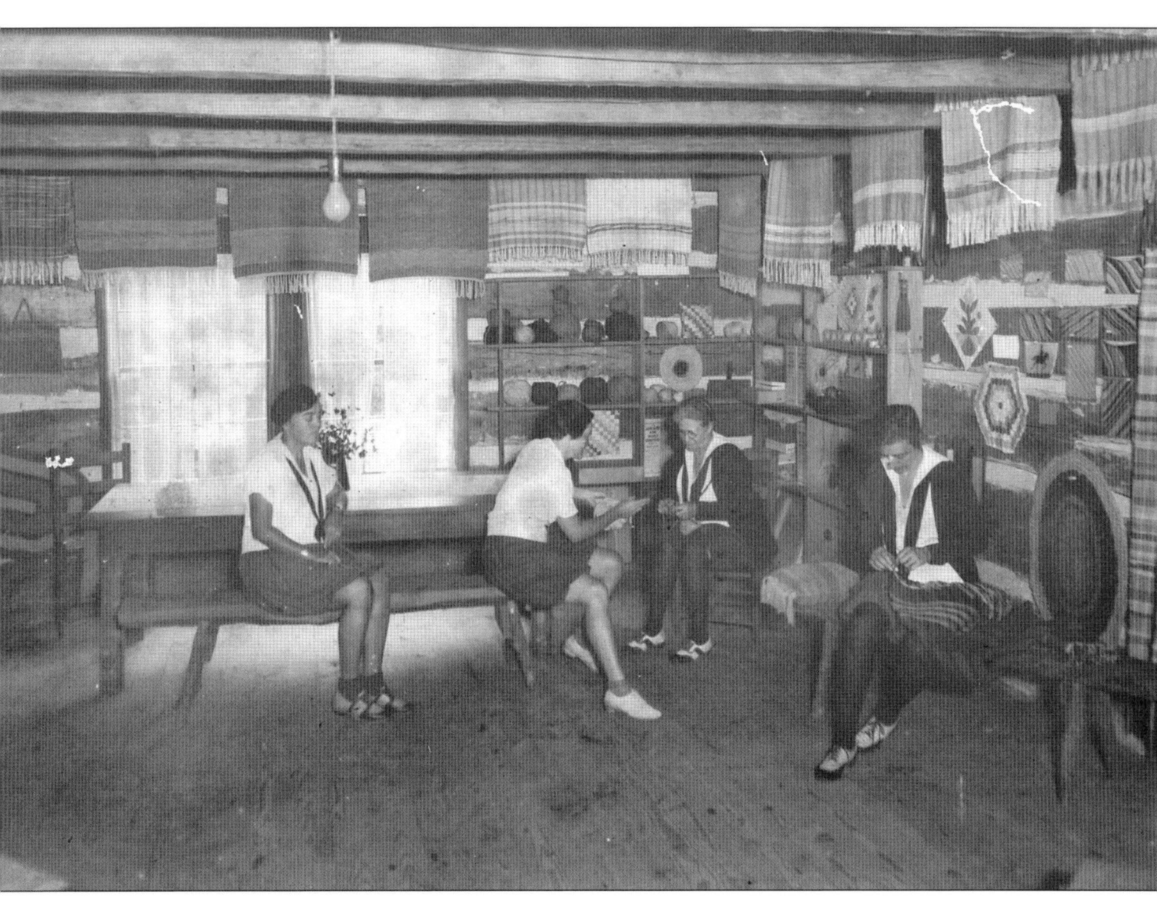

Carrier restored the 200-year-old cabins and made them the center of camp life. She named the buildings Goodwill and Curosty—a colloquial mountain word for crafts. This 1930s photograph shows the interior of Curosty, which houses wide floor looms and smaller tabletop looms still used by campers today, harkening back to traditional Appalachian crafts. The walls display examples of the campers' weavings. (Courtesy of Rockbrook Camp.)

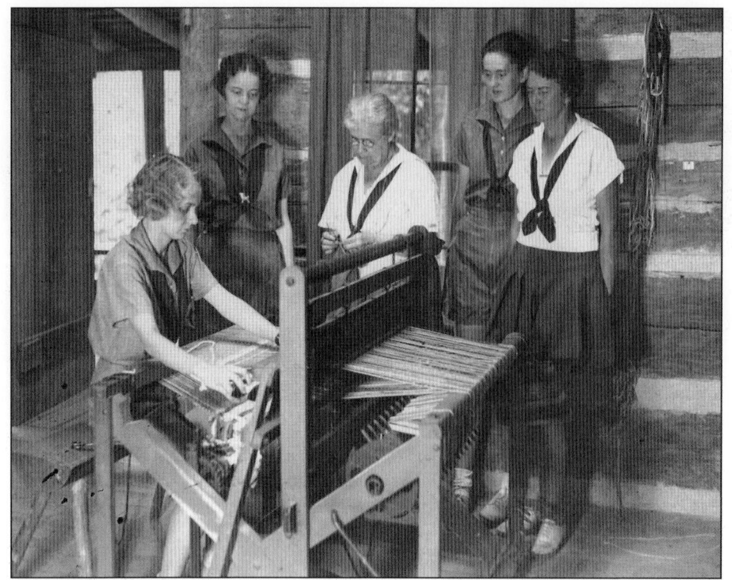

Like area folk schools such as the John C. Campbell Folk School, founded in 1925 by widow Olive Dame Campbell in Brasstown, camps participated in the Appalachian craft revival. Skilled instructors taught girls preindustrial crafts. At Rockbrook's log cabin, "the lore of the mountains is preserved in the indigenous craft of weaving," according to the 1935 camp brochure. (Courtesy of Rockbrook Camp.)

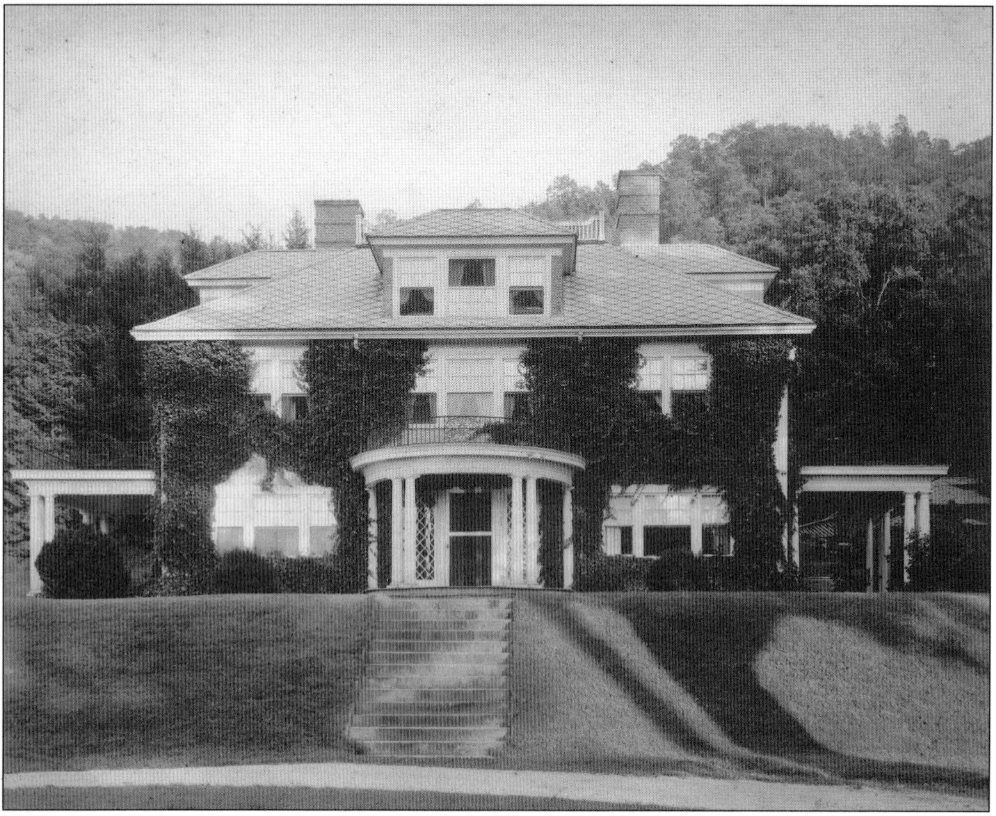

English-born Richard Sharp Smith designed the house at the center of Rockbrook Camp in 1895, home to camp owners and directors Henry and Nancy Carrier. Smith was the supervising architect of the Biltmore Estate and one of the most influential architects in the Asheville area through the 1920s. The house thrilled campers with displays of circus artifacts inherited from P.T. Barnum, including Tom Thumb's chair. (Courtesy of Rockbrook Camp.)

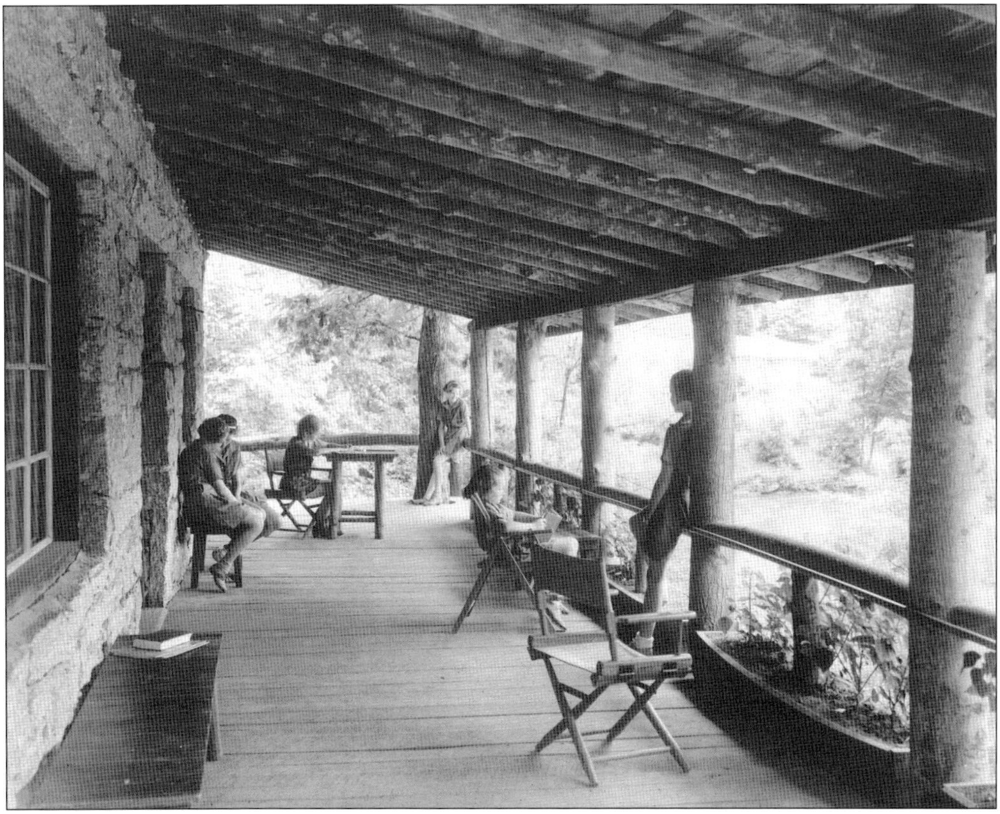

This 1930s photograph shows campers passing their free time on the wide porch of the Lakeview Lodge, reading and writing letters home. This is one of three lodges, along with Castle Rock and Hillside, constructed at Rockbrook in the 1920s from rock quarried from the mountain above the camp. Evidence of this natural resource are two prominent rock outcroppings—Castle Rock and Dunn's Rock—that rise above the camp. (Courtesy of Rockbrook Camp.)

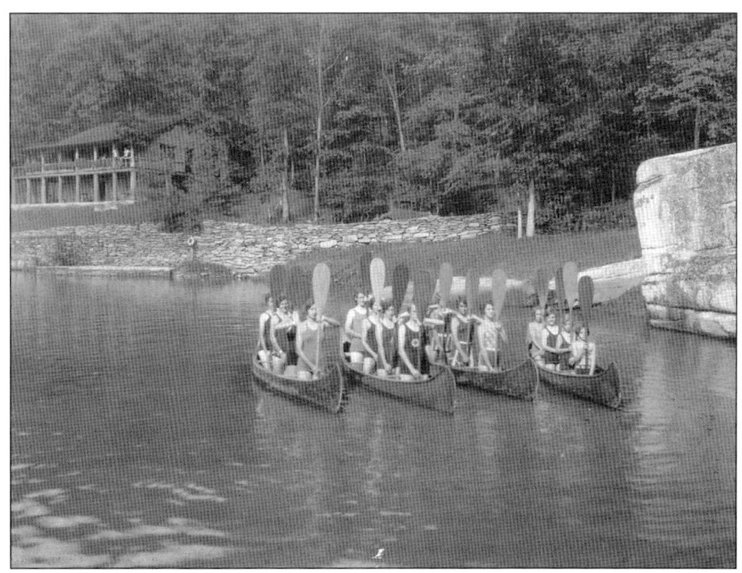

This 1920s photograph shows girls canoeing on the lake in front of Lakeview Lodge. While the lake is man-made, many natural features, including two waterfalls, Stickbiscuit Falls and Rockbrook Falls; the French Broad River; and Vesper Rock, a distinctive large rock jutting out of the water, distinguish the camp. (Courtesy of Rockbrook Camp.)

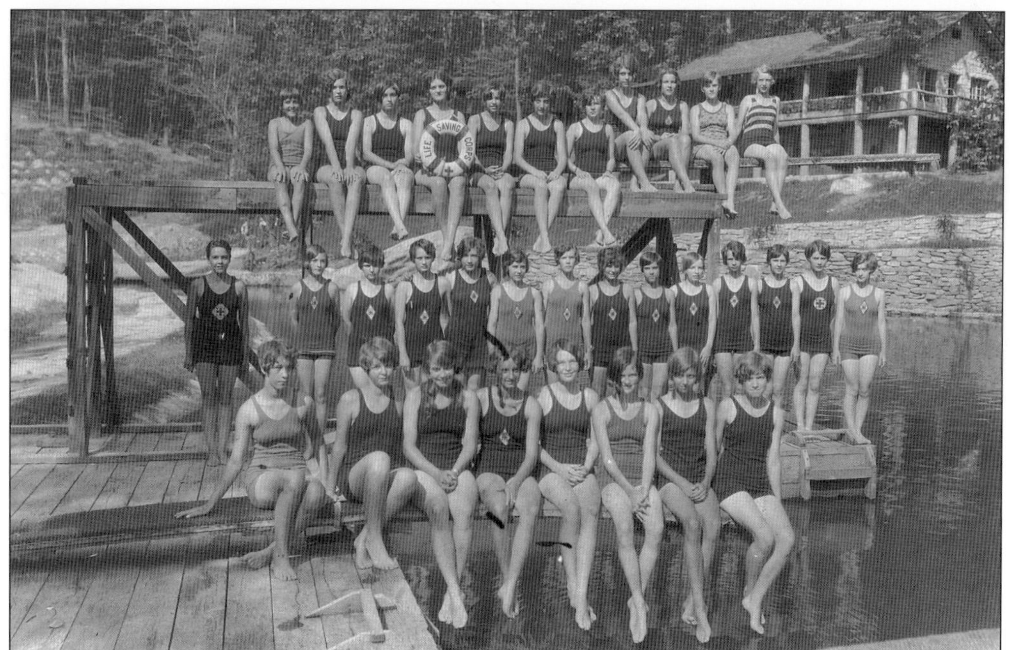

Rockbrook's swimming program included synchronized swimming, water ballet, water safety, basic rescue, and advanced lifesaving. During free time, girls played with kickboards, swam relays, and participated in other water games. Camp activities encouraged sportsmanship but also forged deep and lasting friendships. (Courtesy of Rockbrook Camp.)

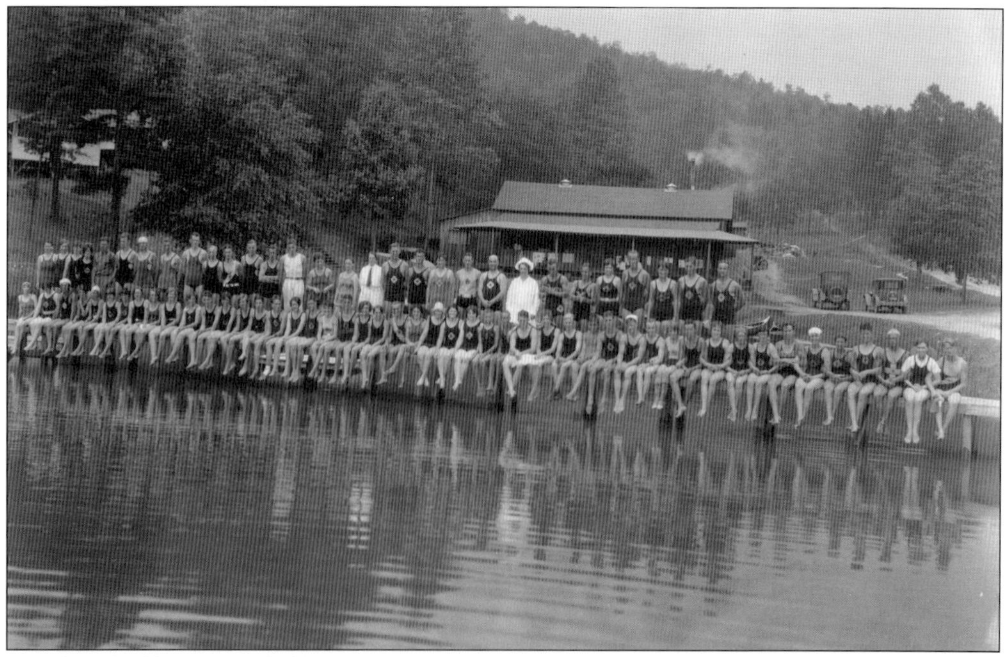

One hundred boys attended Camp Carolina, near Brevard, its first summer in 1924. By the next summer, word had spread and 200 boys registered for camp. There is a saying that goes, "If you want to get to heaven, go to Brevard and take a left, and pretty soon your car gets drenched by a water balloon and you know you're there—heaven—better known as Camp Carolina."

Two

The Boys and Girls of Summer

Summer Camps around Hendersonville

In 1921, the Asheville *Citizen-Times* reported on the opening of yet another boys' camp in Henderson County, which, the paper claimed, was "rapidly becoming the center of camps in the South." Encircled by the Blue Ridge Mountains to the east, the Pisgah Ledge to the west, and the Saluda Mountains to the south, Henderson County has served as a summer colony for coastal and Deep South inhabitants driven by oppressive heat, humidity, yellow fever, and malaria epidemics to the cool climates afforded by the higher elevations since the early 19th century. The *French Broad Hustler* reported on the community's amenities in 1909, dubbing the county seat of Hendersonville "THE resort of the mountains." By the summer of 1926, the population of Hendersonville quadrupled from 10,000 permanent residents to over 40,000.

The burgeoning resort destination also boasted many well-known private educational institutions, such as the Blue Ridge School for Boys and Fassifern School for Girls. The earliest summer camps, founded in Hendersonville and the surrounding communities of Flat Rock, Green River, Tuxedo, and Laurel Park, as well as the nearby towns of Chimney Rock and Lake Lure in Rutherford County, proffered a well-balanced education "where students will rebuild used-up energies and where the aesthetic senses will be developed along with physical resuscitation."

Located just west of Hendersonville, the planned resort of Laurel Park featured Rhododendron Lake with a sandy beach, diving boards, slides, and canoe rentals. The recreation destination was home to Laurel Park Camp for boys and Rhododendron Camp for girls in the 1910s and 1920s. To the northeast, Lake Lure, created in 1927, enhanced the natural attraction of Chimney Rock. Camp Minnehaha was established in 1912, followed by Chimney Rock Camp for Boys in 1917. To the south, the damming of the Green River created the largest lake in Henderson County, Lake Summit, in 1920. By 1922, Camp Mondamin and Camp Greystone were established on its shores, followed by Camp Arrowhead in 1937 and Camp Green Cove in 1945. The county's numerous religious conference centers, such as the Presbyterian Bonclarken and the Episcopalian Camp Kanuga also established camps. Following the Second World War, two Jewish camps were founded in Hendersonville, Blue Star Camp and Camp Judaea. These early camps established the Hendersonville area's historic reputation as the Southeast's destination for organized summer camps.

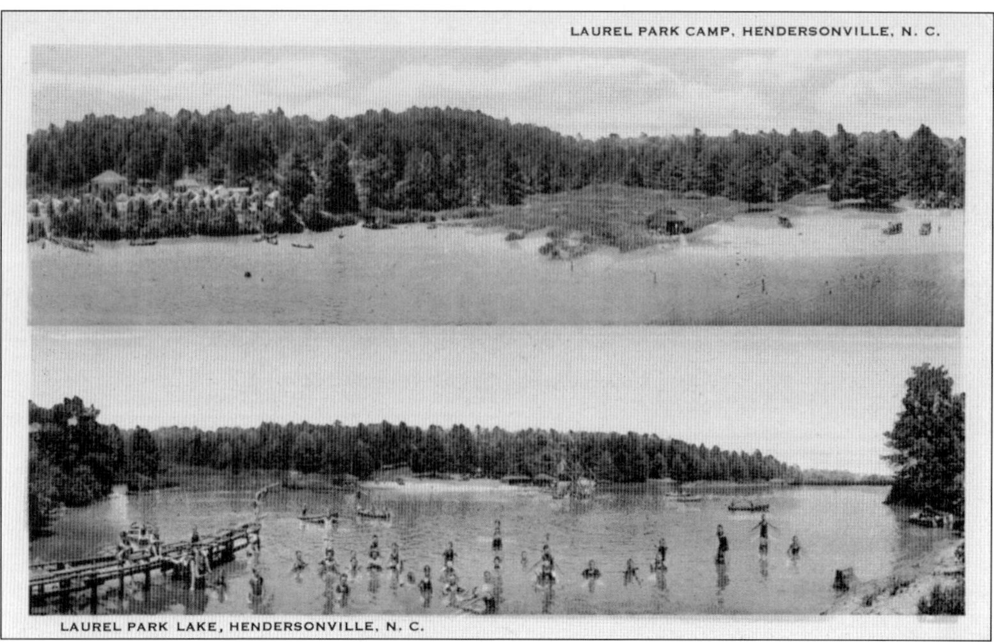

In 1910, Charlestonian Major I.B. Brown established the first of Henderson County's camps, Laurel Park Camp for Boys, in "the most beautiful natural park in America." Though academically focused, the camp offered an array of outdoor sports, contending that "a well-appointed camp is nature's workshop for the all-round development of the young boy." (Courtesy of North Carolina Photographic Archives, Wilson Library, University of North Carolina at Chapel Hill.)

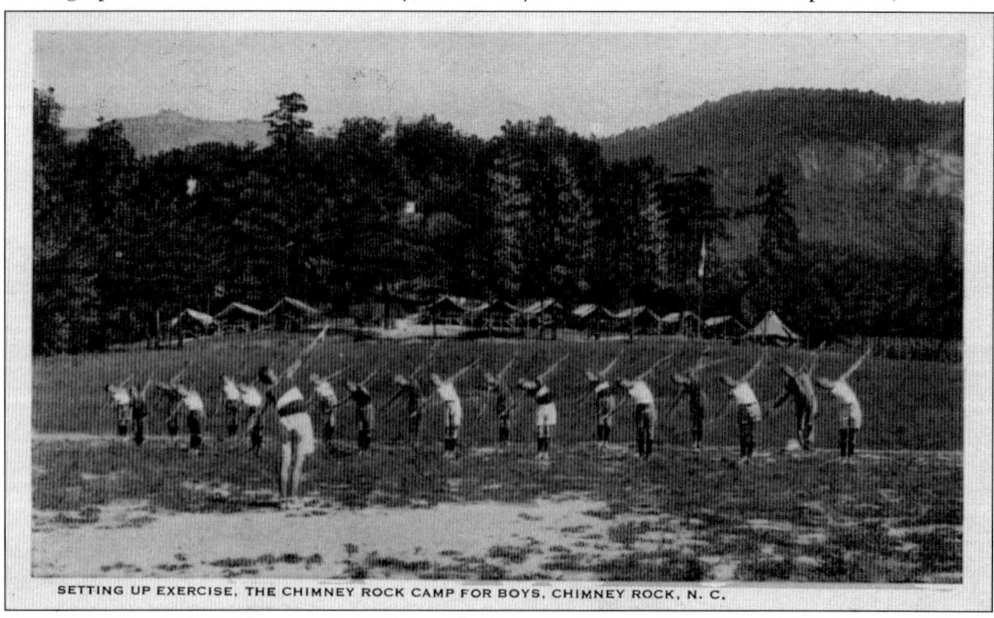

Founded around 1917, Chimney Rock Camp for boys, and later girls, operated until the early 1980s on Lake Lure, after which the camp's original cabins, gym, dining hall, and lakefront served as a filming location for the 1987 blockbuster *Dirty Dancing*. (Courtesy of Durwood Barbour Collection of North Carolina Postcards, North Carolina Photographic Archives, Wilson Library, University of North Carolina at Chapel Hill.)

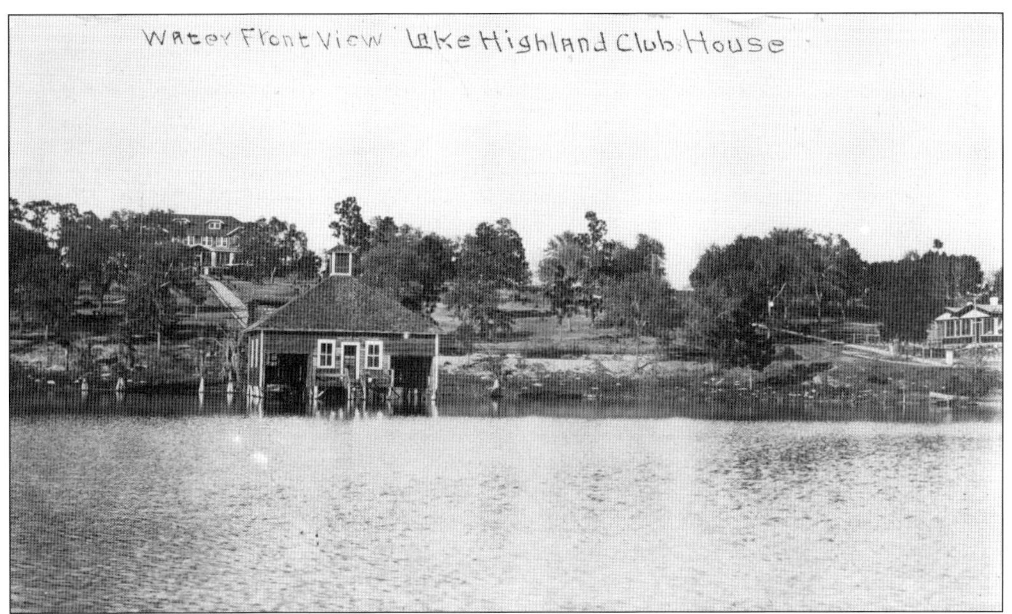

In 1910, South Carolina businessmen founded the Highland Lake Club on 500 acres formerly owned by George Trenholm, secretary of the Confederate treasury, and South Carolina governor William Aiken in Flat Rock, but the venture failed after two years. Col. J.C. Woodward established Camp Highland Lake in 1919. The camp continued under the direction of his son until 1947. (Courtesy of North Carolina Collection, Pack Memorial Public Library.)

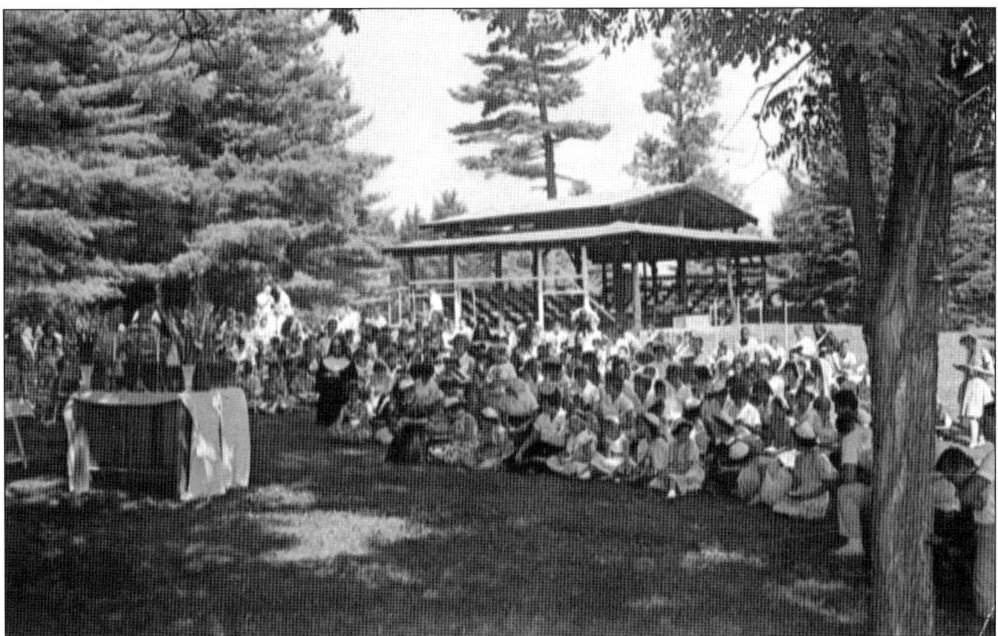

From 1956 to 1985, the Catholic Church operated Our Lady of the Hills Camp at Highland Lake, the second Catholic camp in Henderson County after Little Flower Camp. Campers recited the rosary and attended Mass. It was one of the first racially integrated camps in the region. (Courtesy of Durwood Barbour Collection of North Carolina Postcards, North Carolina Photographic Archives, Wilson Library, University of North Carolina at Chapel Hill.)

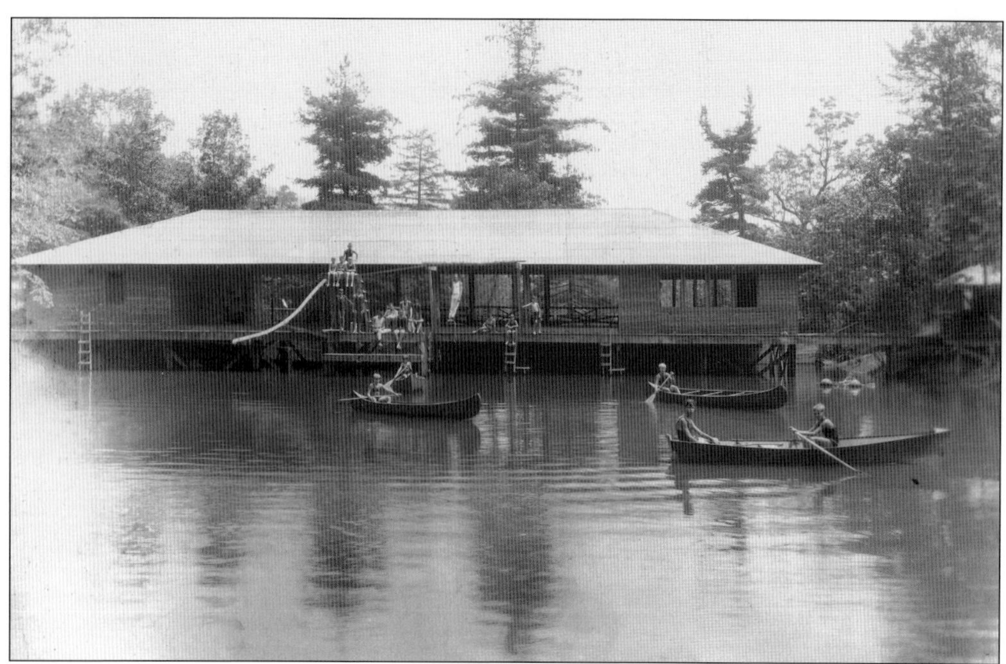

Located roughly 10 miles north of the North Carolina–South Carolina state line and equidistant from the cities of Asheville and Greenville, Lake Summit was formed in 1920 after the damming of the Green River to harness its power for South Carolina textile mills. With 10 miles of shoreline, the lake proved an ideal setting for summer camps. Shown here are the docks at Camp Tawasentha in the 1920s. (Courtesy of Camp Mondamin.)

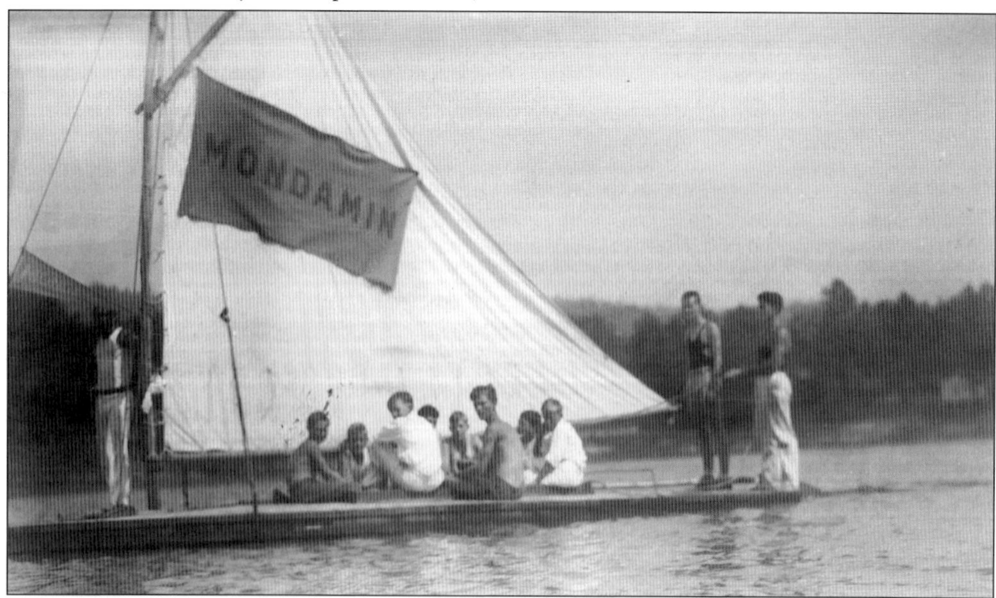

The 350-acre Lake Summit boasts advantageous winds for sailing, as this 1920s photograph shows. Camp Mondamin aims to instill lifelong skills and values through adventures. As 19th-century American theologian William Shedd averred, "A ship in harbor is safe, but that is not what ships are built for." The waterfront property and surrounding 800 acres of wilderness are "a magnificent playground and great university," according to the camp. (Courtesy of Camp Mondamin.)

The son of state senator Joseph Oscar Bell Sr., Frank Bell Sr., also known as "Chief," founded Camp Mondamin in 1922 along Lake Summit. In Longfellow's "The Song of Hiawatha," Mondamin taught his people self-sufficiency so they could gain independence. The staff and campers shown in this 1927 photograph came from different parts of the Southeast. (Courtesy of Camp Mondamin.)

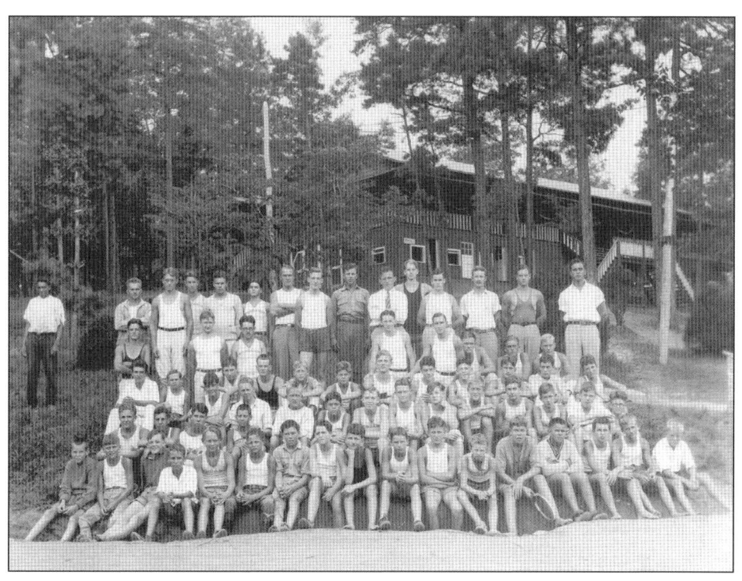

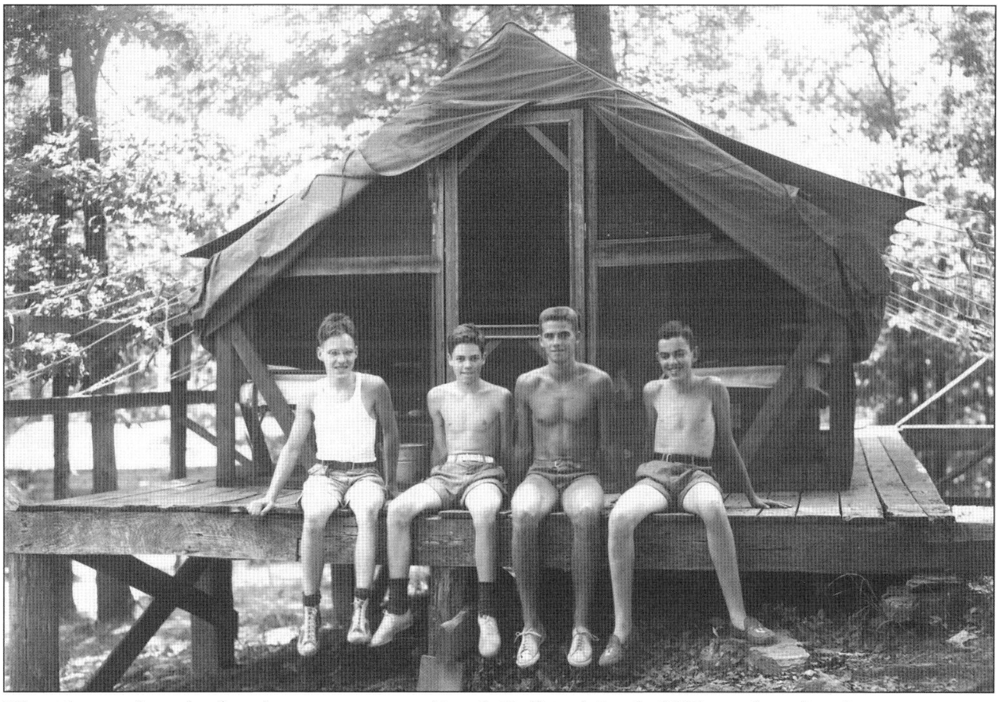

The idea to found a boys' camp came to Frank Bell in March 1922, and in April, construction commenced on the dining hall, the only permanent building aside from the wood stove kitchen. Lodging for the campers and staff consisted of tents. Bell and his inexperienced staff of six welcomed 31 campers in late June. This is a later photograph from the 1940s. (Courtesy of Camp Mondamin.)

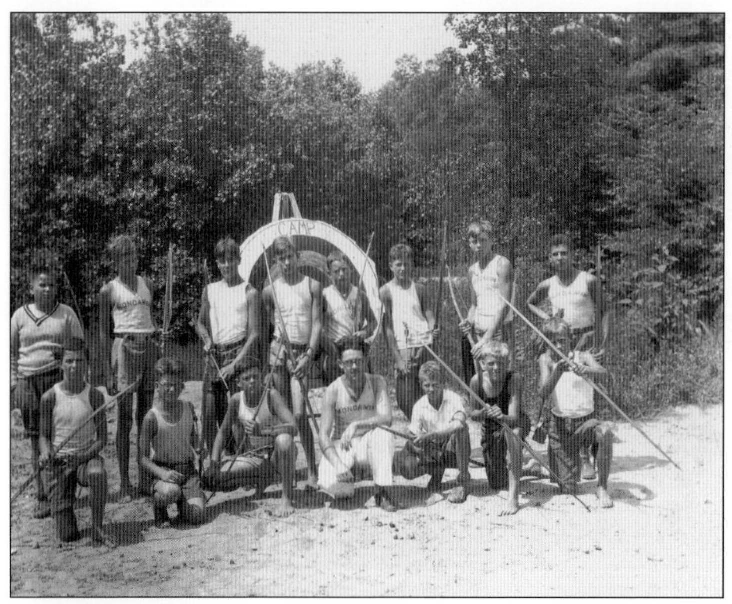

Mondamin endorsed John Ruskin's ideals of education by "training [boys] into the perfect exercise and kingly continence of their bodies and souls. It is a painful, continual, and difficult work to be done by kindness, by watching, by warning, by precept, and by praise, but above all—by example." This 1927 photograph shows the camp's archery squad. The campers constructed their own bows. (Courtesy of Camp Mondamin.)

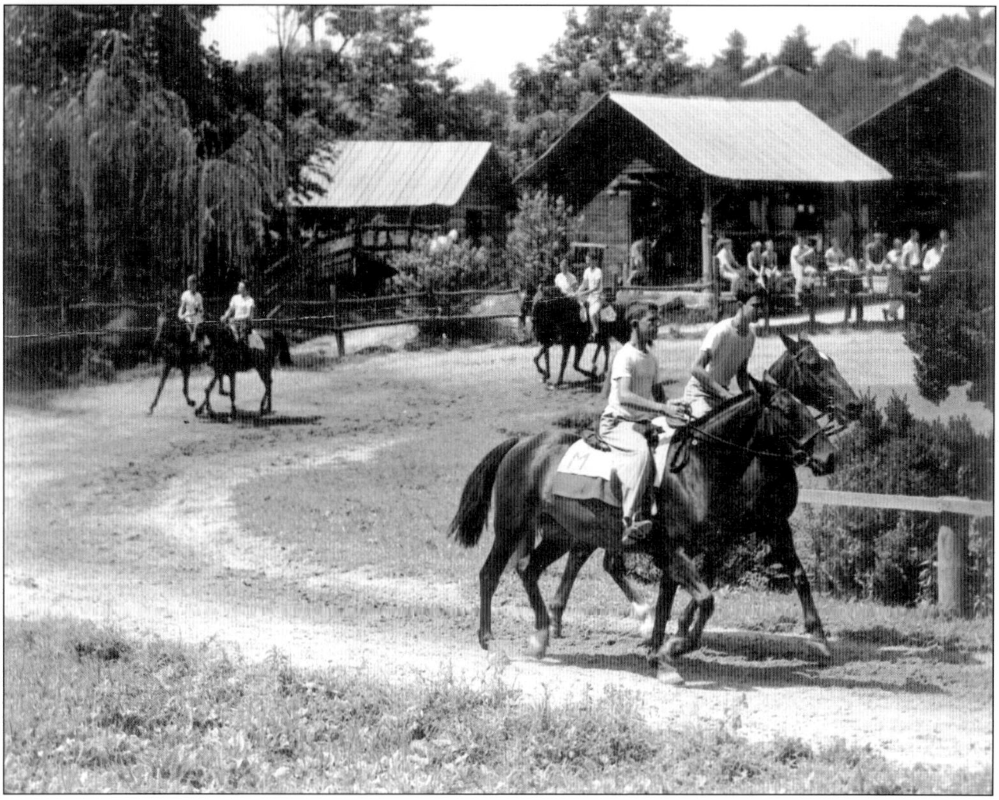

By the late 1920s, Mondamin added more facilities and modern amenities, including an open-air gymnasium, log cabins, wooden-floor tents, a screened dining hall with ice boxes, a complete moving picture machine, a Victrola, long-distance telephone lines, flush toilets, a library, museum, nine-hole golf course, five tennis courts, a large barn with saddle horses, a fleet of about 20 boats, and a five-room infirmary. (Courtesy of Camp Mondamin.)

The 1927 camp brochure stated that "physical sturdiness, mental resourcefulness, a happy social adjustment, spiritual growth—cleanliness, generosity, and courage in all things—these are the goals of Mondamin—and happiness is a natural by product." These boys dance with girls from Mondamin's sister camp, Camp Green Cove. (Courtesy of Camp Mondamin.)

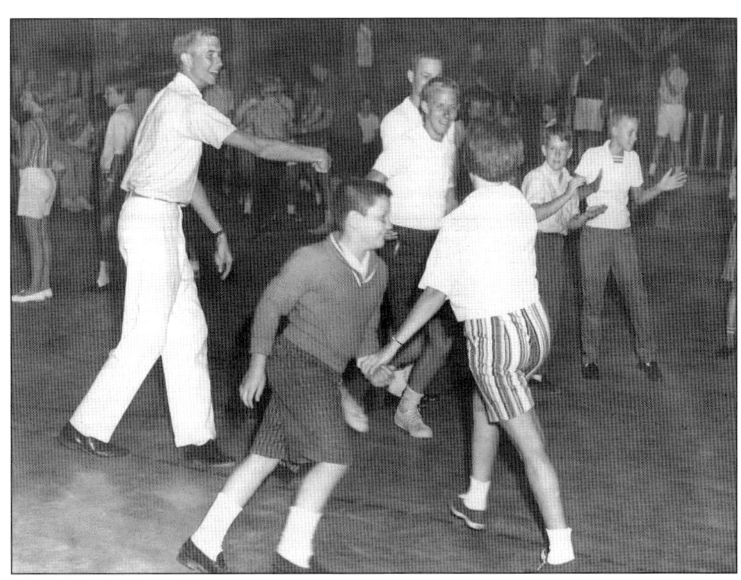

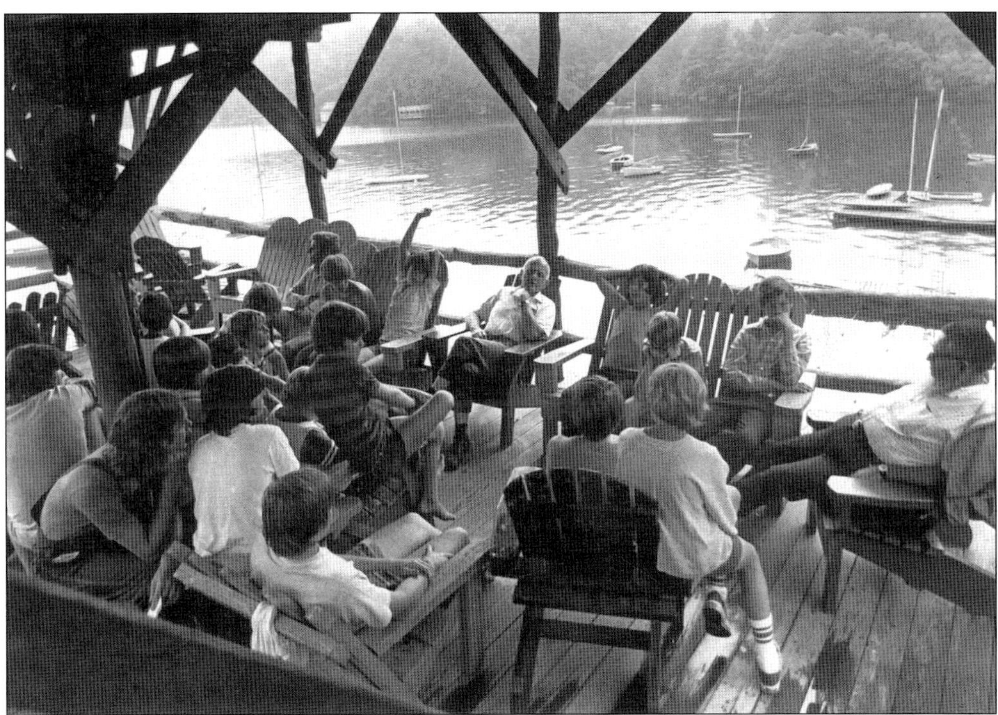

Chief, pictured in the center of this 1970s photograph, coined the phrase "bull sessions" for his open discussions on "the tower," a three-story edifice on the lake. The top deck displays a flagpole and bell to summon campers for wake up and meals. The second deck is furnished with Adirondack chairs, as shown here. The lower level features swimming lanes, a diving board, and a rope swing. (Courtesy of Camp Mondamin.)

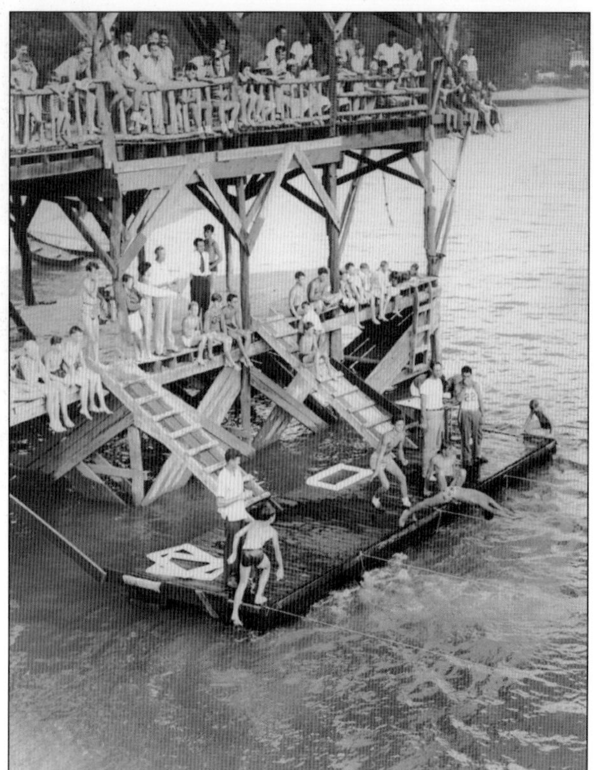

This mid-20th-century photograph clearly shows the wooden tower's three stories as boys jump into Lake Summit. (Courtesy of North Carolina Collection, Pack Memorial Public Library.)

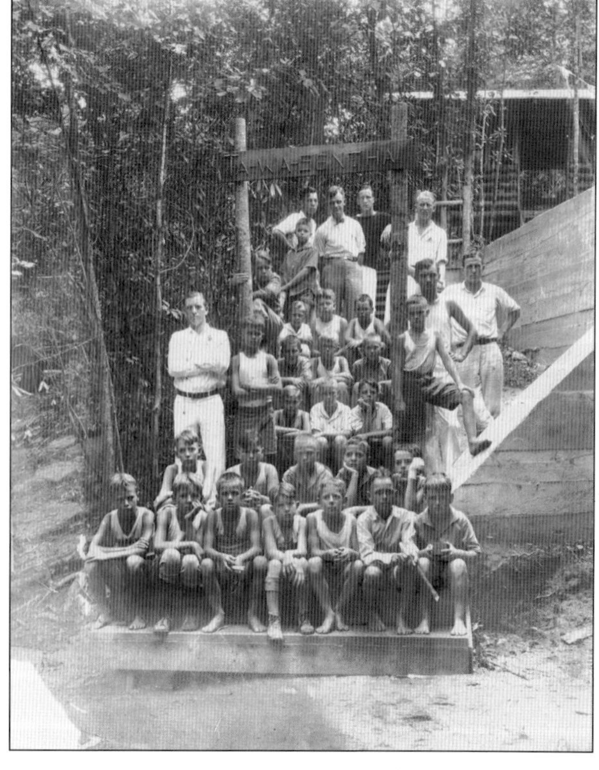

Affiliated with Camp Mondamin, Camp Tawasentha was in existence from around 1925 to 1938. The camp hosted boys ages 7 to 11, while boys ages 12 to 18 attended Mondamin. Like many camps formed in the interwar period, the camp drew upon frontier and Indian motifs, with log cabins and a name derived from Longfellow's "Song of Hiawatha." (Courtesy of Camp Mondamin.)

Campers have long explored rivers near and far by canoe. In 1933, campers and staff paddled from Mud Creek in Hendersonville to the French Broad, down to the Tennessee, and on to the Ohio to its confluence with the Mississippi in Cairo, Illinois. A few years later, campers paddled from the Green River to the Atlantic Ocean. (Courtesy of Camp Mondamin.)

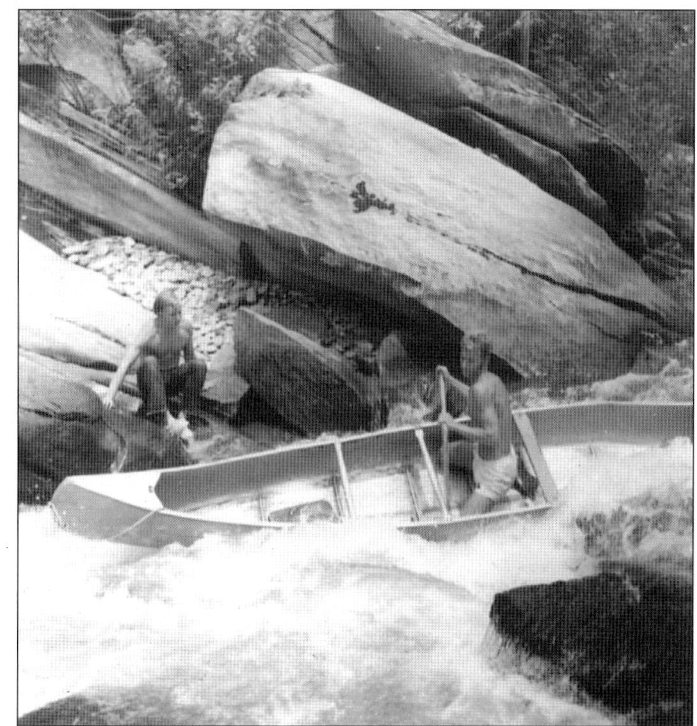

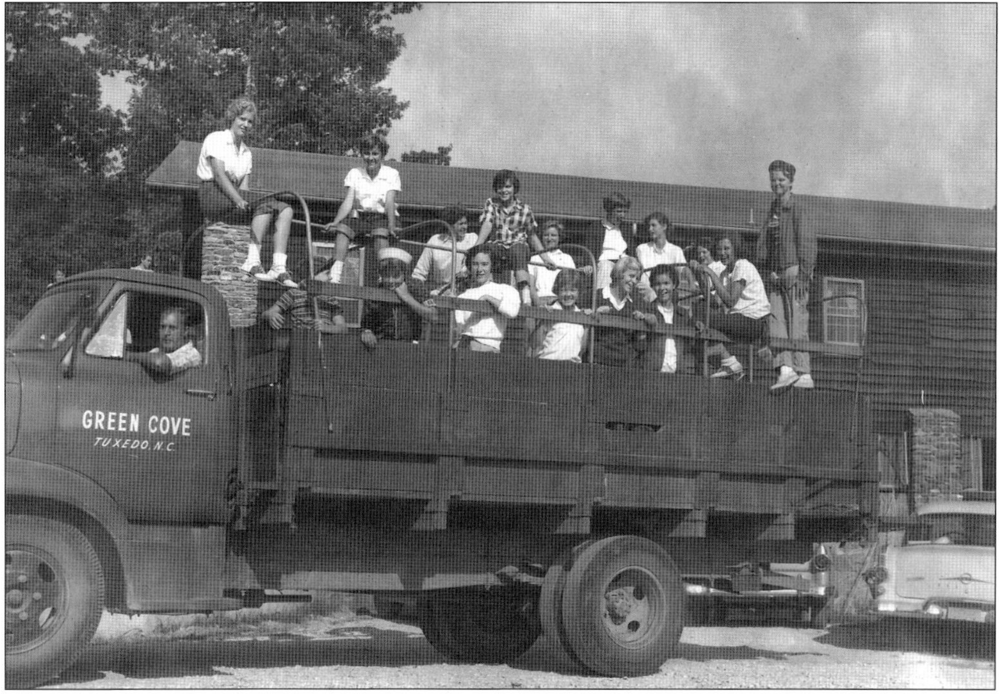

In 1945, Frank Bell opened a camp for girls at Rockbrook Camp in Brevard. The camp was renamed Camp Green Cove and moved to its present location at the upper end of Lake Summit, about a mile from Mondamin, in 1949. Like Mondamin, the camp has been owned and operated by generations of the Bells for its entire history. (Courtesy of Camp Green Cove.)

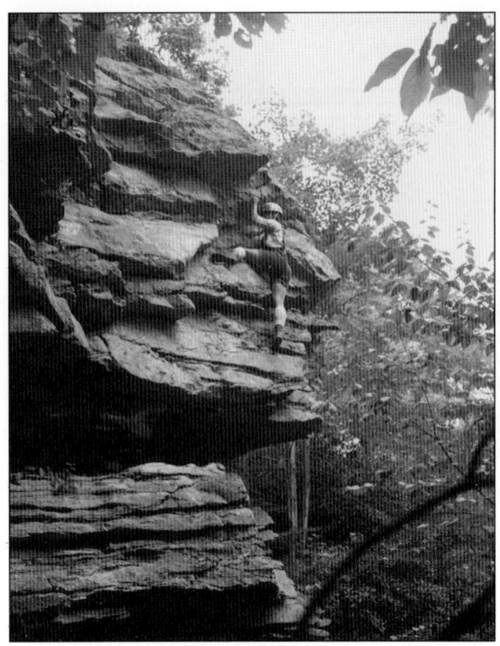

Chief said "education is not a diploma" but instead extends to experiences outside the classroom that build skills, values, and wisdom that enrich living. Mondamin and Green Cove campers spend part of each session at camp and the remainder on wilderness excursions, rock climbing, backpacking, hiking, whitewater canoeing, and mountain biking throughout western North Carolina. (Courtesy of Camp Green Cove.)

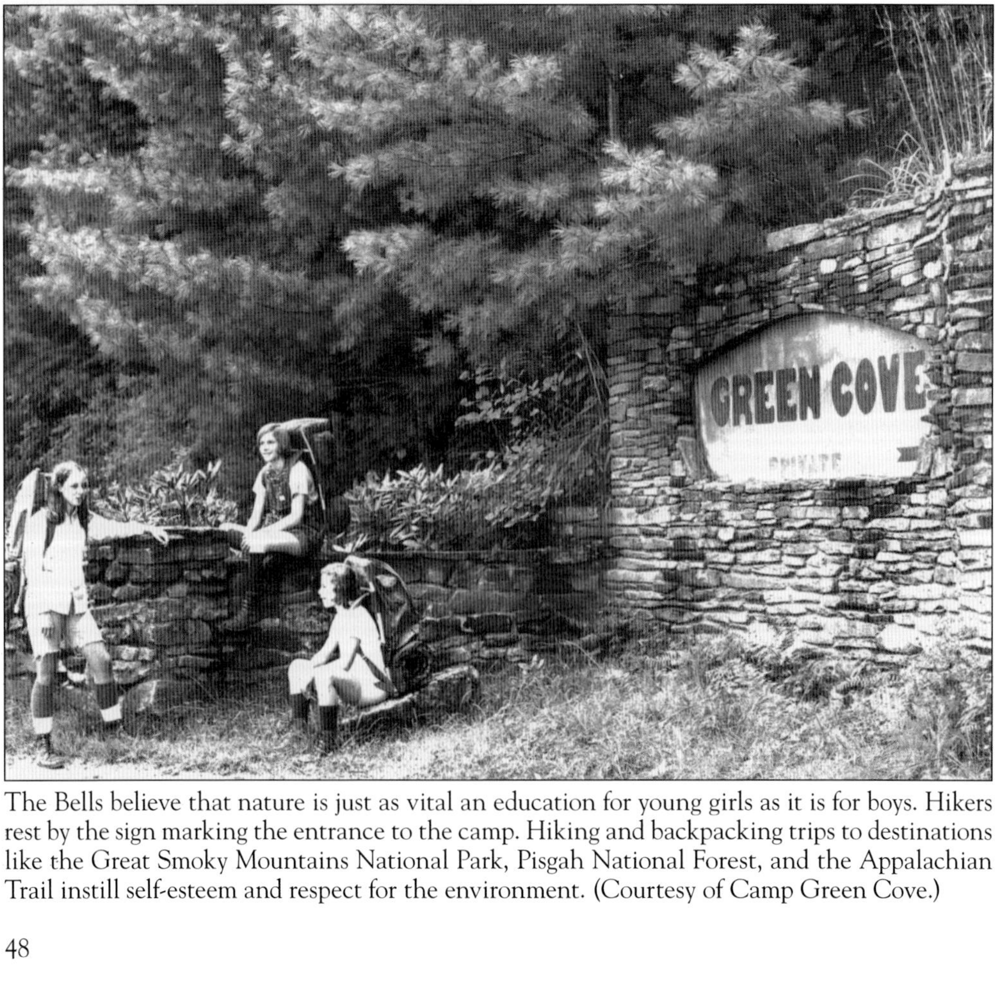

The Bells believe that nature is just as vital an education for young girls as it is for boys. Hikers rest by the sign marking the entrance to the camp. Hiking and backpacking trips to destinations like the Great Smoky Mountains National Park, Pisgah National Forest, and the Appalachian Trail instill self-esteem and respect for the environment. (Courtesy of Camp Green Cove.)

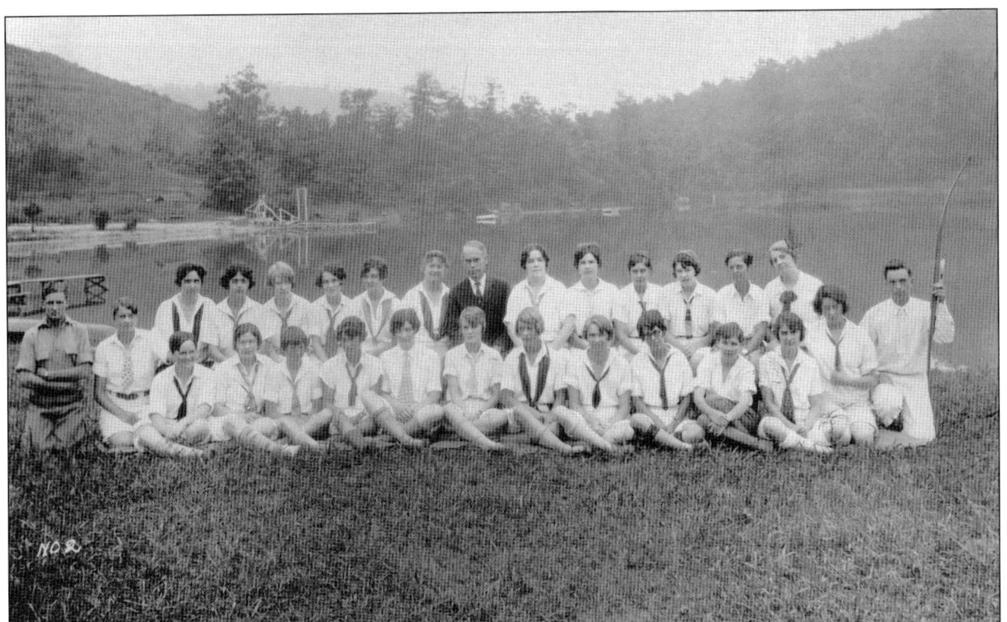

In 1920, Dr. Joseph R. Sevier, a Presbyterian pastor from Augusta, Georgia, and a descendant of Tennessee's first governor, pictured wearing a dark suit, founded Camp Greystone for girls ages 7 to 17. After hearing eyewitness accounts of New England summer camps, Sevier sought to expose girls to the outdoors, where they could have fun and sharpen their athletic skills while growing as Christians. (Courtesy of Camp Greystone.)

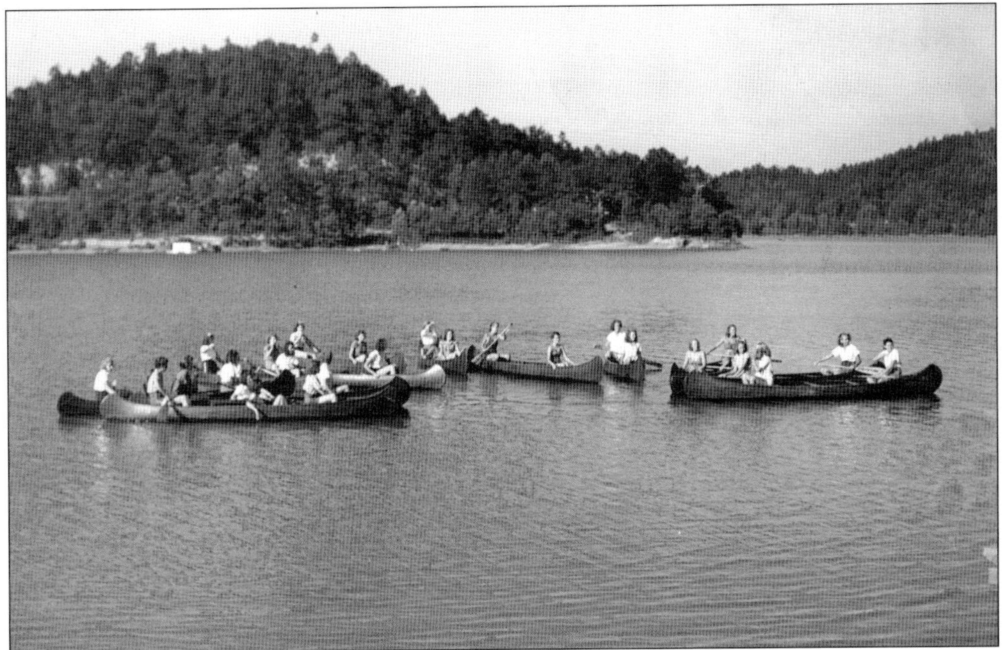

In the era of women's suffrage, bobbed hair, and shorter hemlines, Sevier was concerned about the lack of activities for young women and shocked that in the entire city of Augusta, with a population of 60,000, not one woman knew how to swim. To remedy this, he organized Camp Hickman across the Savannah River in 1919. (Courtesy of Camp Greystone.)

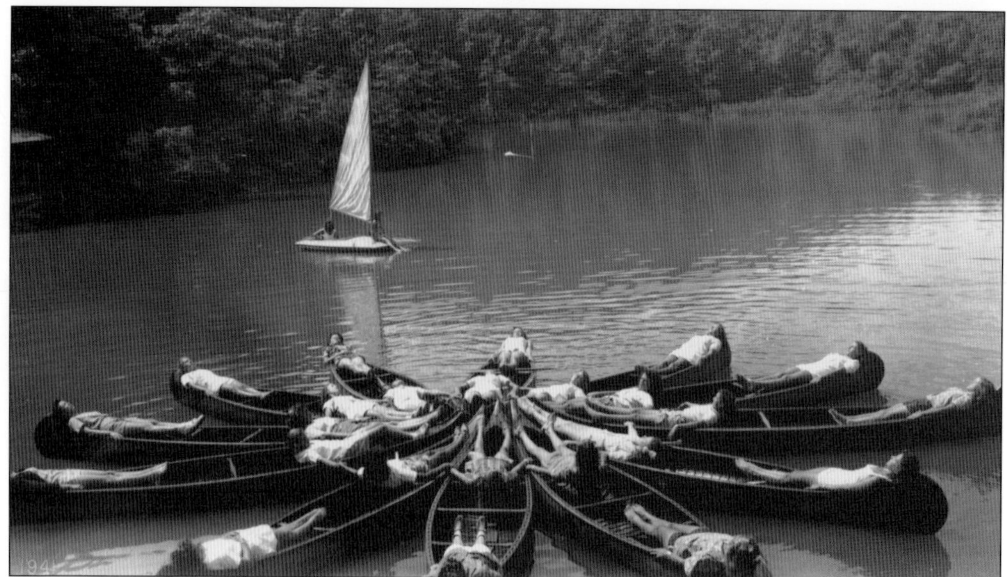

In 1920, Sevier relocated the camp to Greystone Mountain in Tennessee, due to Augusta's heat. Yet, the elevation made the camp too cold. The summit also lacked a lakefront. Sevier spotted Lake Summit on a train to Augusta. When the train stopped at Saluda, he hired a taxi to Tuxedo and purchased 15 acres on the waterfront from mill owner Joseph O. Bell on the spot. (Courtesy of Camp Greystone.)

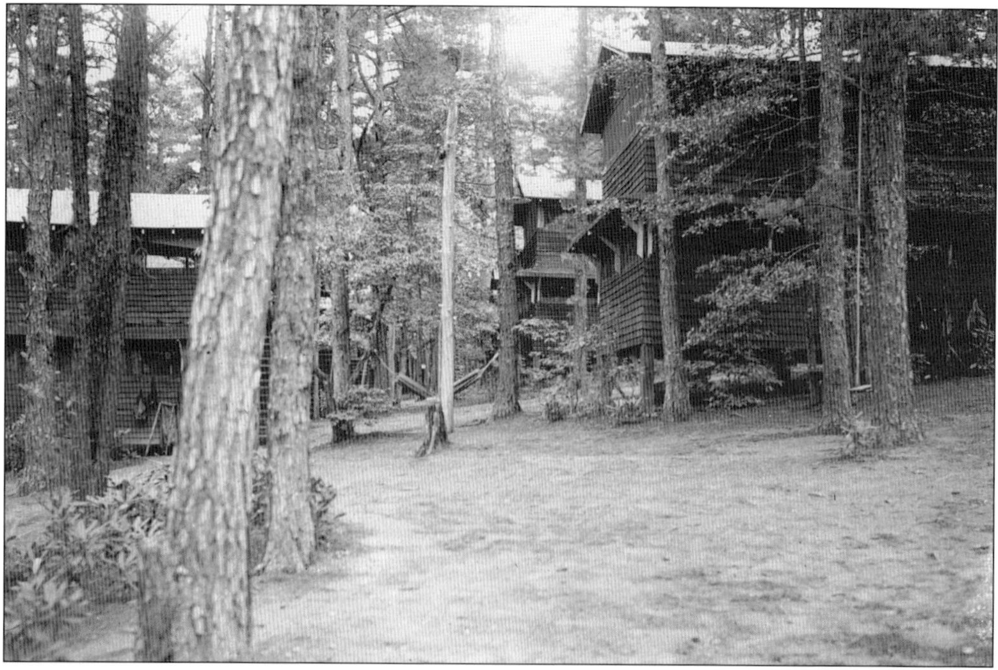

Sevier got to work straightaway preparing the site for the 1922 camping season, and his first priority was constructing camp buildings. He used the lumber from barracks at Camp Sevier, a World War I Army training camp in South Carolina, to build simple two-story cabins, which he called "tentalows," a combination of the words tent and bungalow, to house the campers. (Courtesy of Camp Greystone.)

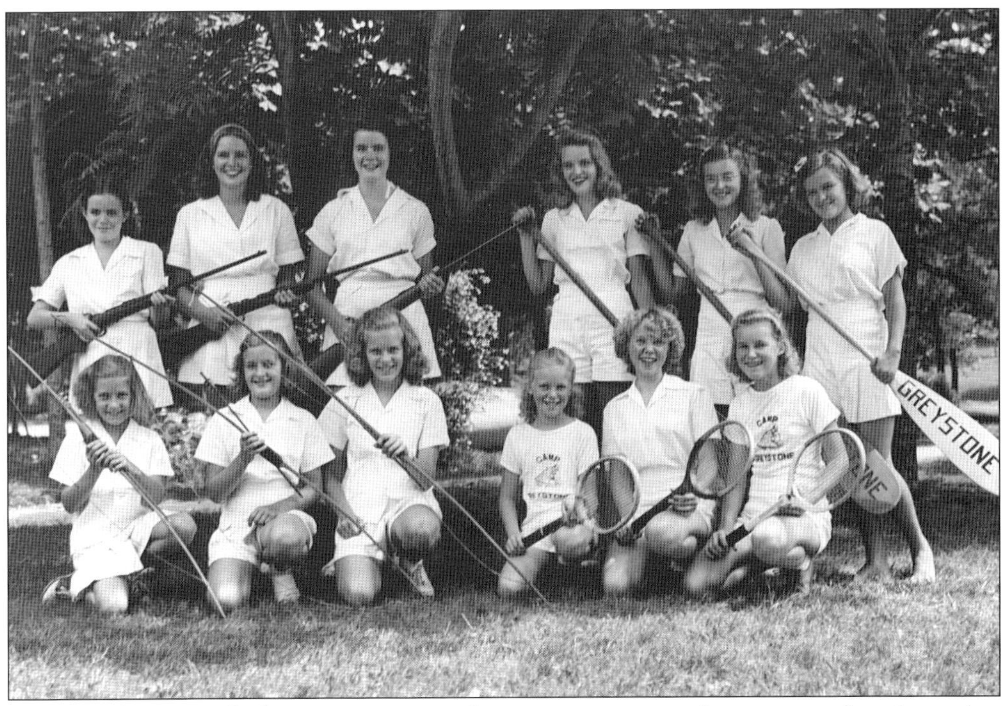

The tentalows were laid out in two rows. Campers in one tentalow competed against other tentalows to encourage teamwork and sportsmanship. (Courtesy of Camp Greystone.)

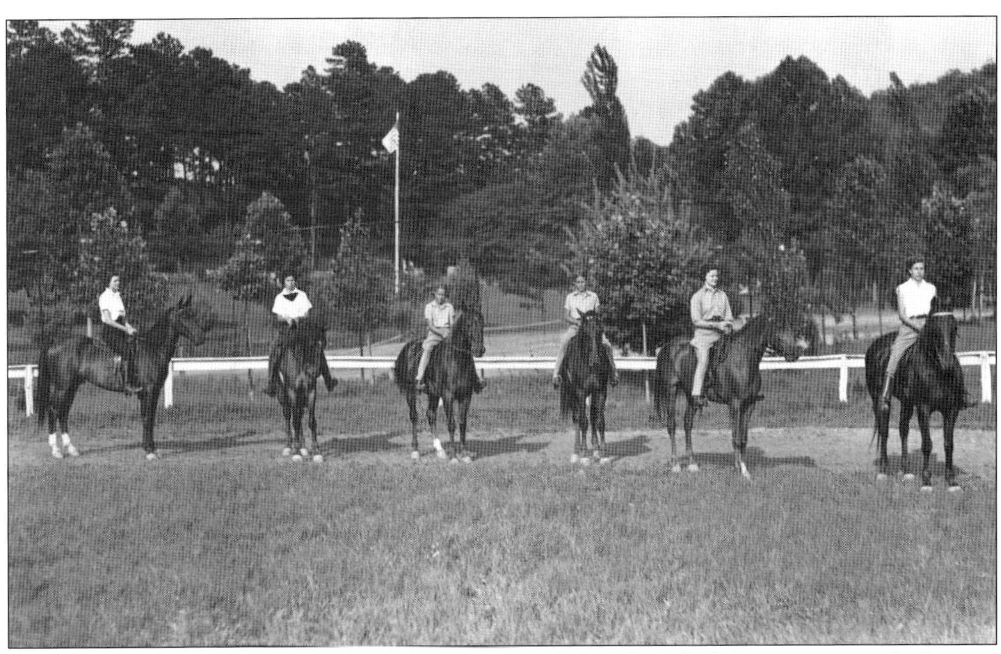

Girls who in the first weeks were clumsy on horseback soon handled their mounts with the ease of seasoned horsewomen after riding at Camp Greystone. (Courtesy of Camp Greystone.)

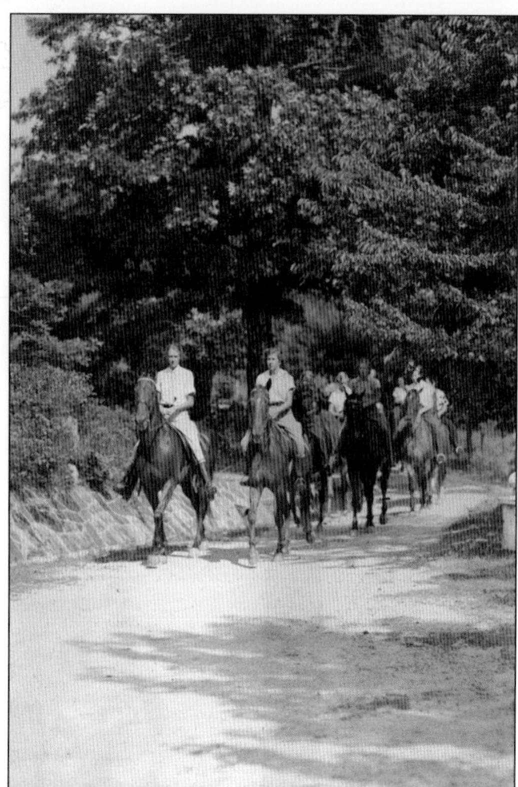

In the first summer, campers took a 10-mile horseback ride to Hendersonville, where they rode down Main Street and stopped at the ice cream parlor and took in a movie. (Courtesy of Camp Greystone.)

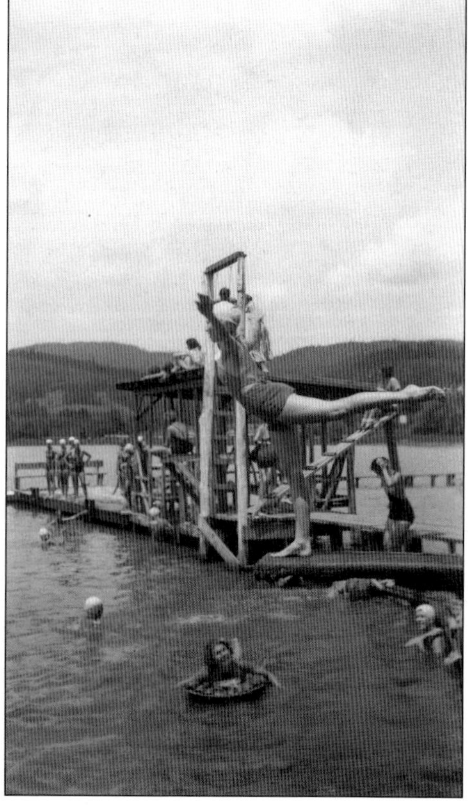

A former Greystone camper recalled, "This place is pure delight—a miracle in the mountains. These days are the closest thing to heaven I can imagine." Girls "blush and learn to be ladies. They put their napkins in their laps and still catch frogs in the afternoon. Here they are alive and full of life." (Courtesy of Camp Greystone.)

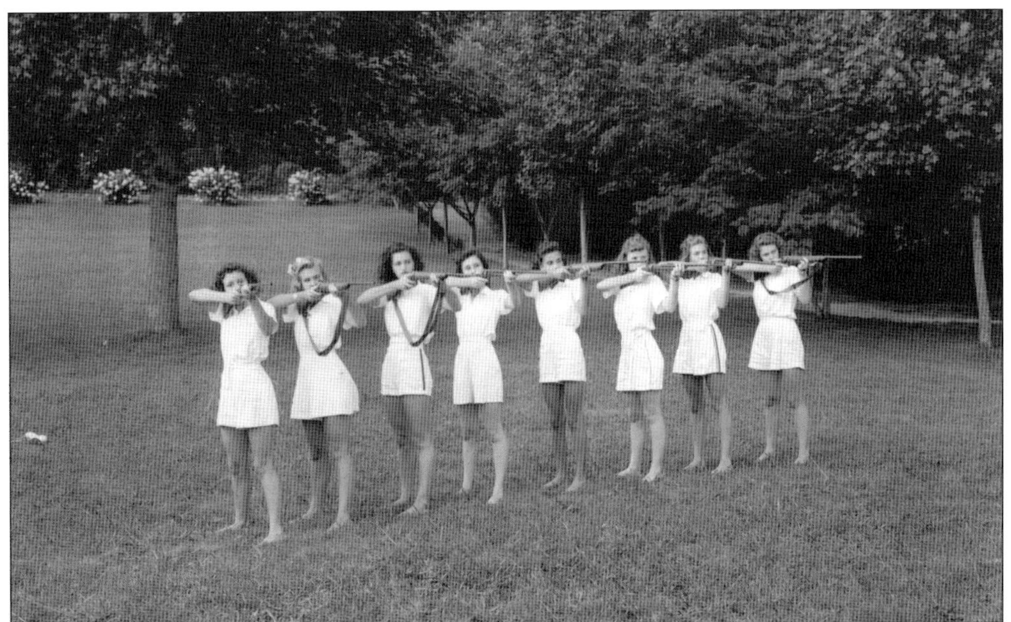

Southerners had long summered in the mountains to escape the heat and yellow fever. In the early 1920s, the influenza epidemic of 1918, which killed more Americans than World War I, was fresh on parents' minds. The fresh air, physical exercise, and nourishing food brought color to young girls' cheeks. (Courtesy of Camp Greystone.)

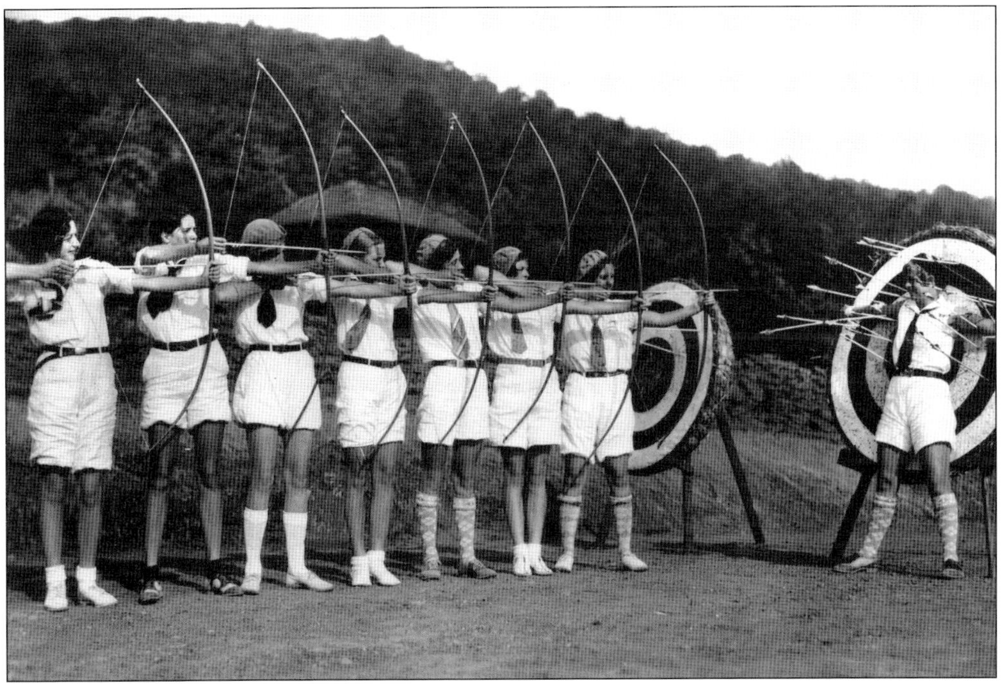

In 1932, a photograph of Camp Greystone's archery exhibition at the Grove Park Inn in Asheville appeared in *Cosmopolitan* magazine. The following year, Fox Movietone shot a newsreel of the archers. As the camp's renown spread, Greystone was the subject of a *Life* magazine feature story in 1941. (Courtesy of Camp Greystone.)

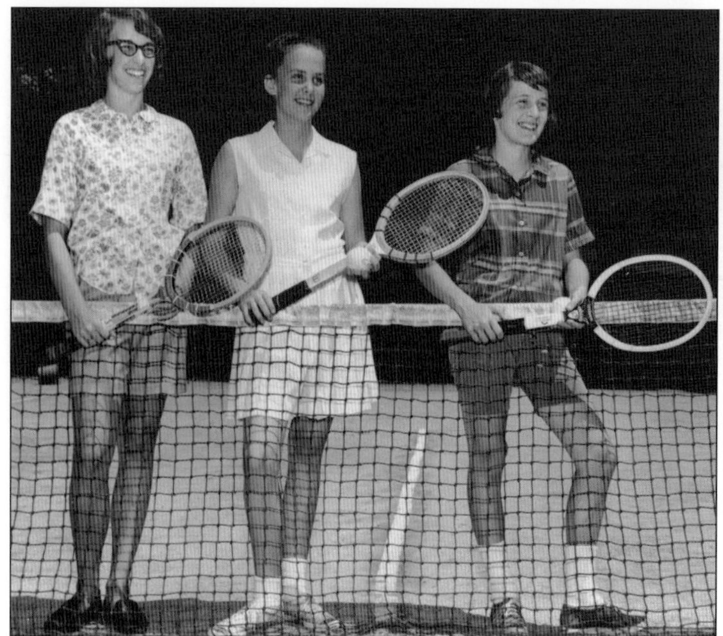

Greystone campers make lasting friendships participating in a wide variety of activities, including water sports, land sports, adventure programs, horseback riding, fine arts, performing arts, and even farming and gardening. (Courtesy of Camp Greystone.)

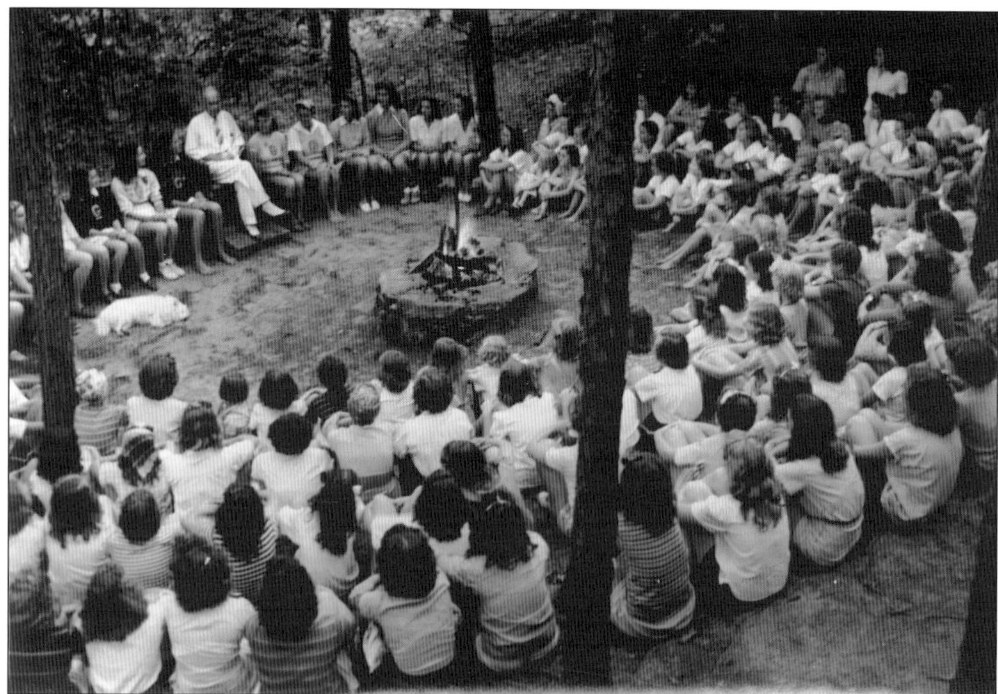

The long-standing ritual of the council fire sparks a flurry of emotions ranging from reverence to excitement for campers. The timing of the fire is a closely guarded secret until the director makes an announcement at supper. Based on the oral tradition of the Bible, the fire is an opportunity for storytelling across generations. The night ends with camp songs and "Taps." (Courtesy of Camp Greystone.)

Four generations of the Sevier family have operated the camp over the years. Sevier's daughter Virginia Sevier Hanna of Spartanburg, South Carolina, assumed the directorship in 1945. Hanna's daughter Libby Miller and her husband, Jim, took over in 1968, and their son Jim "Jimboy" Miller Jr. currently operates the camp. (Courtesy of Camp Greystone.)

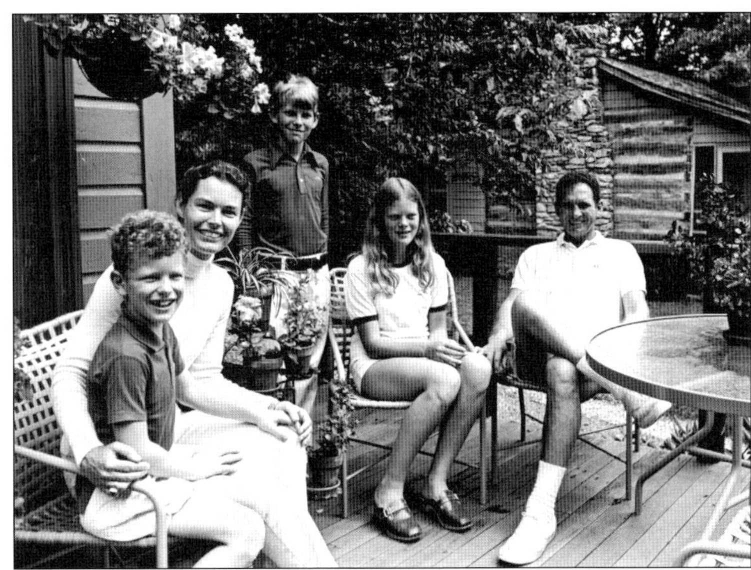

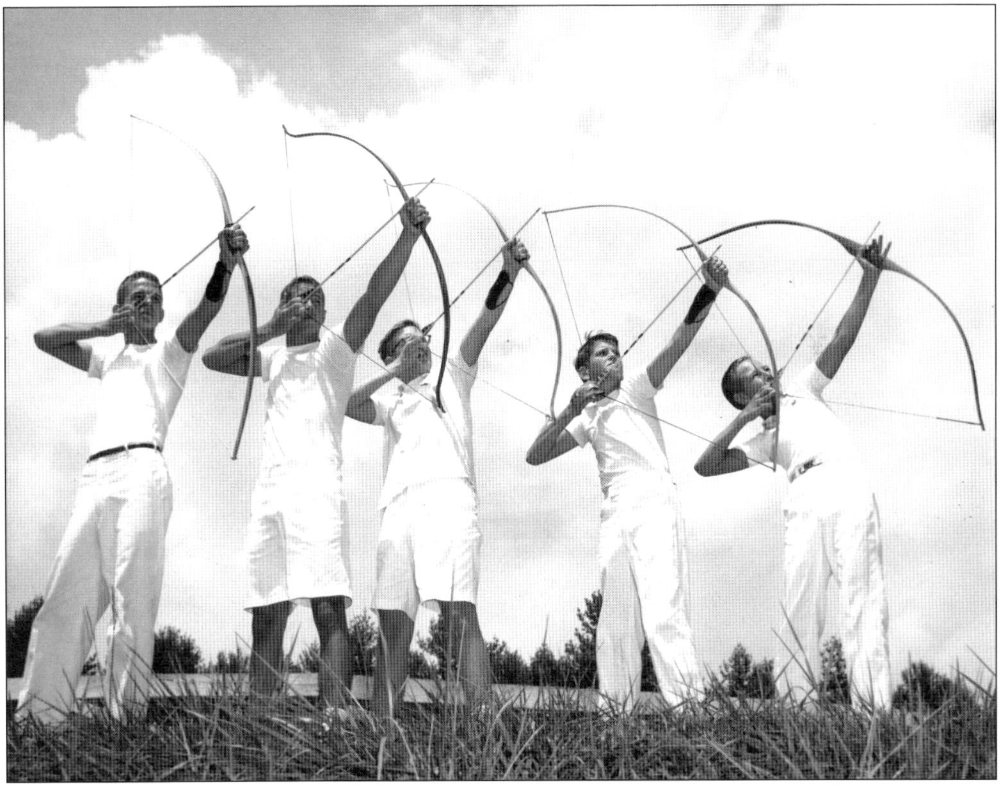

In the summer of 1927, South Carolina high school football coach H.R. Dobson took his team to Wolfe Lake, near Hendersonville, to train for the upcoming football season. The next summer, he founded Camp Pinnacle on the site, so called because it was the highest and the best. Miami businessman Van Kussrow agreed to finance the camp the following year. (Courtesy of Camp Pinnacle.)

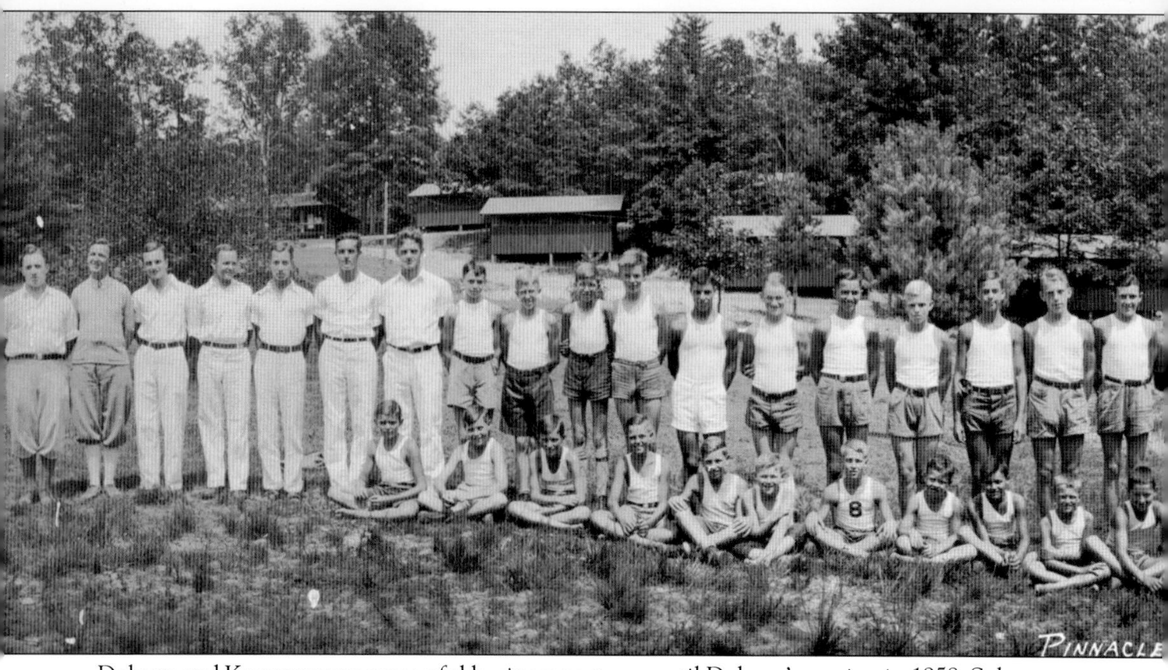

Dobson and Kussrow were successful business partners until Dobson's passing in 1958. Subsequent directors included Walt Cottingham, Roger Smoak, Tom Good, Chappy Hollis, and Glen Gray. Kussrow remained president until his death in 1990 and was succeeded by his son Van C. Kussrow

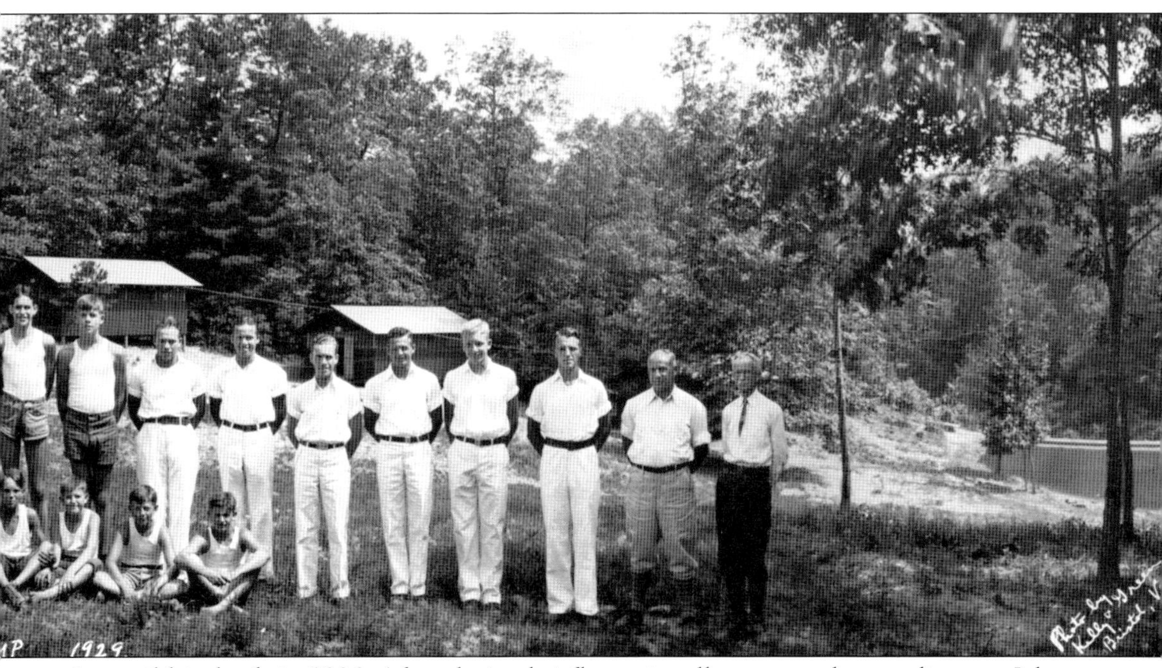

Jr., until his death in 2006. After closing briefly, nationally renowned camp directors John Dockendorf and Steve Baskin reopened Pinnacle in 2011. (Courtesy of Camp Pinnacle.)

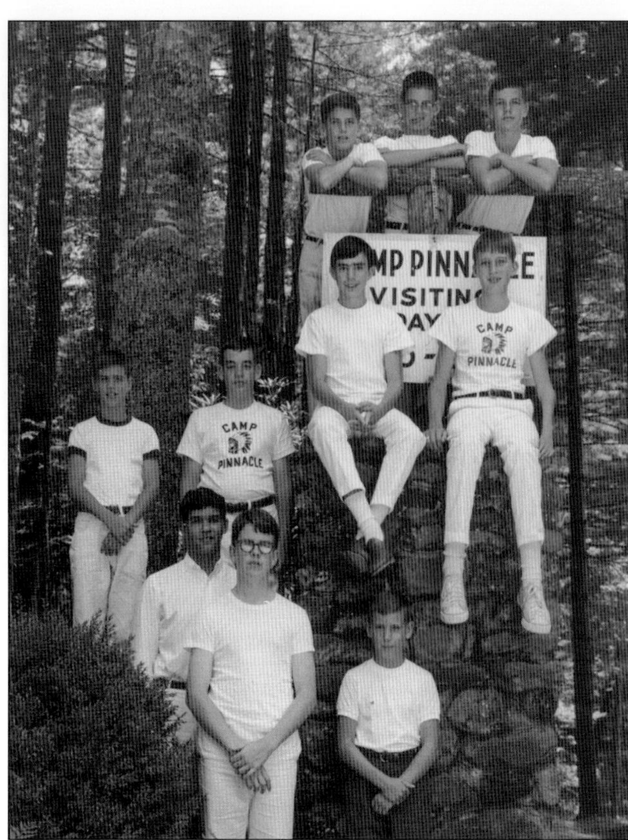

The typical Camp Pinnacle uniform consisted of a stark white shirt and light-colored slacks. (Courtesy of Camp Pinnacle.)

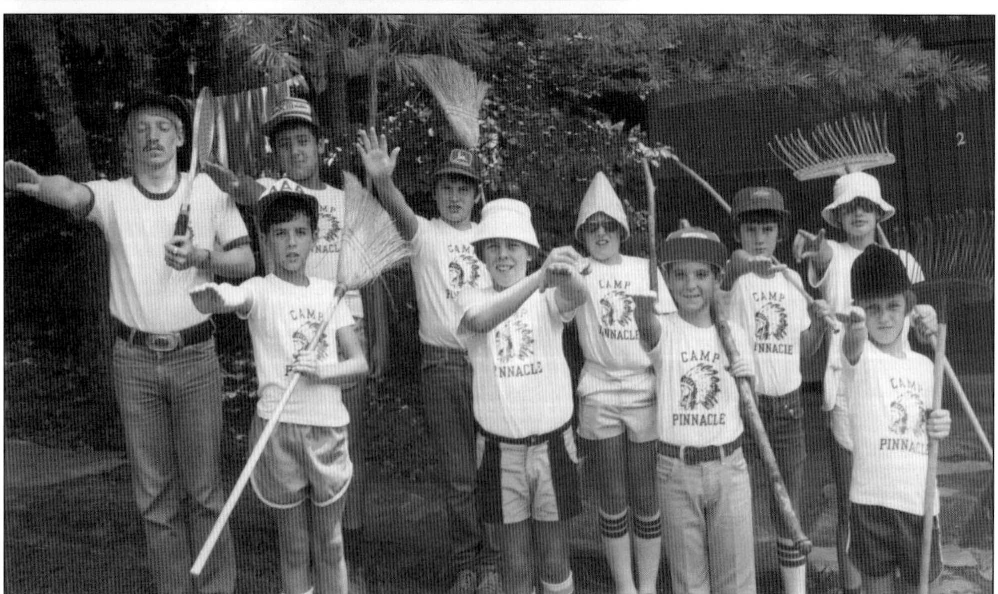

Camp Pinnacle, located on 126 wooded acres on the shores of the 20-acre Wolfe Lake between Little River and Crab Creek Roads, offered a range of activities, including swimming, boating, sports, arts and crafts, mountain biking, and climbing, allowing boys to build confidence, improve social skills, develop new abilities, and, foremost, have fun. (Courtesy of Camp Pinnacle.)

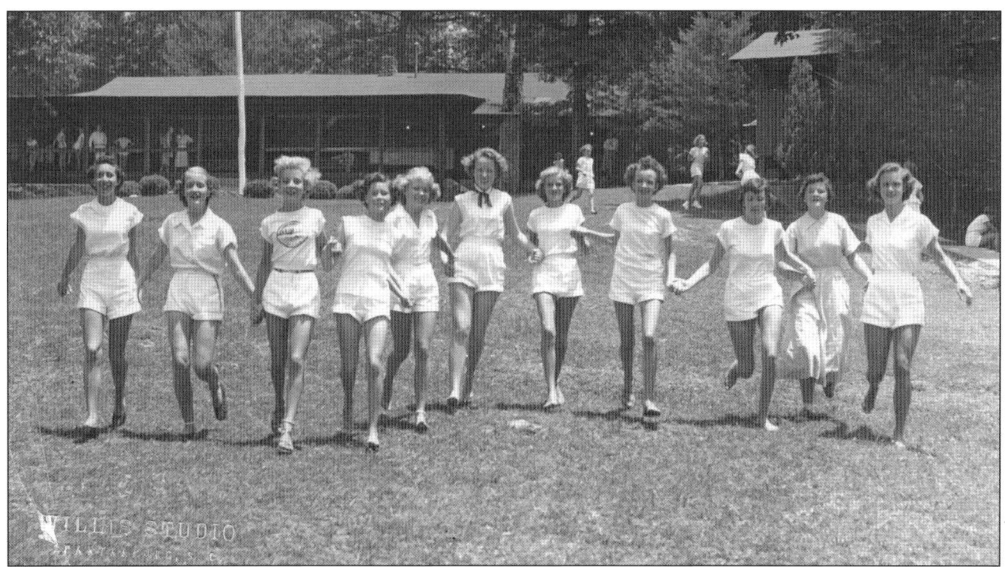

In 1931, Camp Pinnacle began a camp for girls directed by Dobson's wife, Laura Mae. Other directors included Francis Major, Nelle Carr, Beth Blackwell, Mary Lanier, Linda Reeves, and Jean Cochran. (Courtesy of Camp Pinnacle.)

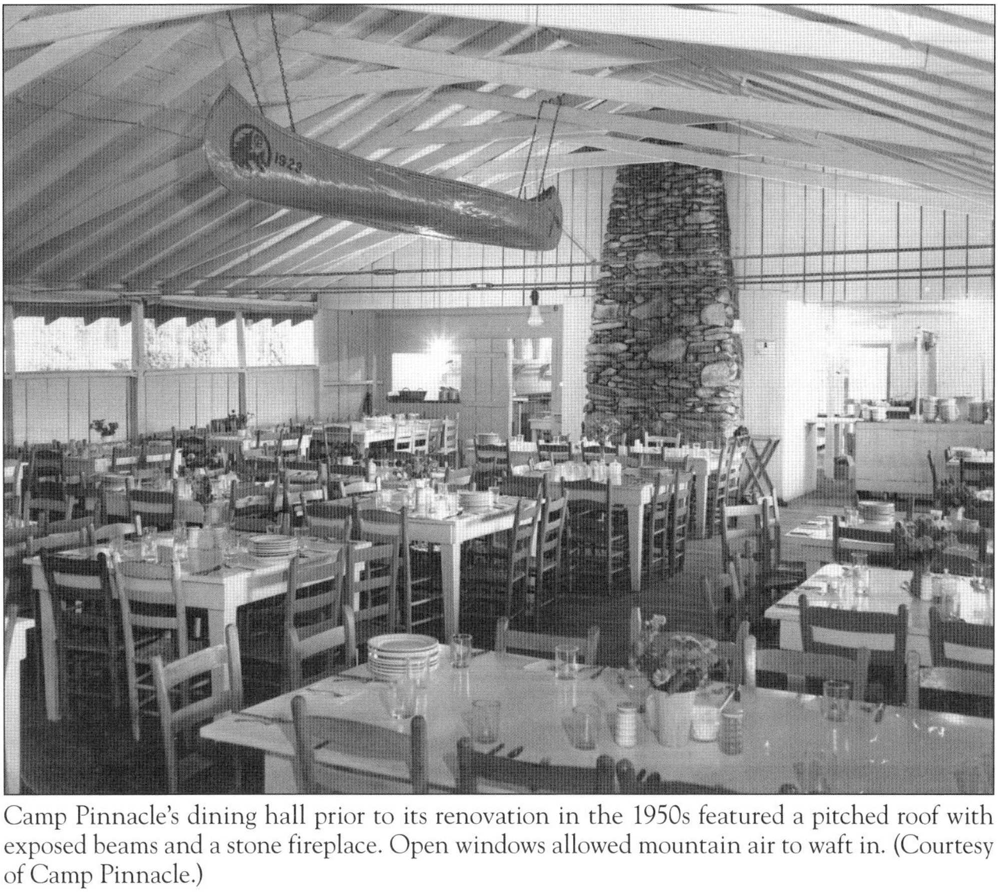

Camp Pinnacle's dining hall prior to its renovation in the 1950s featured a pitched roof with exposed beams and a stone fireplace. Open windows allowed mountain air to waft in. (Courtesy of Camp Pinnacle.)

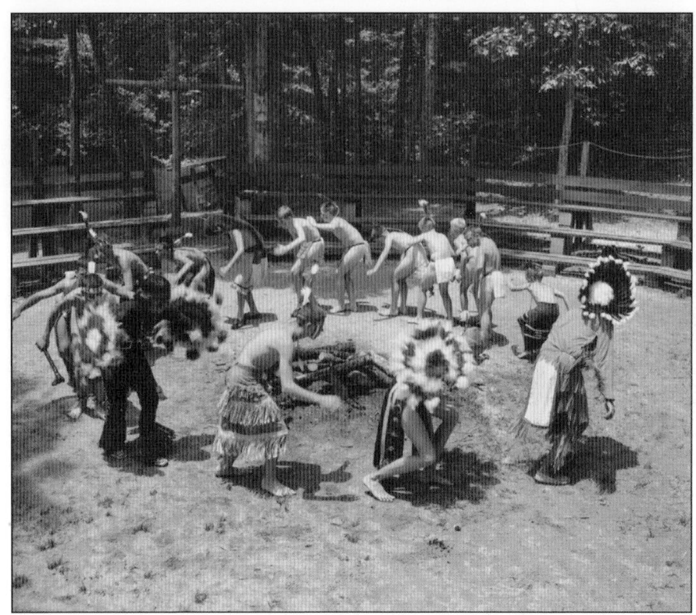

Like many camps founded in the 1920s, Camp Pinnacle incorporated Native American rituals and motifs influenced by Ernest Thompson Seton's Woodcraft Indian movement, such as council rings, tepees, and Native American dance. "Playing Indian" was commonplace among white children in the 20th century. Early-20th-century psychologist G. Stanley Hall theorized that children progressed through developmental stages from savagery to civilization. (Courtesy of Camp Pinnacle.)

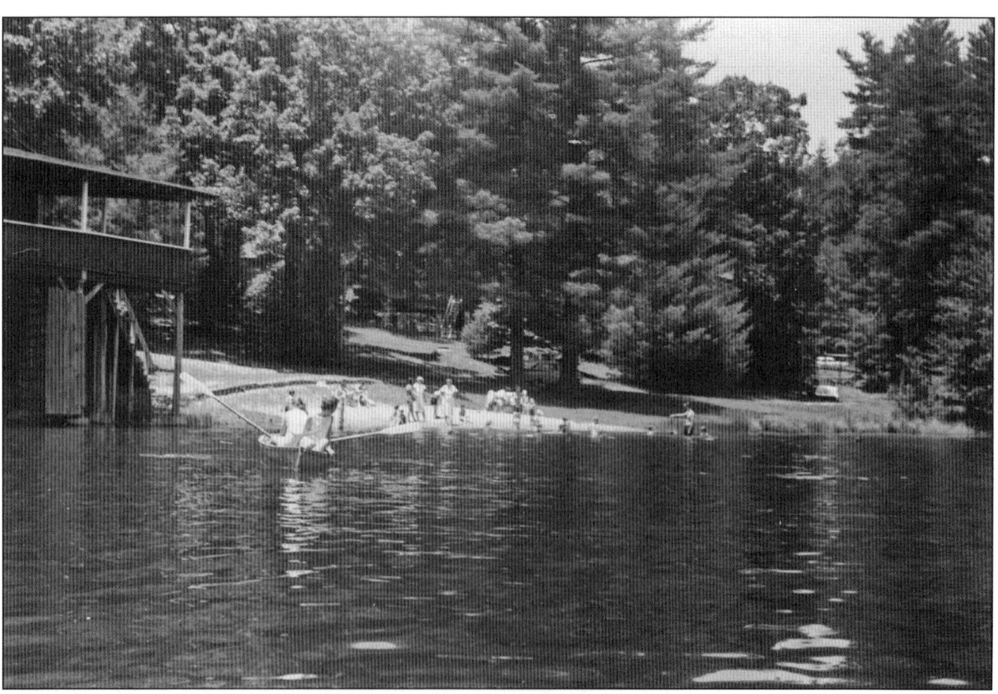

In 1909, George Stephens, a Charlotte banker, real estate mogul, and newspaperman, purchased 950 acres in Henderson County for a summer resort. He dammed Mud Creek to create a 100-acre lake and hired nationally renowned landscape designer John Nolen and architect Richard Sharp Smith to design the Kanuga Lake Club. Kanuga survived the flood of 1916 and four bankruptcies before the Episcopal Church purchased it in 1928. (Courtesy of Camp Kanuga.)

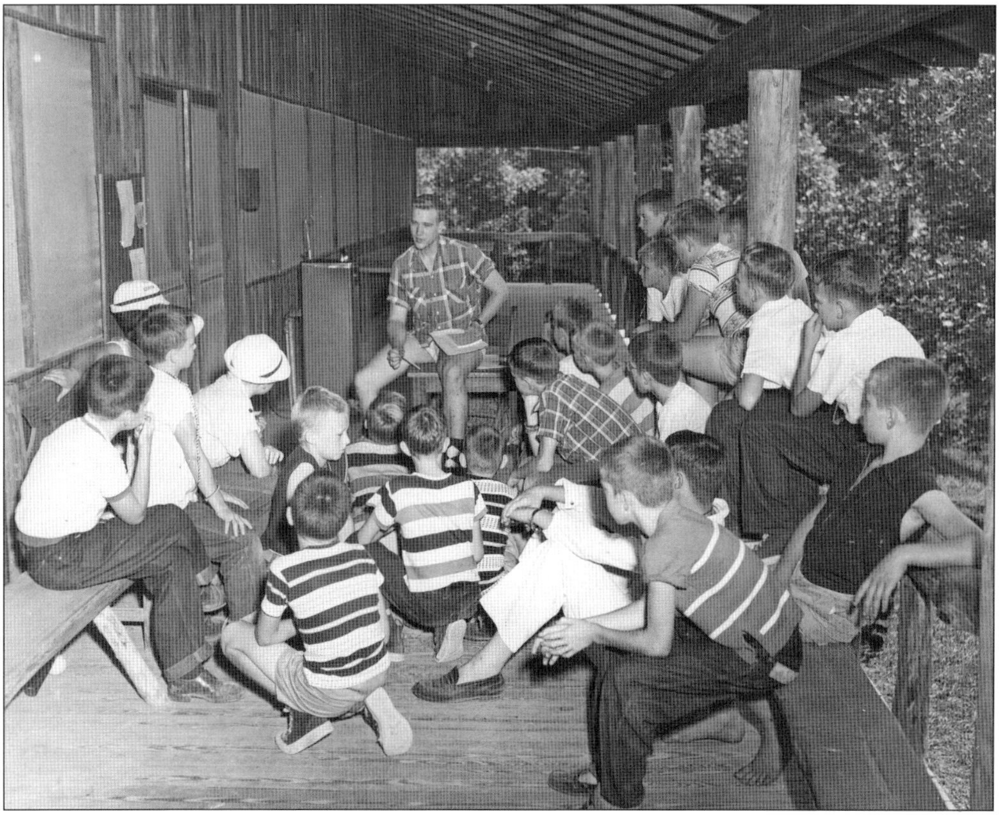

The Episcopal Church acquired Kanuga for religious and education programs and added a boys' camp in 1931. When a new camp opened on the east side of the property in 1968, the original facility became a camp for girls. The two camps merged in the early 1970s. (Courtesy of Camp Kanuga.)

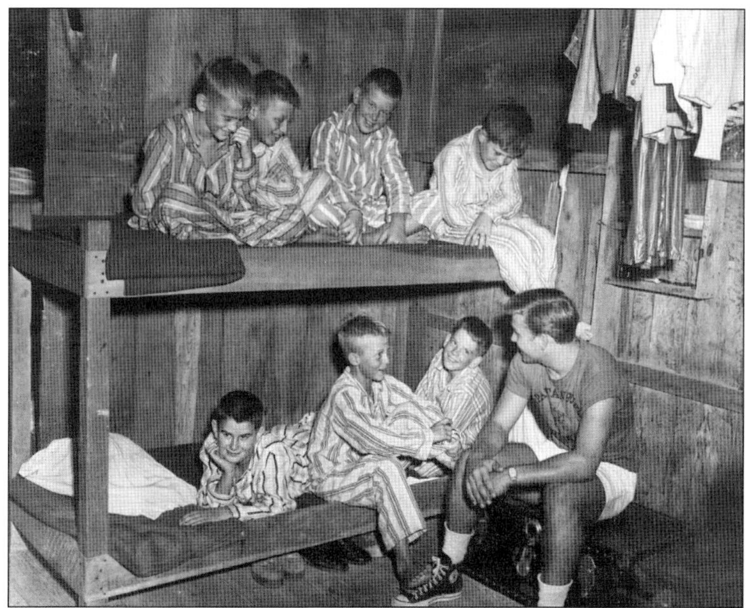

Kanuga's campers are assigned to cabins by age, grade level, and sex. (Courtesy of Camp Kanuga.)

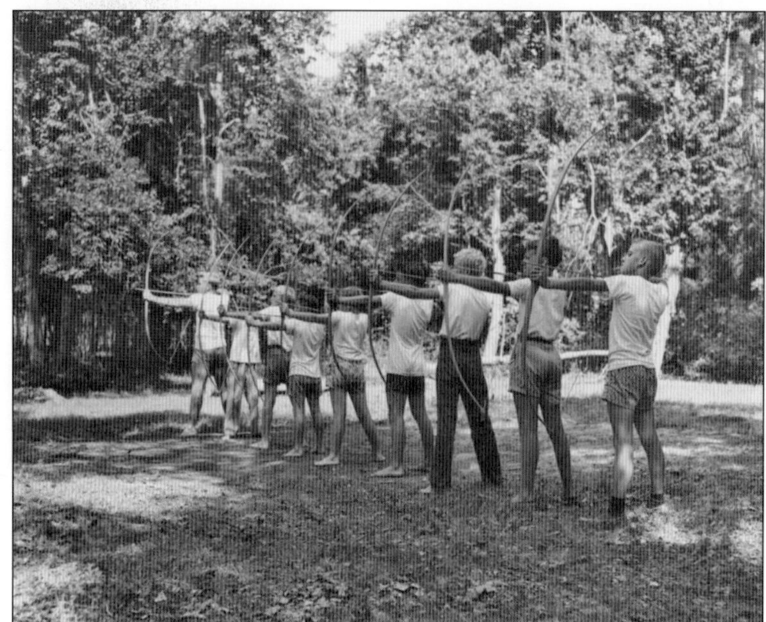

Camp Kanuga offers a traditional camp program of archery, swimming, boating, handicrafts, hiking, camping out, cooking out, and fishing, along with worship. (Courtesy of Camp Kanuga.)

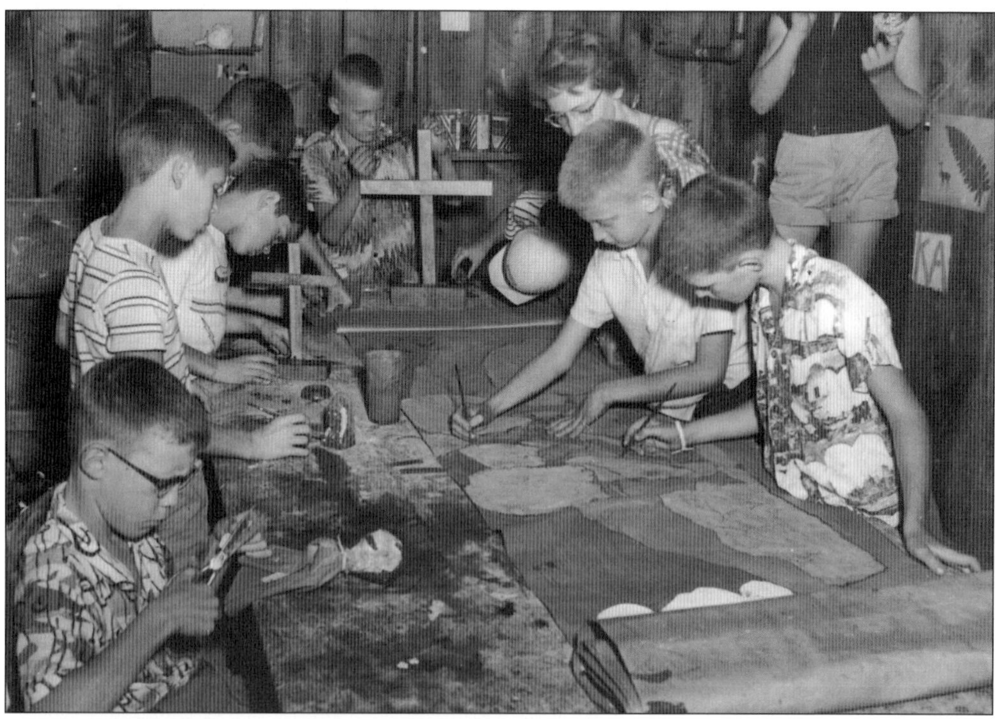

Camp Kanuga was just one of the religiously affiliated camps in Henderson County, which historically included the Camp Tekoa, Our Lady of the Hills, Bonclarken, Fruitland Baptist Camp, Blue Star Camp, Camp Judaea, and Nazarene Camp, among others. In this 1950s photograph, campers make crosses in the crafts cabin. (Courtesy of Camp Kanuga.)

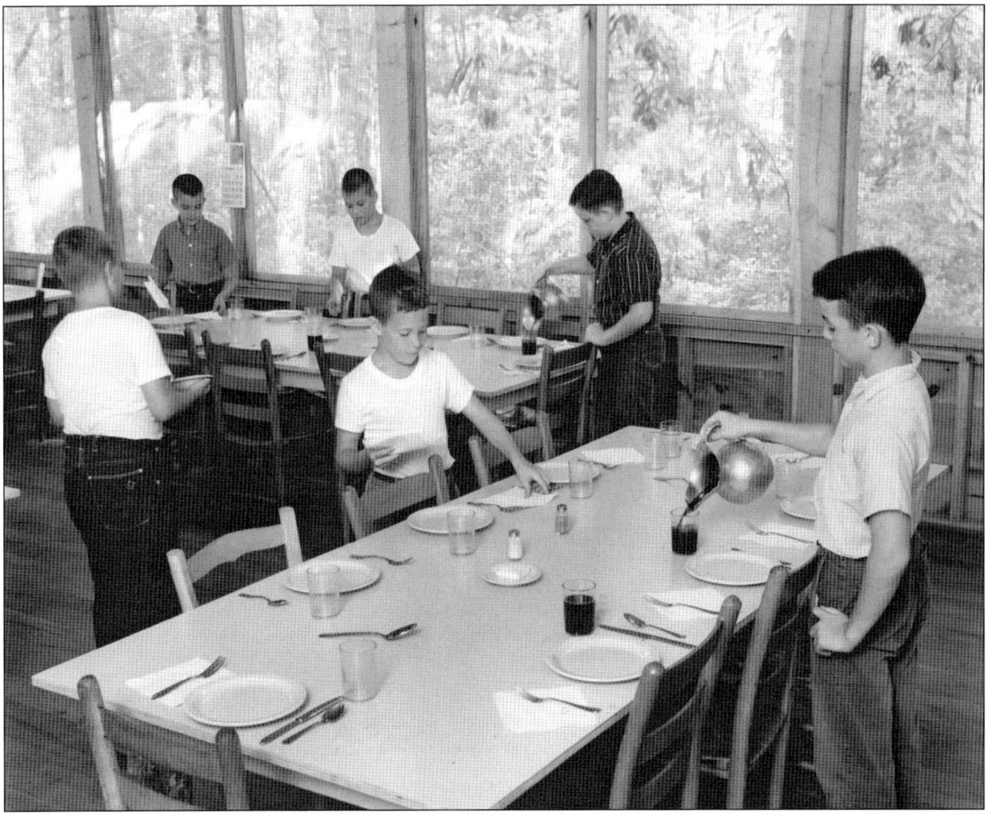

Campers partook of "Kanuga Toast" in the dining hall. The legendary toast gave "breaking bread" a new meaning. Cooks toasted white bread until it was completely dry and so hard, it shattered when picked up to butter. Although some joked that one could play Frisbee with it, the kitchen once made 500 slices a day during the height of summer. (Courtesy of Camp Kanuga.)

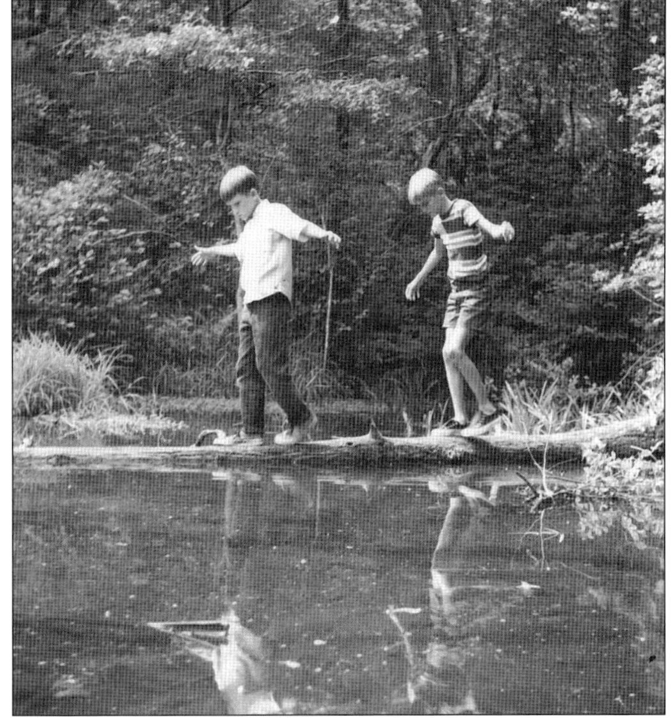

In 1998, Kanuga founded Camp Bob on the site of the historic camp, to provide a summer camp experience for disadvantaged youth, thanks to the financial support of more than 20 churches and other organizations throughout the Southeast. (Courtesy of Camp Kanuga.)

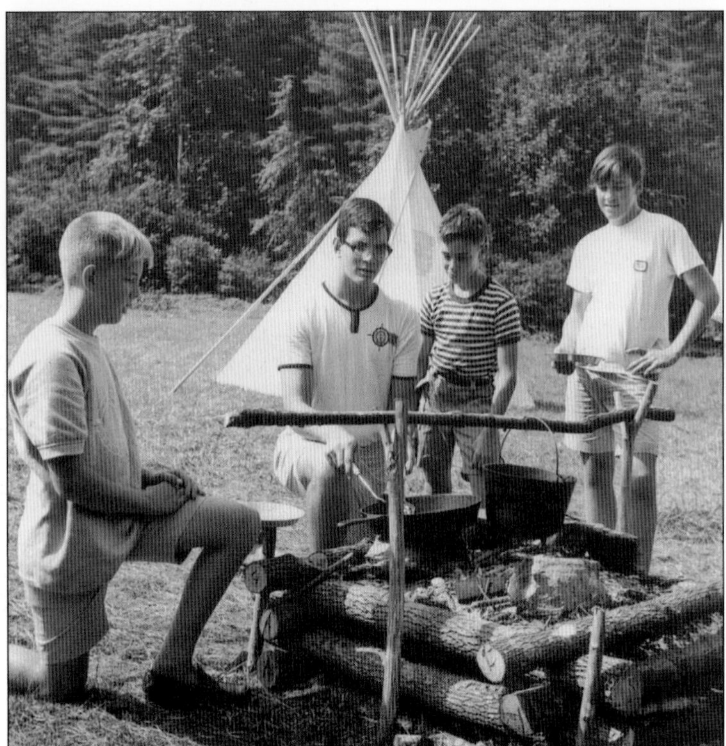

Located on the lakefront, Camp Kanuga also encompasses over 1,000 acres of woodlands and a playing field. (Courtesy of Camp Kanuga.)

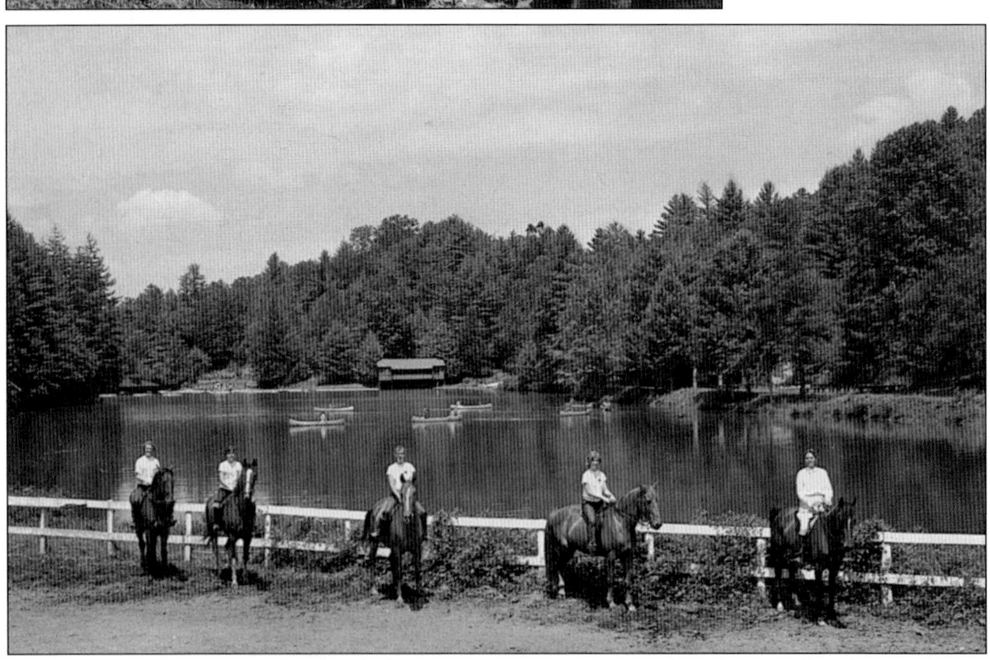

In the midst of the Great Depression in 1933, Dottie Haynes, a widowed schoolteacher from Spartanburg, South Carolina, founded Camp Ton-a-Wandah for girls near Flat Rock. The name means "by the fall of water," and the camp features a crystal-clear lake, streams, and its own waterfall. The dining hall is even built right over the lake, and campers dine to the soothing sound of flowing water. (Courtesy of Camp Ton-a-Wandah.)

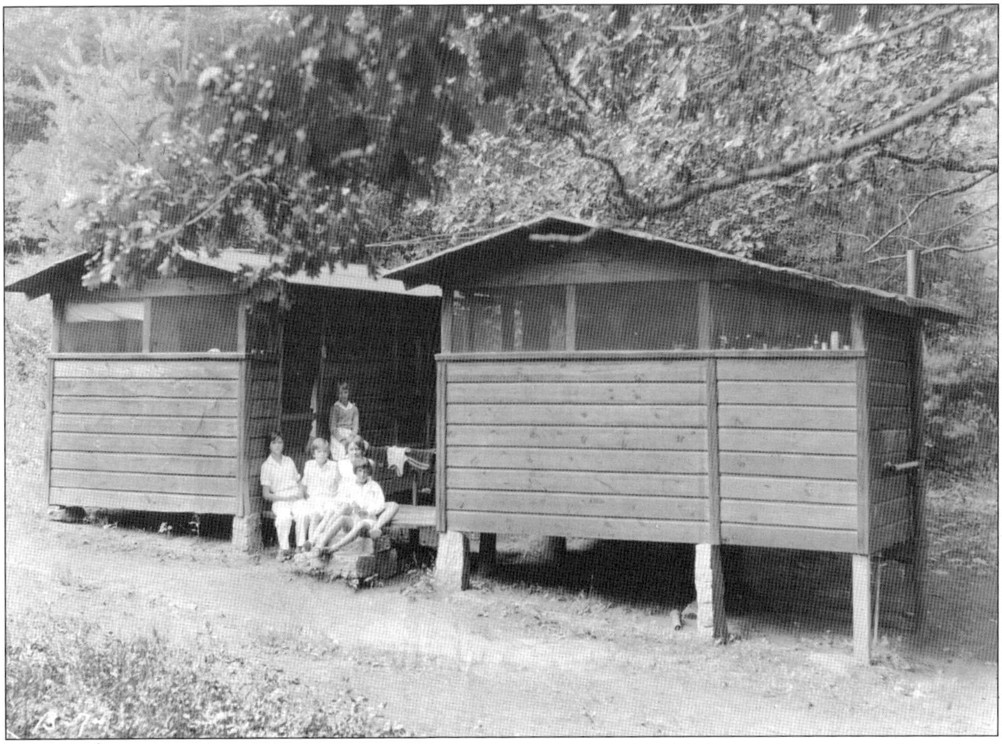

Camp Ton-a-Wandah's mountainous setting at an elevation of 2,500 feet and rustic wooden cabins instilled a reverence for nature in the girls. The camp's creed espoused: "I believe in the whisper of leaves, the strength of the trees, the call of birds, the inspiration of towering mountains and in every great lesson nature teaches." (Courtesy of Camp Ton-a-Wandah.)

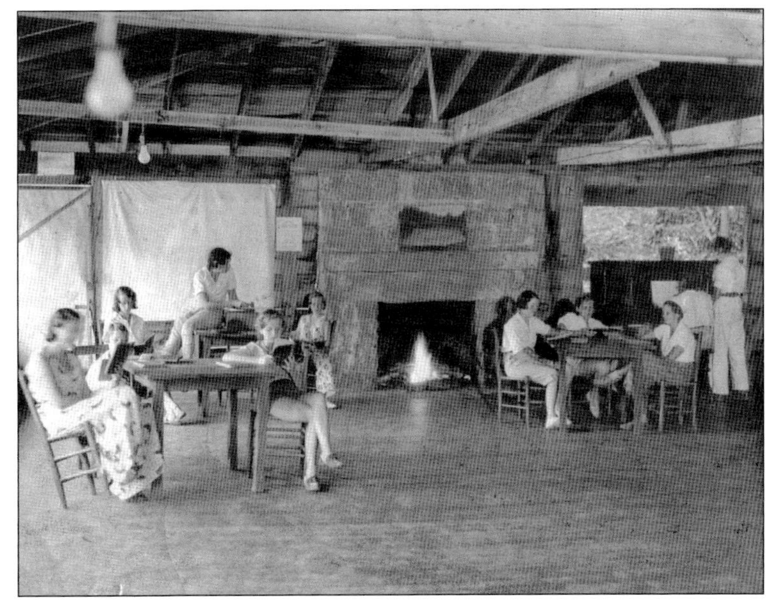

Three generations of the Haynes family have owned and operated Camp Ton-a-Wandah for girls ages 6 to 15. In addition to emphasizing character building, community, sportsmanship, work, and fun, the camp gives the girls moments of silence "to question her soul and find herself." (Courtesy of Camp Ton-a-Wandah.)

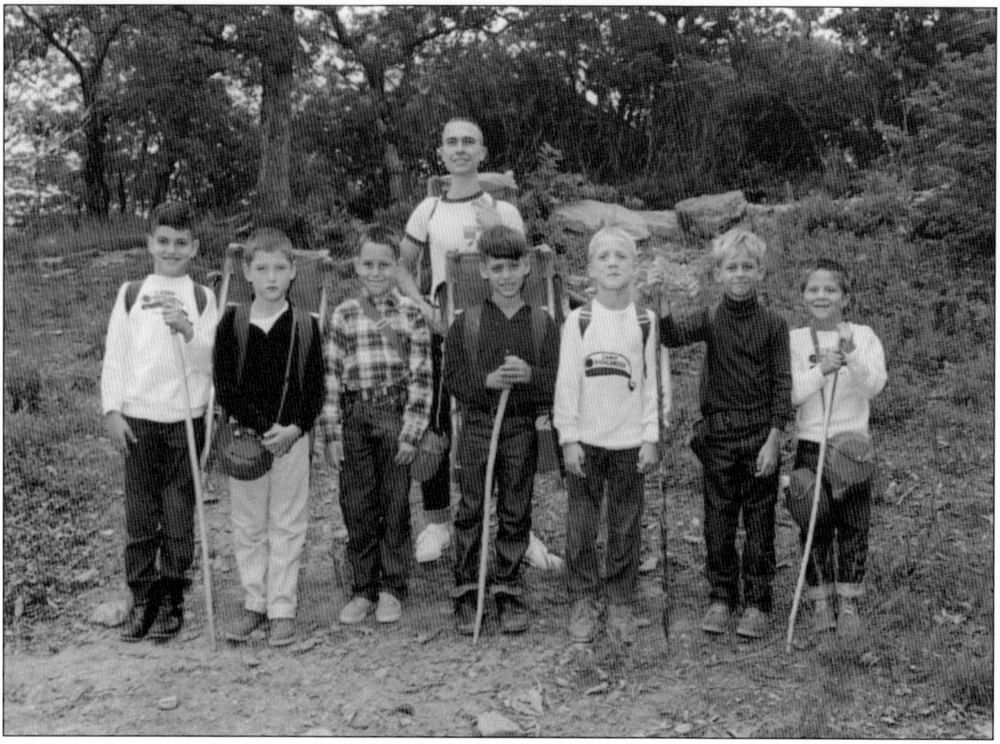

High school coach Ben Wax and his wife, Polly, founded an after-school program and day camp for boys in their hometown of Baton Rouge, Louisiana. In 1957, they purchased the former girls' camp, Camp Parrydice, in Highlands, North Carolina, and renamed it Camp Highlander. It was an all-boys' camp until the early 1960s and was relocated to Old Forge Mountain in Mills River in 1968. (Courtesy of Camp Highlander.)

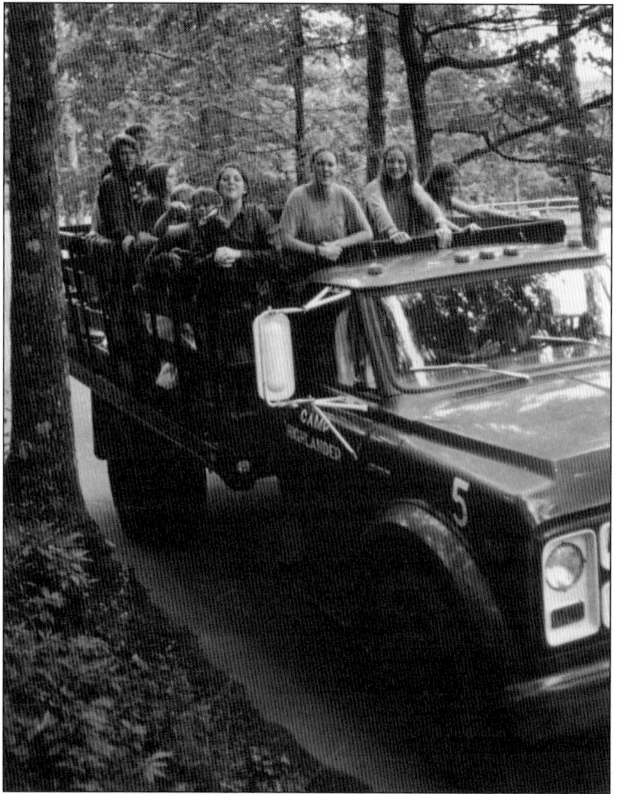

Campers take off-site trips to explore the great outdoors, including Sliding Rock in Pisgah National Forest, whitewater rafting on the Nantahala River, and hiking the Appalachian Trail. (Courtesy of Camp Highlander.)

Floating in the clouds at an elevation of 4,200 feet at its original location in Highlands, Camp Highlander lived up to its motto of being "a place like no other." With fog not breaking until noon, each day began with four bell tolls to signify the values of courage, honesty, integrity, and faith. This tradition continues at the camp today. (Courtesy of Camp Highlander.)

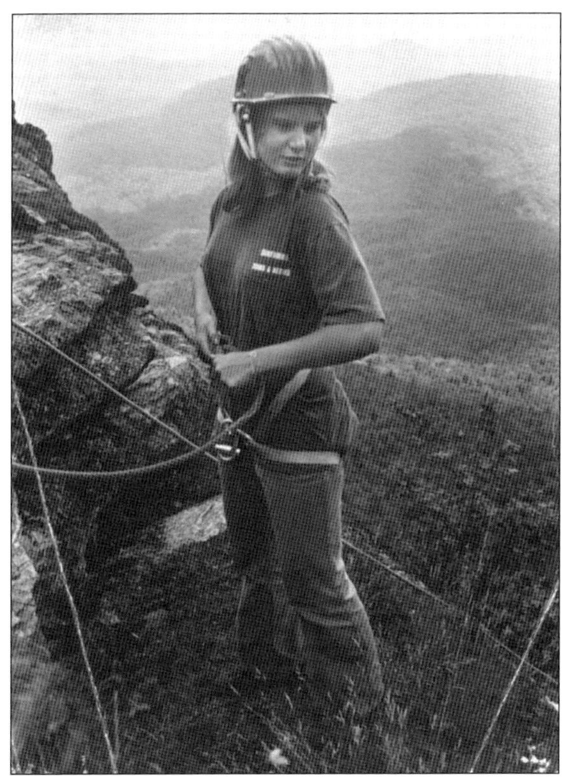

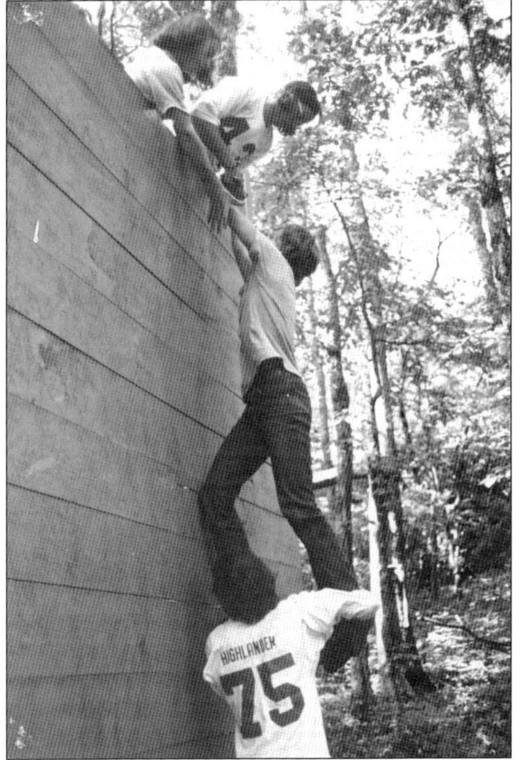

The staff divides campers into cabin unit groups. The units provide an encouraging environment for campers as they face challenges and accomplish individual goals through a range of activities, including wilderness activities, overnight camping, arts and crafts, theater, horseback riding, and water and land sports. The units participate in popular camp-wide games such as Elephant Ball; Dwarfs, Wizards, and Giants; and Bombardment. (Courtesy of Camp Highlander.)

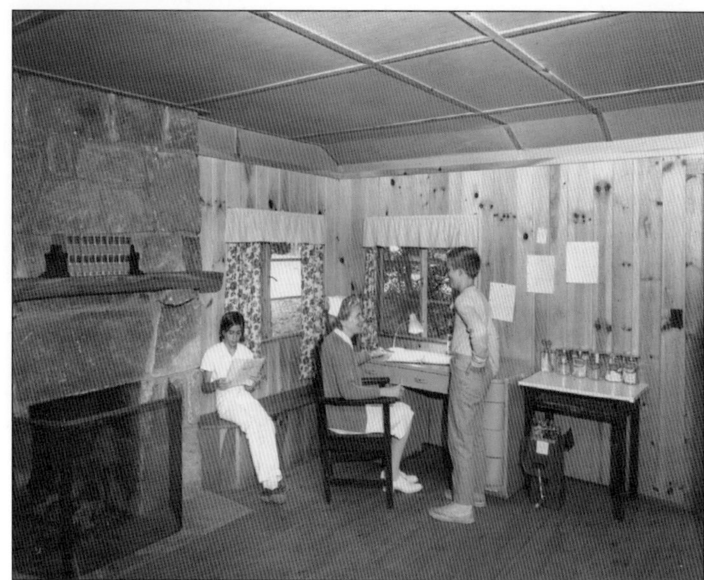

Trained and certified staff serve as role models and mentors for campers at Camp Highlander, ensuring their safety, well being, skill development, and personal growth. The majority of the staff were former campers themselves. (Courtesy of Camp Highlander.)

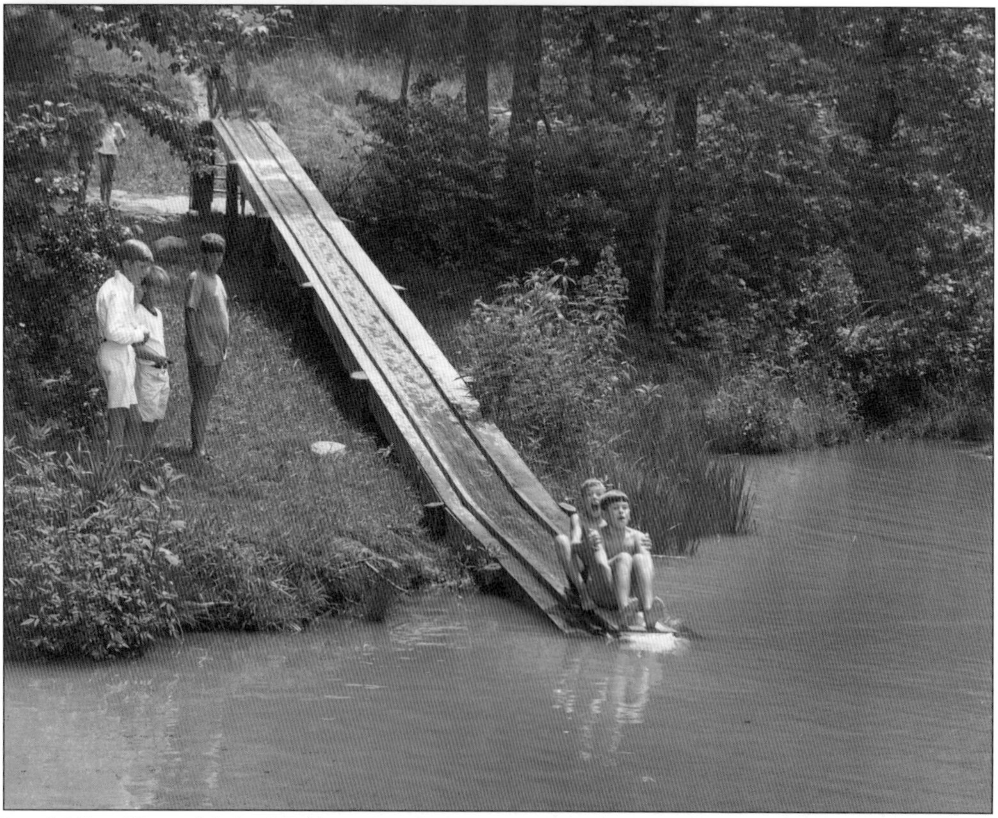

Jim Miller III established Falling Creek Camp near Tuxedo, North Carolina, in 1969. The Christian camp for boys was meant to serve as the brother camp for the girls' Camp Greystone, which Miller also directed. The property, with an elevation of roughly 3,000 feet, features two spring-fed lakes with diving boards, docks, a zip line, and a unique slide, pictured here. (Courtesy of Falling Creek Camp.)

Miller left a successful business career to work full time with youth as the director of Camp Sequoyah and later Camp Greystone with his wife, Libby Hanna Miller, before founding Falling Creek Camp to instill boys with abiding virtues like loyalty and good sportsmanship in a changing world. He sought to "build character and develop the finest leaders of the future from the young men of today." (Courtesy of Falling Creek Camp.)

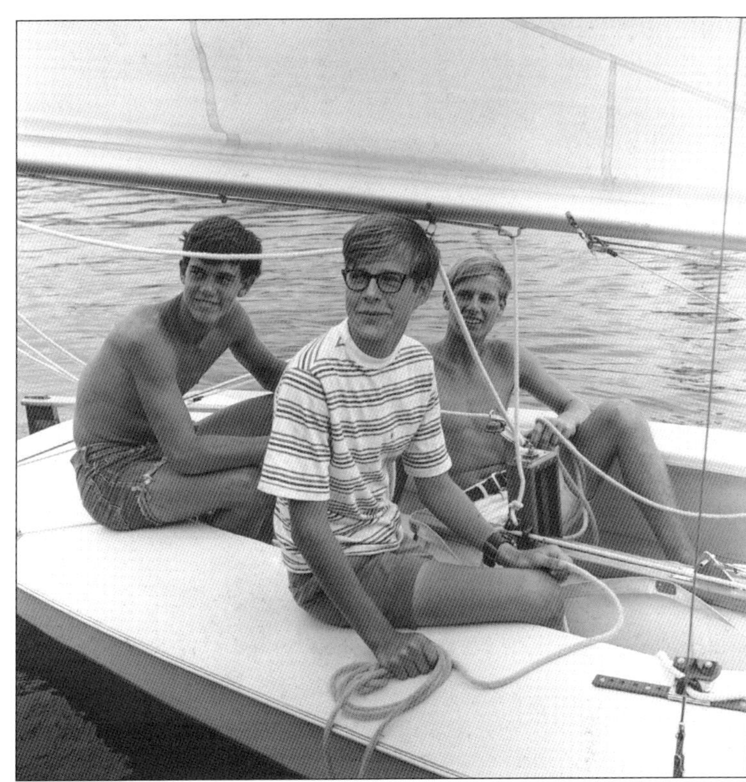

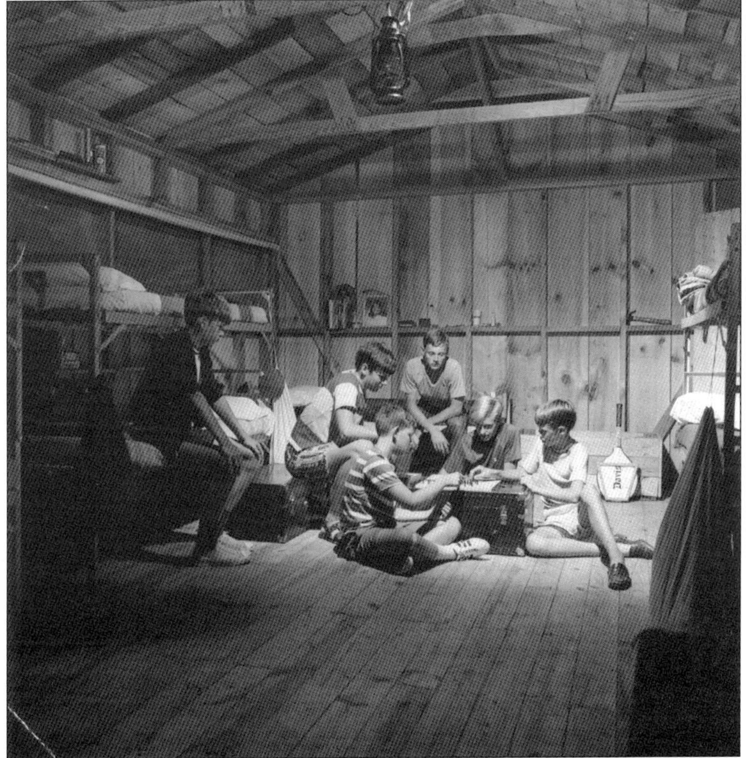

At Falling Creek Camp, "Boys make new friends and learn the secret of keeping them through life. They learn how to live with other boys and learn the give and take of life," according to the 1969 camp brochure. (Courtesy of Falling Creek Camp.)

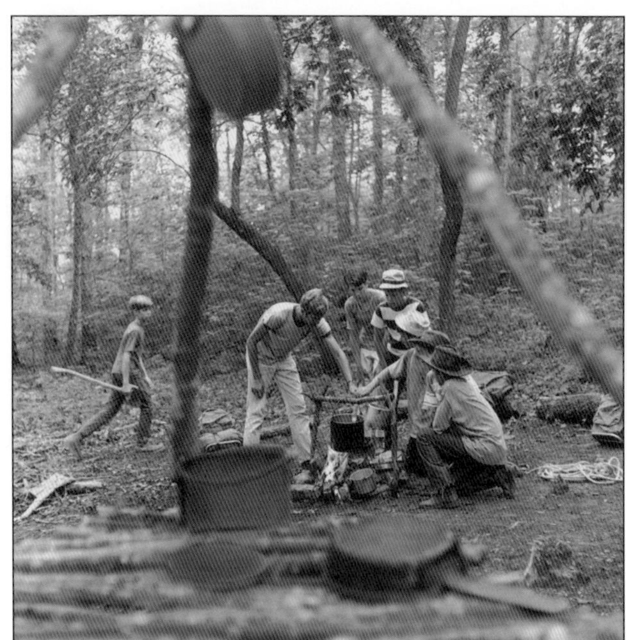

Falling Creek Camp's over 500 undisturbed woodland acres provide an ideal setting for teaching and practicing woodcraft and wilderness skills. Activities including backpacking, hiking, overnight camping, and trail riding offered ample opportunity for Boy Scouts to earn merit badges. Today, the camp's expedition trips extend these outdoor adventures out West and abroad. (Courtesy of Falling Creek Camp.)

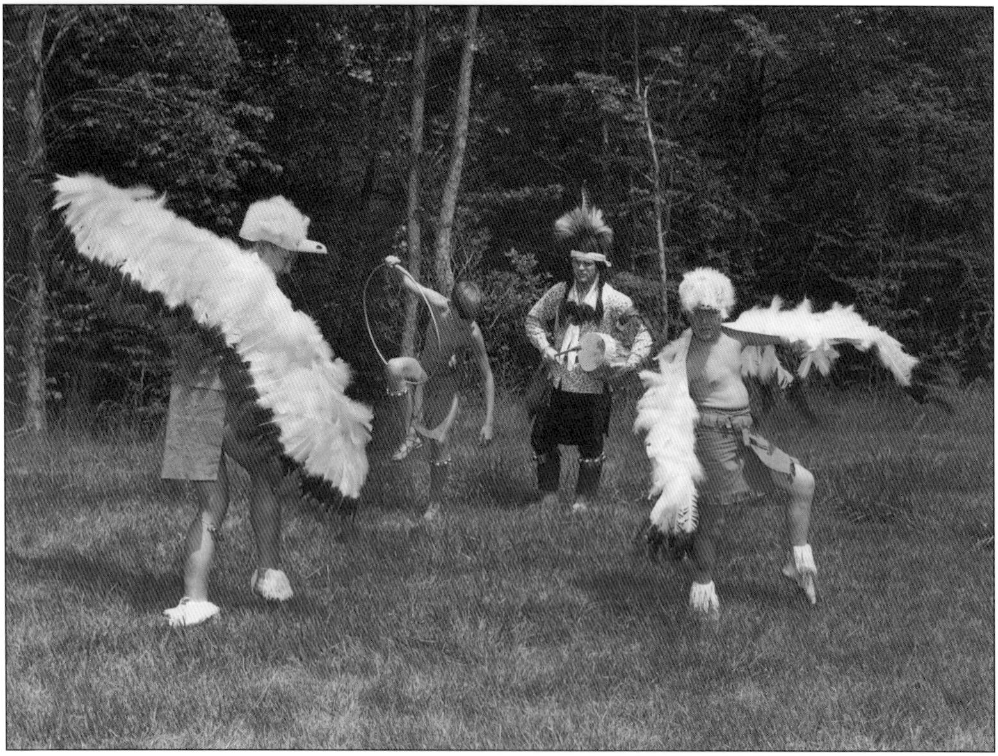

Falling Creek maintains many long-standing traditions, including the Grand Council, a drama modeled on southeastern Native American rituals, as shown in this photograph. Other traditions include campfires, overnight camping trips, and Ebenezer Rock, a meandering wall composed of rocks dropped by campers on their way to the last campfire of the session. The rocks symbolize God's presence and Falling Creek campers past and present. (Courtesy of Falling Creek Camp.)

Three

The Land of the Sky

Summer Camps around Asheville

The 1876 novel *The Land of the Sky; or Adventures in Mountain By-Ways* by Christian Reid, the pen name of Frances Christine Fisher Tiernan, tells the story of the summer visitors to western North Carolina. The alluring title has hence been appropriated as a regional tourism slogan. Since the 19th century, tourism has been the lifeblood of the Asheville area's economy. The lofty elevations of the Blue Ridge Mountains, the moderate climate, and scenic attractions enticed vacationers from the lowland Carolinas and Georgia, as well as convalescing tuberculosis patients during the antebellum period. Tourism is an oft overlooked major sector of the New South economy, particularly in southern Appalachia. In the wake of rapid social and economic change, tourists sought rejuvenation from the perils of modernity in the great outdoors. Abetted by the arrival of the railroad in 1880 and the burgeoning Gilded Age consumer culture, Asheville became a "playground for the wealthy." Inns, boardinghouses, hotels, and resorts cropped up to accommodate the swelling numbers of tourists. Around the turn of the 20th century, religious retreats arose around the Asheville area, concentrated particularly in the Swannanoa Valley to the east, including Montreat, Ridgecrest, and YMCA Blue Ridge Assembly. The rise of automobile culture brought more visitors to the newly established Blue Ridge Parkway and Great Smoky Mountains National Park. Many of the area's first summer camps opened for the children of upper- and middle-class tourists. Today, summer camps are a tourist draw in their own right as throngs of campers converge each summer in "The Land of the Sky."

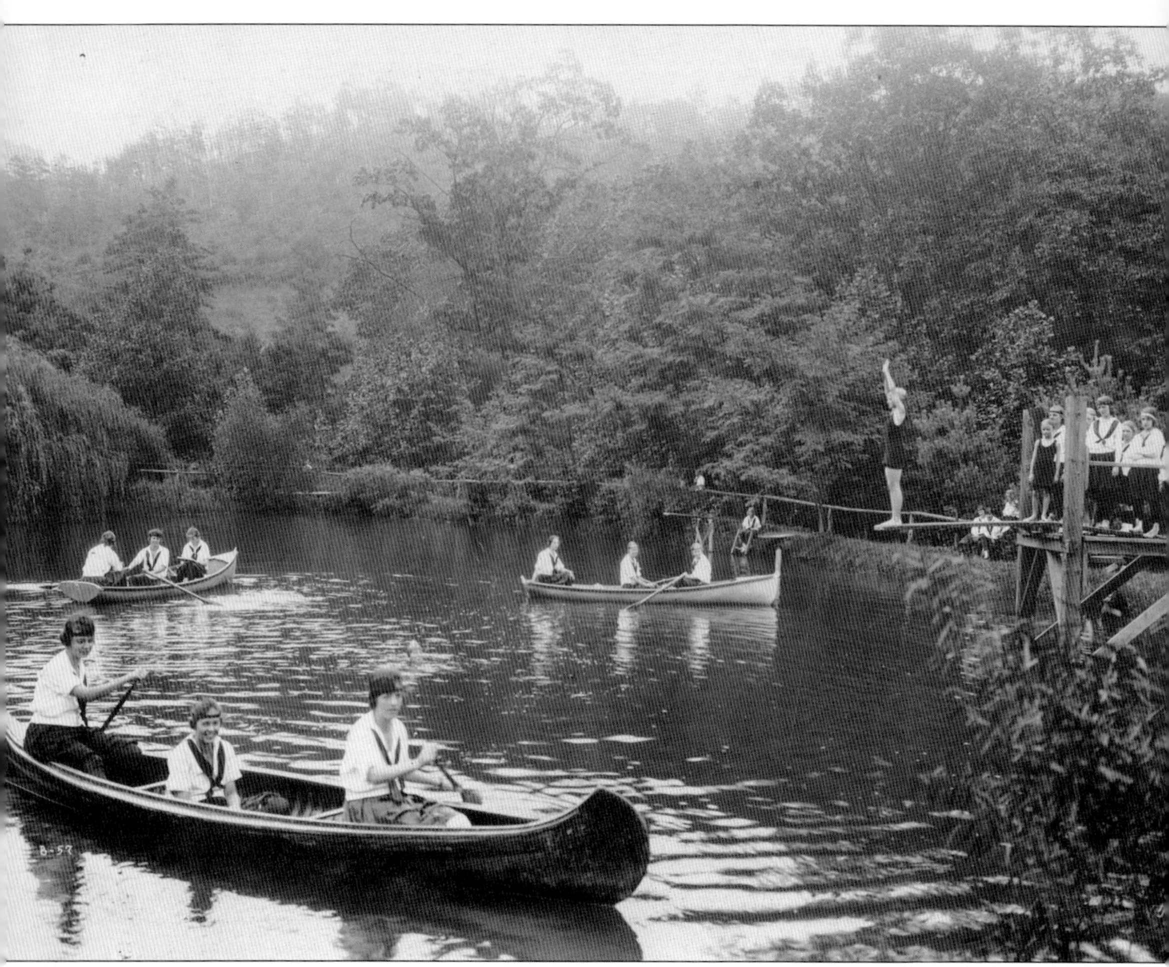

East Asheville's Chunns Cove Camp, founded in 1916, welcomed girls ages 9 to 18. Activities at Chunns Cove Camp included swimming, diving, lifesaving, boating, horseback riding, and overnight mountain trips. This photograph, dating to around 1919, shows three canoes on Lake Little. Campers gather on the dock, and one appears poised to dive into the lake. (Courtesy of North Carolina Collection, Pack Memorial Public Library.)

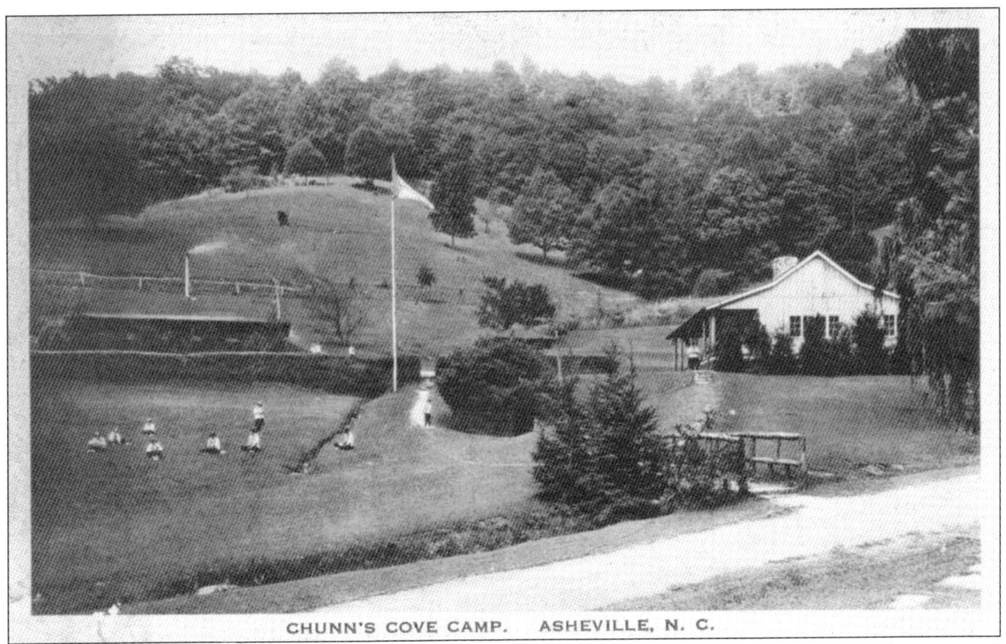

The 65-acre camp featured a spring-fed lake. E.W. Grove hosted Sunday picnics on the pastoral grounds with guests from his Grove Park Inn. (Courtesy of North Carolina Collection, Pack Memorial Public Library.)

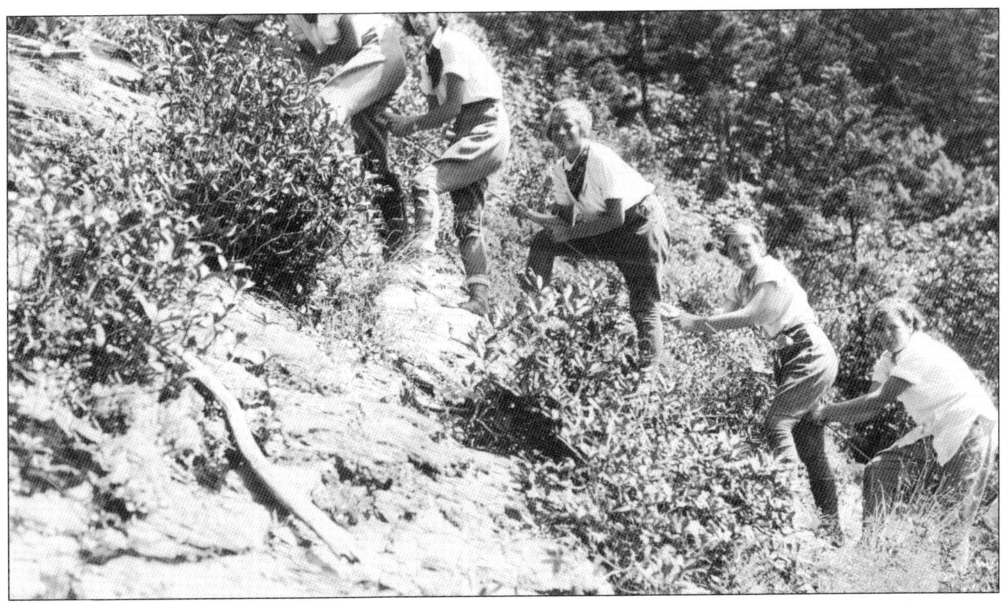

This 1934 photograph shows a group of Chunns Cove campers hiking in the nearby Great Smoky Mountains, the year Congress designated it a national park. (Courtesy of North Carolina Collection, Pack Memorial Public Library.)

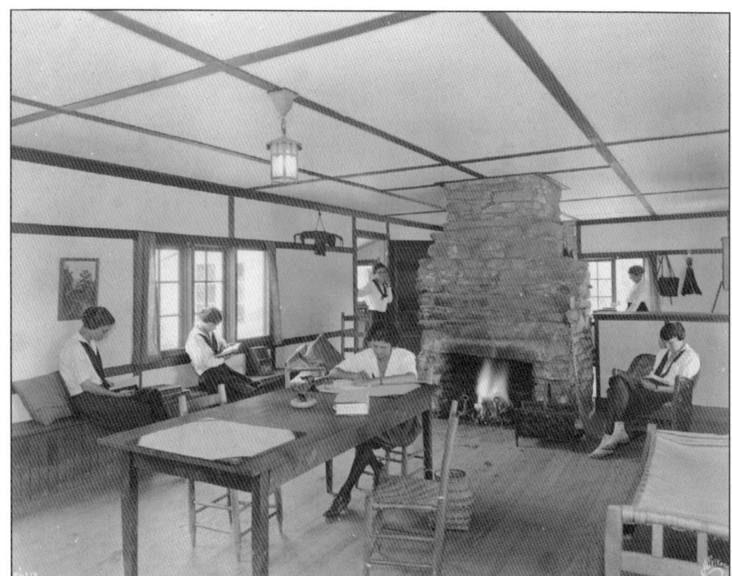

This c. 1919 photograph shows the Art and Crafts–style interior of the craft cabin at Chunns Cove Camp, which featured a central stone fireplace and cane-bottomed chairs. (Courtesy of North Carolina Collection, Pack Memorial Public Library.)

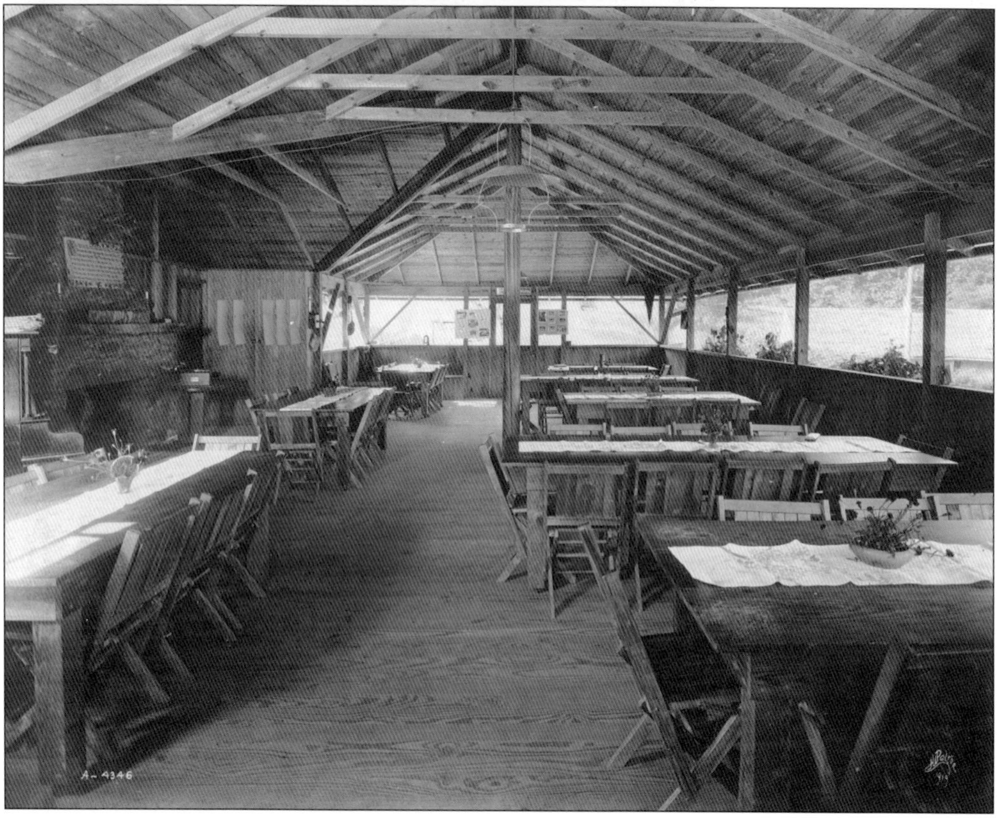

This 1919 photograph affords an interior view of Chunns Cove Camp's dining hall, outfitted with eight tables, which seated 8 to 10 campers each on folding chairs. The hall featured a stone fireplace, open rafters, and hardwood floors. A piano and phonograph provided entertainment. The structure was even equipped with a telephone, seen mounted on the wall. (Courtesy of North Carolina Collection, Pack Memorial Public Library.)

Three Chunns Cove campers are shown inside the "senior kiosk," as the cabins in this 1919 photograph were referred to. One girl reads on the cot, while the camper at center holds a tennis racquet, and the camper on the right strums a small stringed instrument. (Courtesy of North Carolina Collection, Pack Memorial Public Library.)

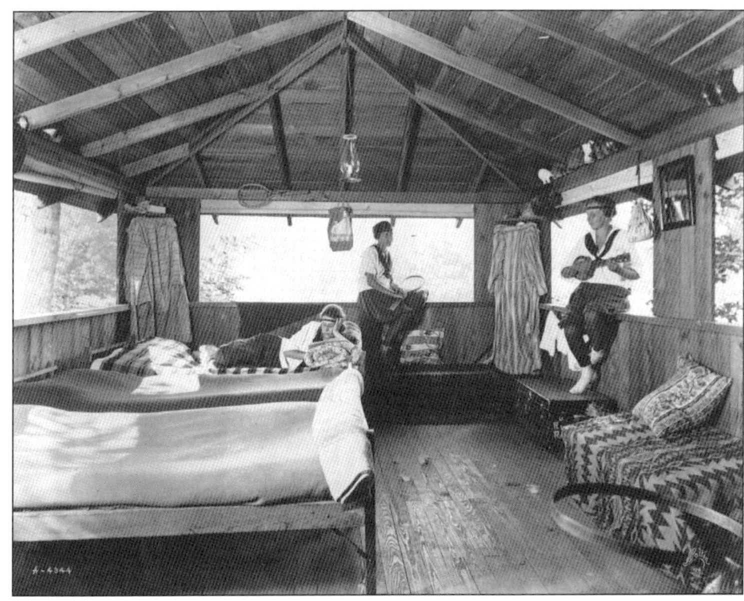

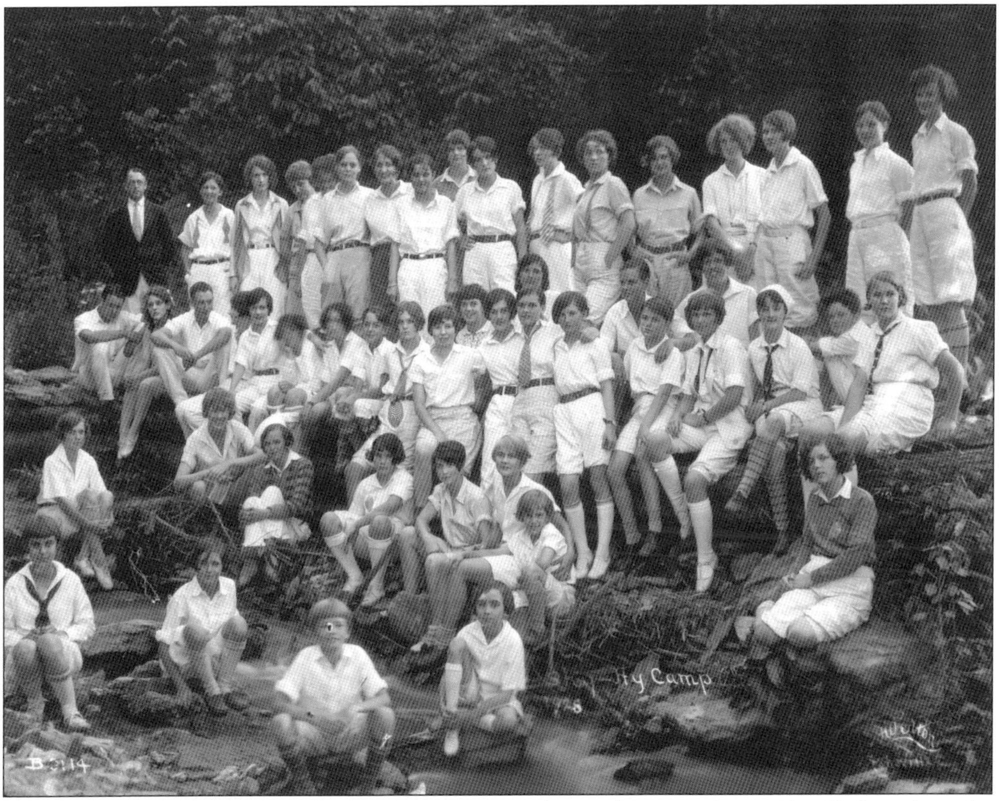

Presbyterian pastor T.E. Simpson of Darlington, South Carolina, ran Camp Sky-Hy for girls in the mountains of North Carolina between the 1920s and 1950s. The camp operated from Marshall on the eastern bank of the French Broad River, north of Asheville, before relocating to a site between Hendersonville and Flat Rock. This 1928 image shows Simpson with campers and counselors. (Courtesy of North Carolina Collection, Pack Memorial Public Library.)

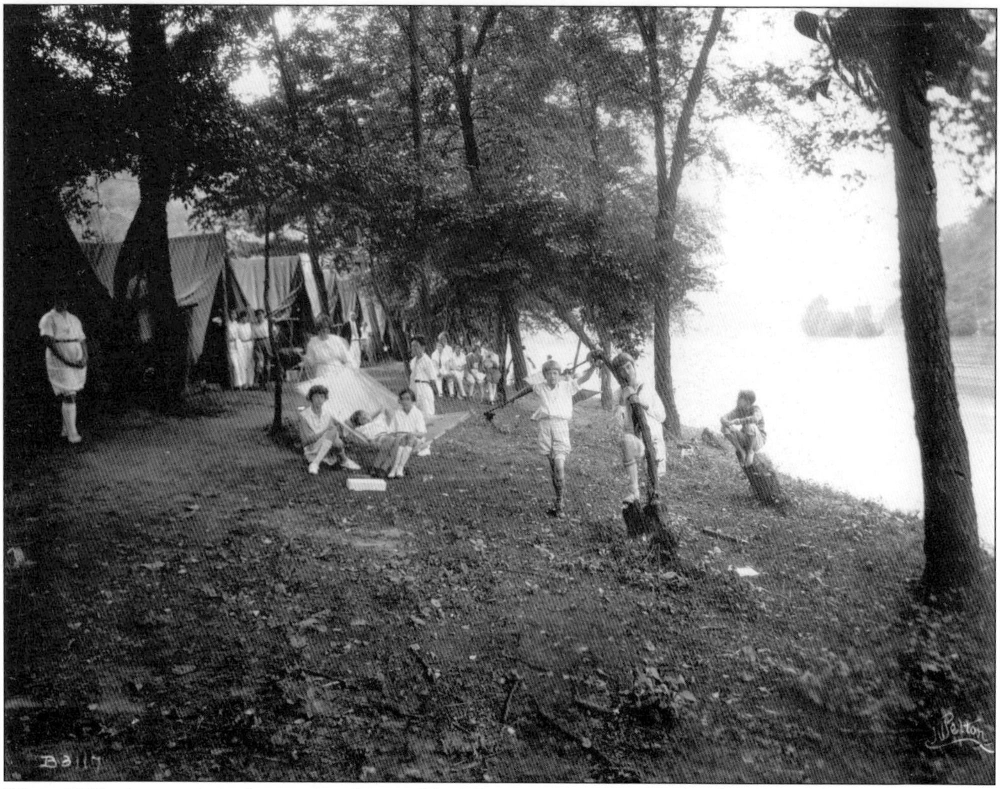

This 1928 photograph shows the Camp Sky-Hy encampment on the banks of the French Broad River, near the small town of Marshall. Campers slept in canvas tents pitched on the riverbank. From its source near the Eastern Continental Divide, the French Broad River flows northeast through the Appalachian Mountains to Tennessee. (Courtesy of North Carolina Collection, Pack Memorial Public Library.)

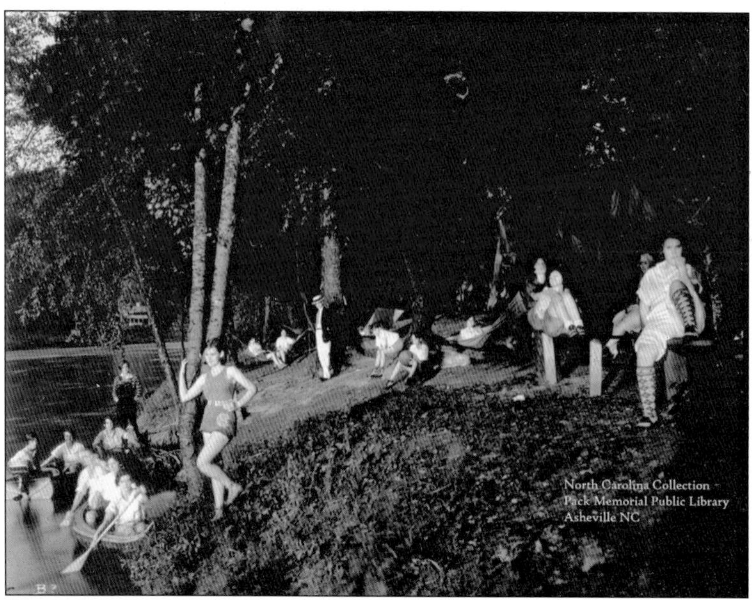

Camp Sky-Hy's location on the banks of the French Broad River afforded natural recreation and idyllic relaxation, as this 1928 photograph shows. (Courtesy of North Carolina Collection, Pack Memorial Public Library.)

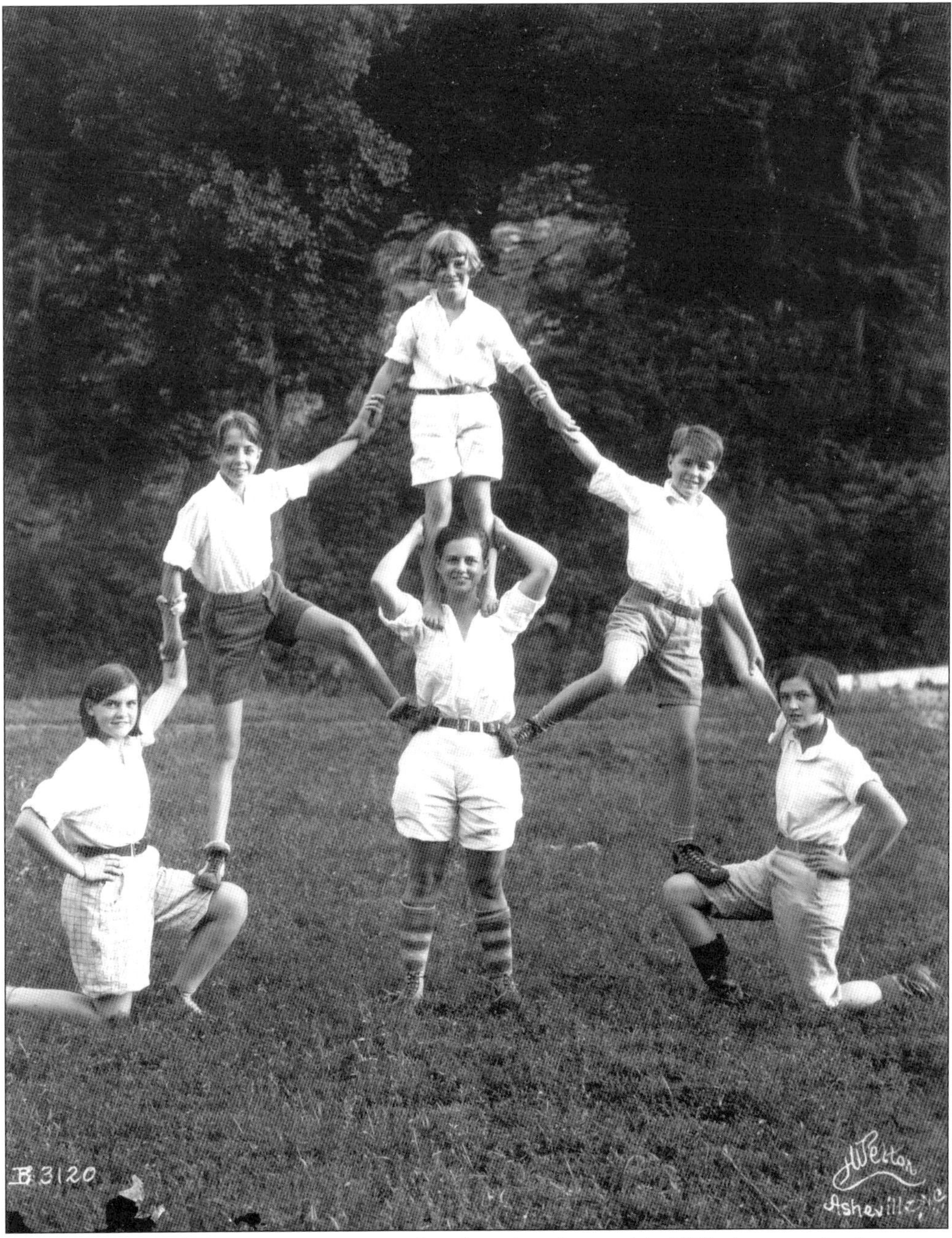

Even a day at a Christian camp was not free from hijinks, as this 1928 photograph of campers poised in a human pyramid demonstrates. (Courtesy of North Carolina Collection, Pack Memorial Public Library.)

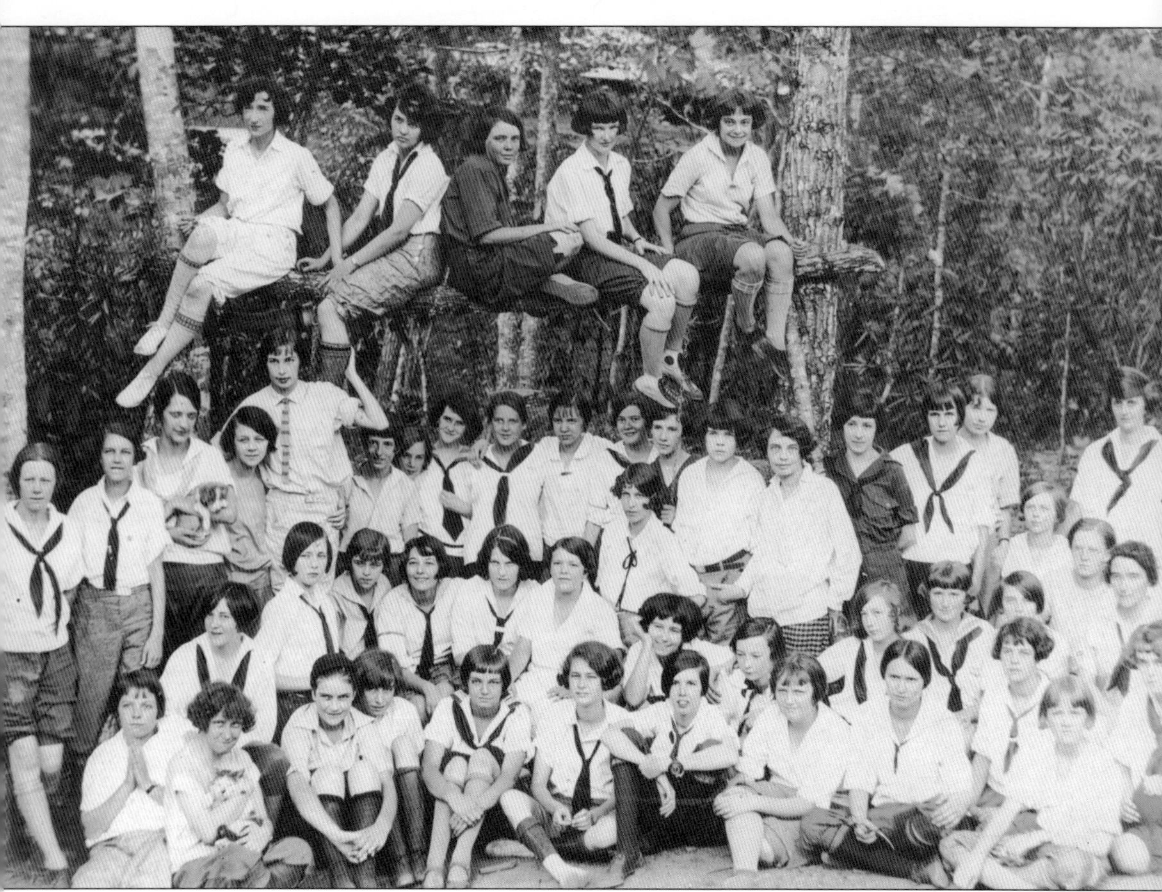

White middie–clad young women with pageboy haircuts pose in this 1920s photograph taken at an unidentified camp. Despite the campers' demure countenances, these girls had playful nicknames for one another like "Bunny," "Bugs," and "Battle Axe." Such names demonstrate the intimate camaraderie that developed at camps, cherished spaces of new experiences and personal transformation away from home. (Courtesy of North Carolina Collection, Pack Memorial Public Library.)

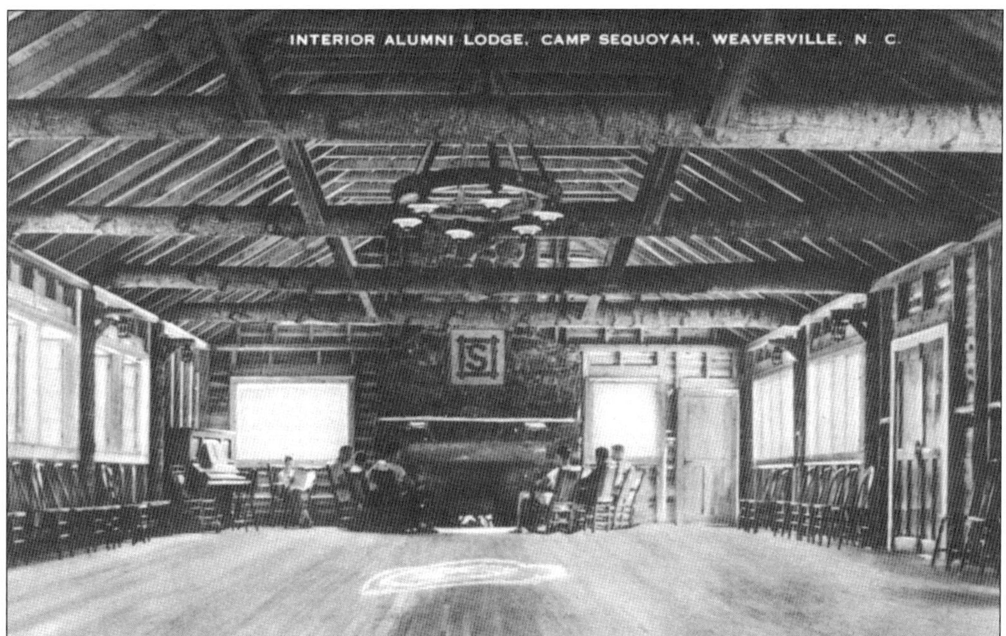

In 1924, C. Walton Johnson founded Camp Sequoyah on 125 acres in Weaverville, North Carolina, as "a real camp for real boys." Sequoyah was "a camp with a purpose," where boys took part in swimming, horseback riding, rock climbing, archery, riflery, canoeing, backpacking, woodcraft, basketry, beading, competing in field games, and camping in tepees. This photograph shows the alumni lodge. (Courtesy of North Carolina Collection, Pack Memorial Public Library.)

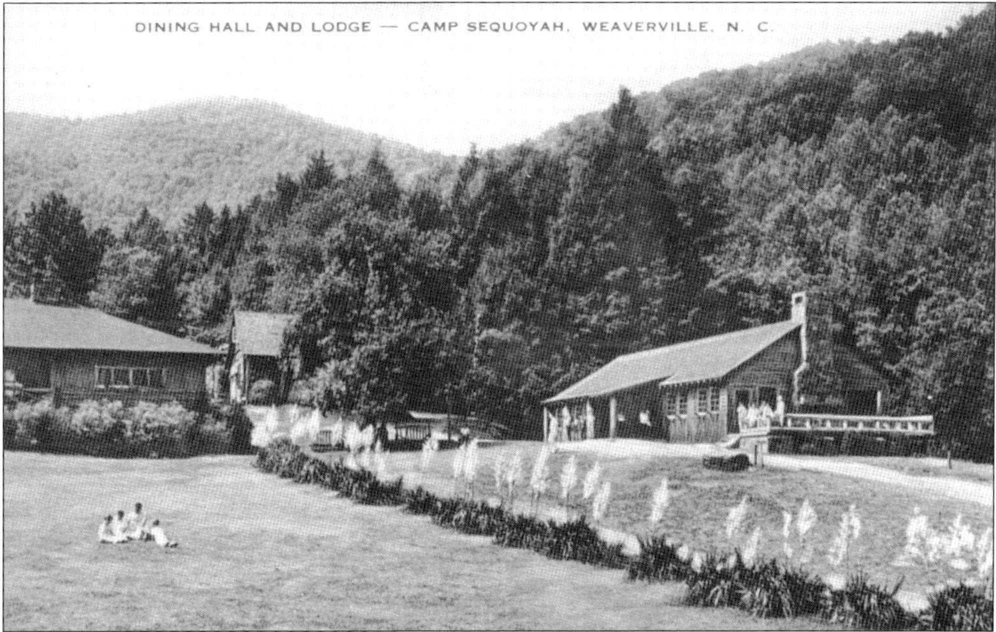

Camp Sequoyah's lodge contained the dining hall, social hall, and a modern kitchen. The dining hall, with its rustic beams, was open on the sides to showcase majestic mountain views as the scent of pine wafted through the fresh air. The social hall boasted comfortable chairs, a large stone fireplace, a Victrola, a piano, and a library at one end.

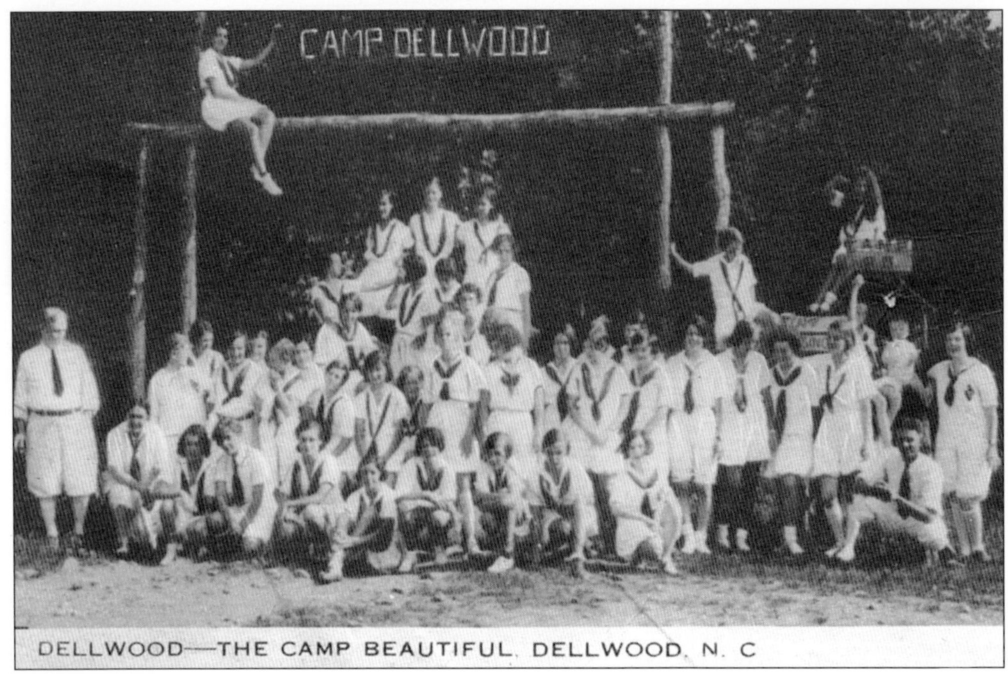

Camp Dellwood was a girls' camp located in Waynesviille, in operation from 1926 to 1973. Mary Mitchell Westall of Asheville attended the camp between 1928 and 1933 and reminisced, "A lovely spot among the hills, a sky of blue above, and trees that bend in graceful form, these make the camp I love." (Courtesy of North Carolina Collection, Pack Memorial Public Library.)

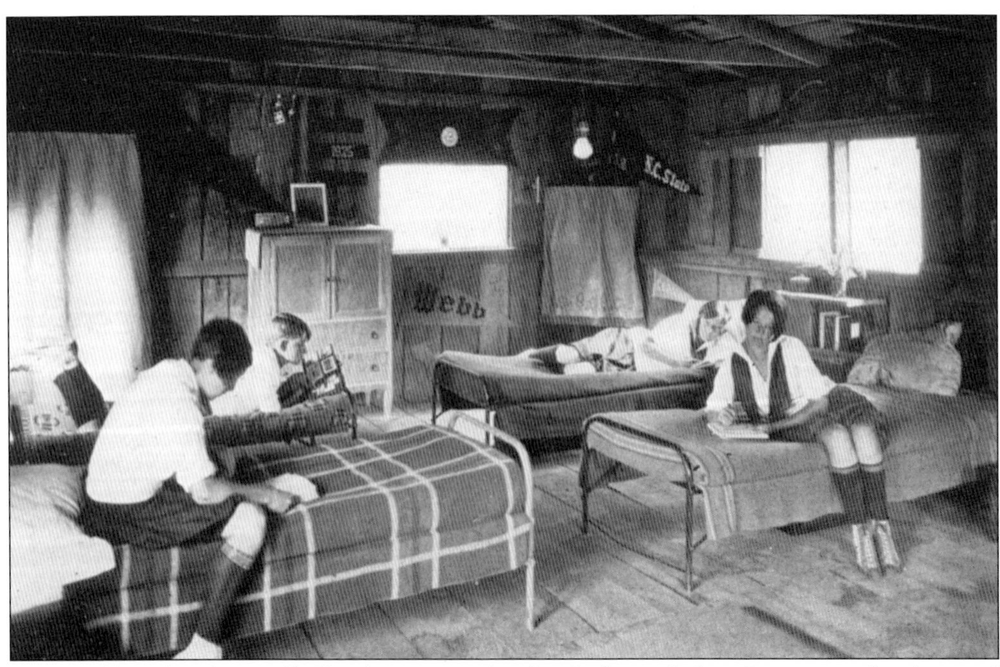

Camp Dellwood's cabins, called kiosks, were outfitted with electric lights. Campers read and penned letters during free time. (Courtesy of North Carolina Collection, Pack Memorial Public Library.)

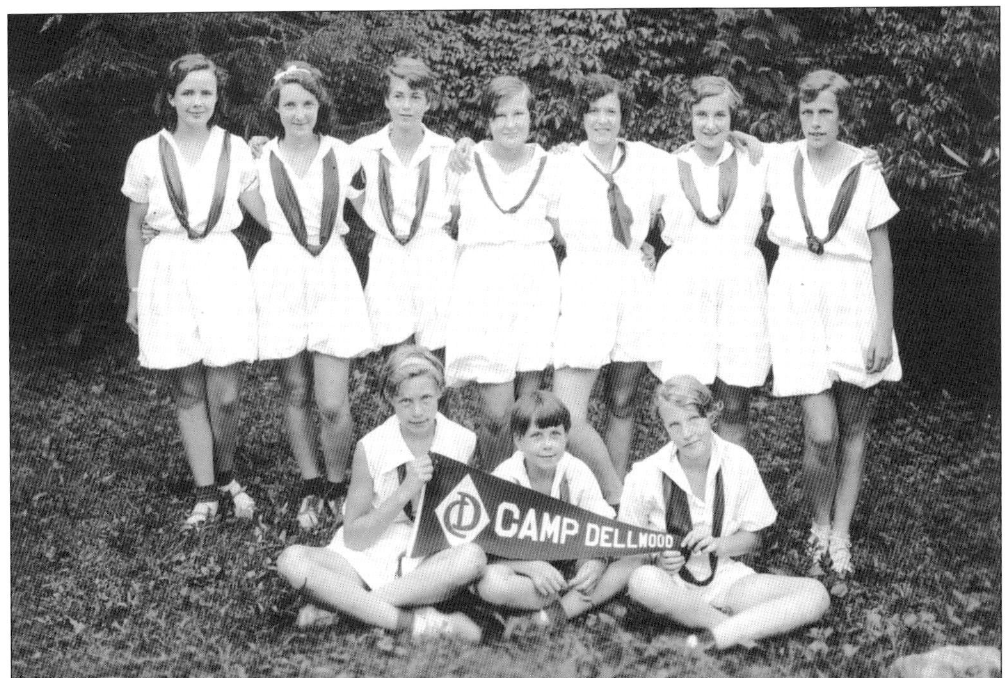

Girls ages 9 to 19 competed as "speedies" and "swifties" in the spirit of friendly rivalry in archery, canoeing, basketball, horseback riding, tennis, and swimming at Camp Dellwood. Campers also engaged in crafts, dancing, dramatics, and nature study. (Courtesy of North Carolina Collection, Pack Memorial Public Library.)

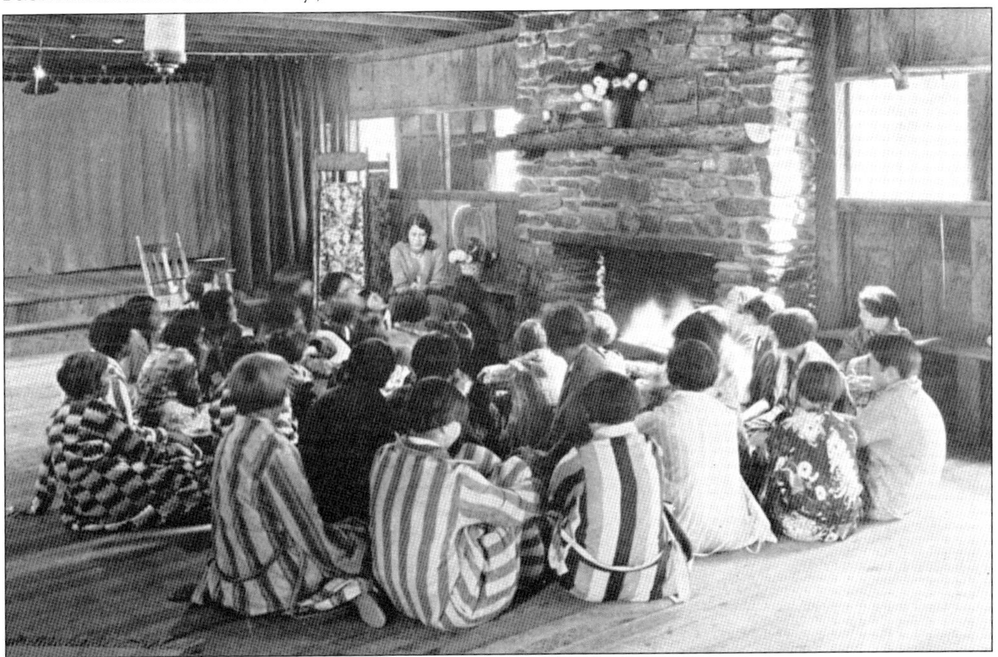

Camp Dellwood's lodge was the social gathering place at camp. In the evenings, campers gathered by the fireside for sing-a-longs, storytelling, and pajama parties, as seen in this 1930 photograph. (Courtesy of North Carolina Collection, Pack Memorial Public Library.)

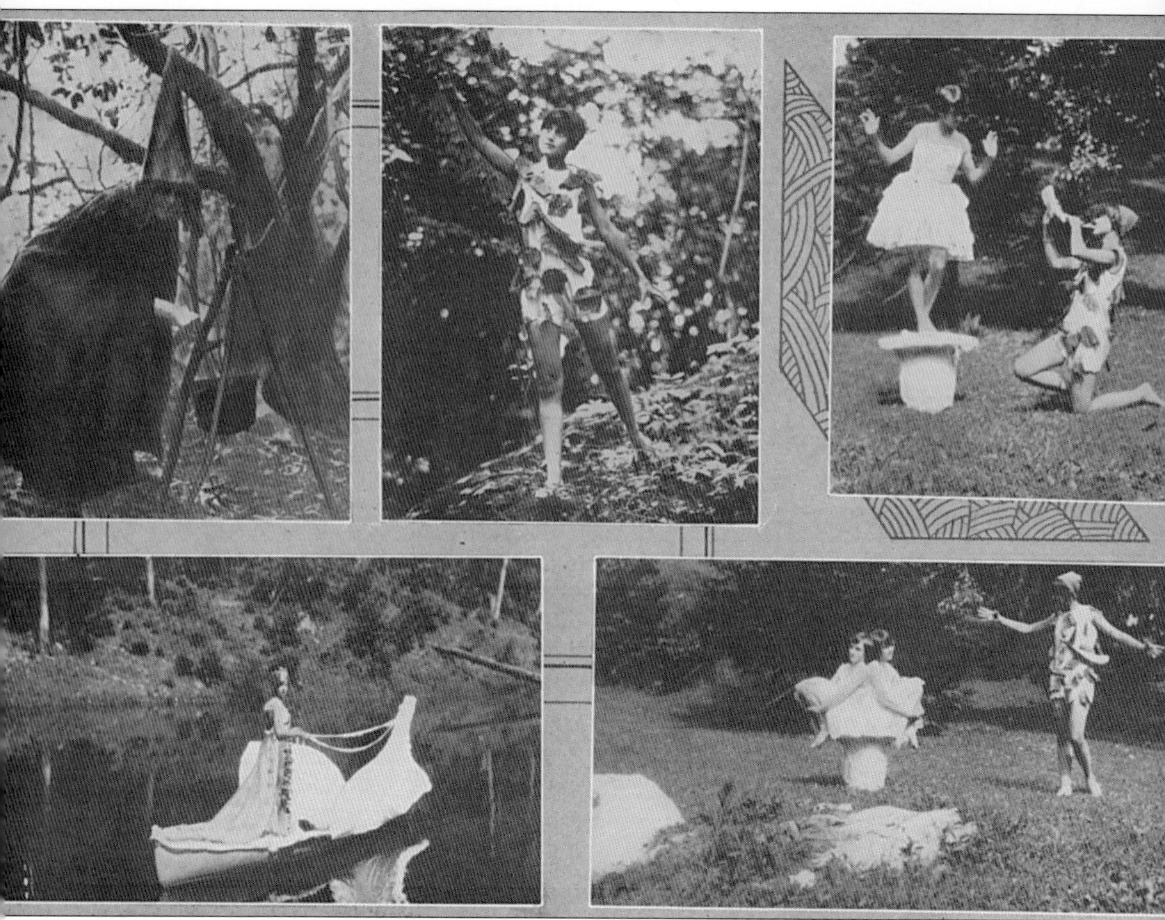

The chimerical Walpurgis Night was a much-anticipated Camp Dellwood tradition held at the close of the summer session. Campers donned costumes to portray fairies, witches, pans, and brownies. (Courtesy of North Carolina Collection, Pack Memorial Public Library.)

Camp Dellwood was like a big family, and girls returned year after year. They kept autograph books to remember their friends and the good memories of camp. This photograph from the late 1920s or early 1930s was mounted in a scrapbook with the handwritten caption "Idiotic Antics." (Courtesy of North Carolina Collection, Pack Memorial Public Library.)

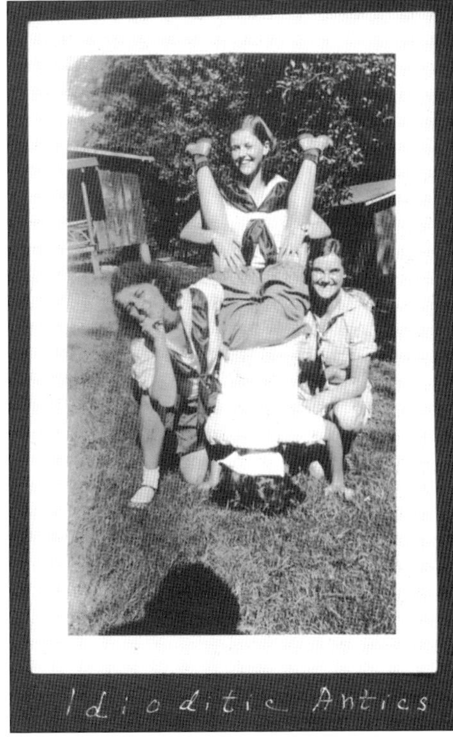

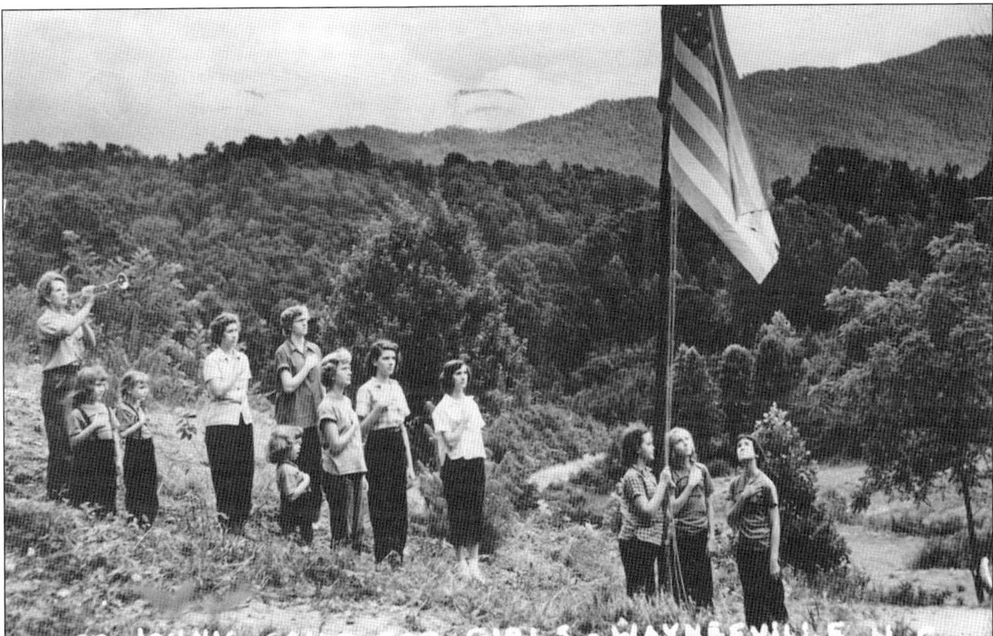

In a 1945 newspaper advertisement, St. John's Camp for Girls, operated by the Sisters of St. Francis, claimed to be the "highest girls camp east of the Rockies." At an altitude of 3,000 feet in Waynesville near the Great Smoky Mountains, the camp also boasted no mosquitoes. (Courtesy of Durwood Barbour Collection of North Carolina Postcards, North Carolina Photographic Archives, Wilson Library, University of North Carolina at Chapel Hill.)

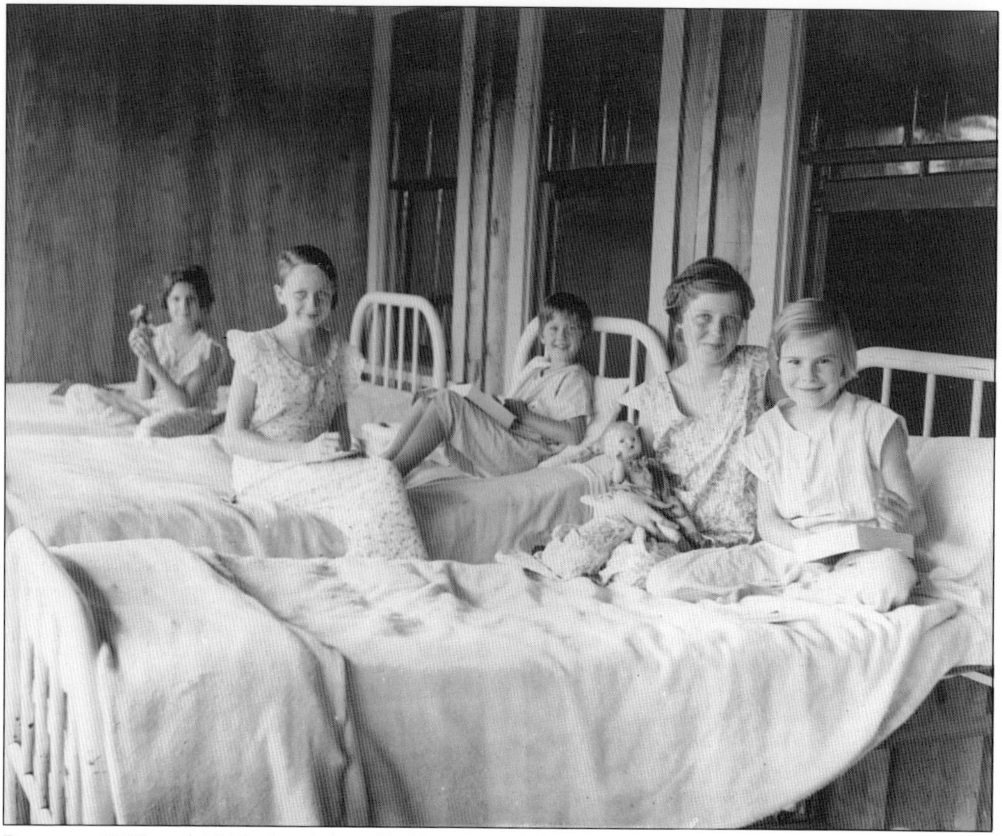

Between 1935 and 1945, the Asheville Kiwanis Club operated a "preventorium" for children at risk of developing tuberculosis on five acres in West Asheville. The preventorium held two six-week sessions each summer. Campers received medicine, rest, and nutrition. (Courtesy of North Carolina Collection, Pack Memorial Public Library.)

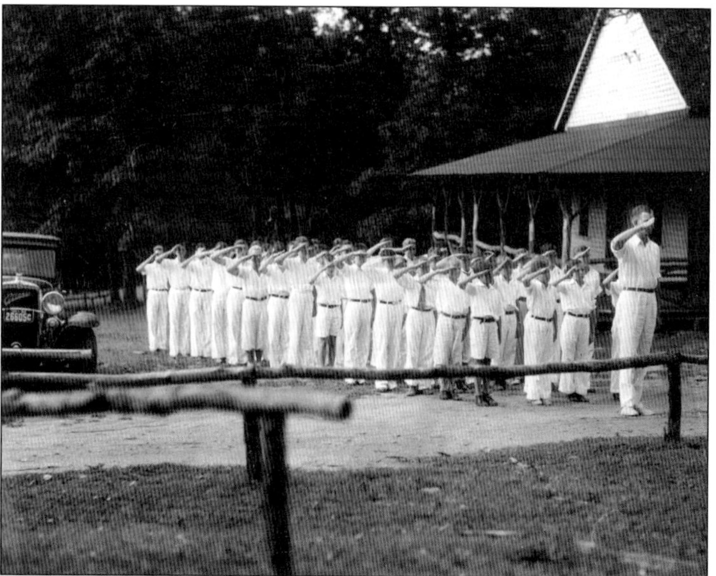

In 1895, Bernard Spilman established Ridgecrest Conference Center, a Baptist retreat east of Asheville. The Baptists acquired land at the present-day site of Camp Ridgecrest in 1924. Camp Swannanoa for boys operated until 1928, and Camp Star Note for girls held sessions in 1926 and 1927. The Sunday School Board founded Camp Ridgecrest at the site in 1929. (Courtesy of Camp Ridgecrest.)

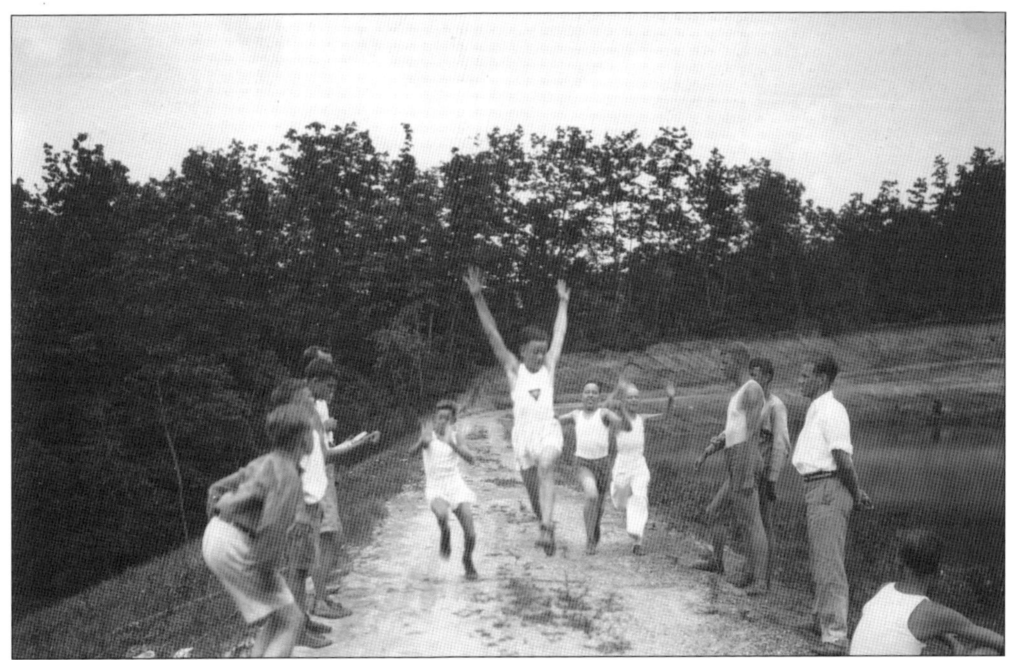

Camp Ridgecrest lets boys be boys, free to get dirty and fraternize without the pressure to impress the opposite sex. This photograph was taken during one of the camp's first seasons. (Courtesy of Camp Ridgecrest.)

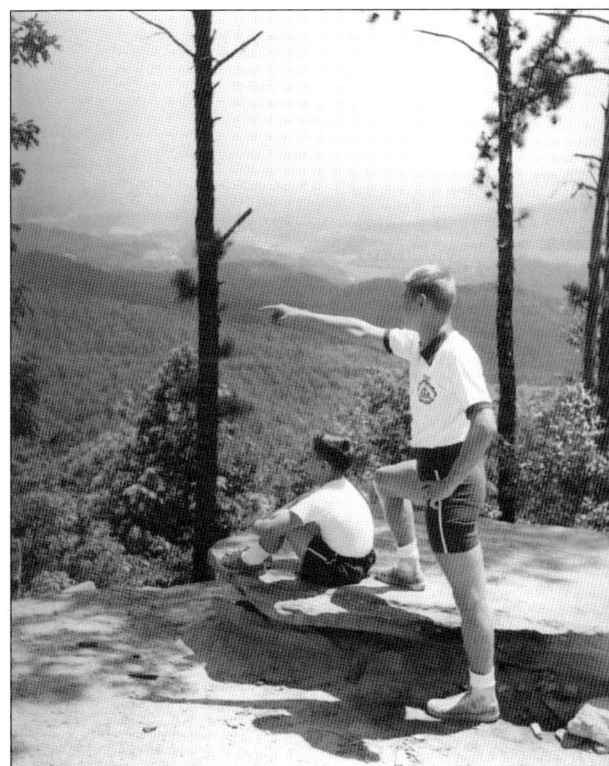

Spilman felt the call to found a Baptist retreat as early as 1895, scouting the southern Highlands before settling on Ridgecrest, where white oaks, red maples, and evergreens extend into the clouds over hiking trails lined with lush mountain laurel that lead to scenic vantage points like the one shown here. (Courtesy of Camp Ridgecrest.)

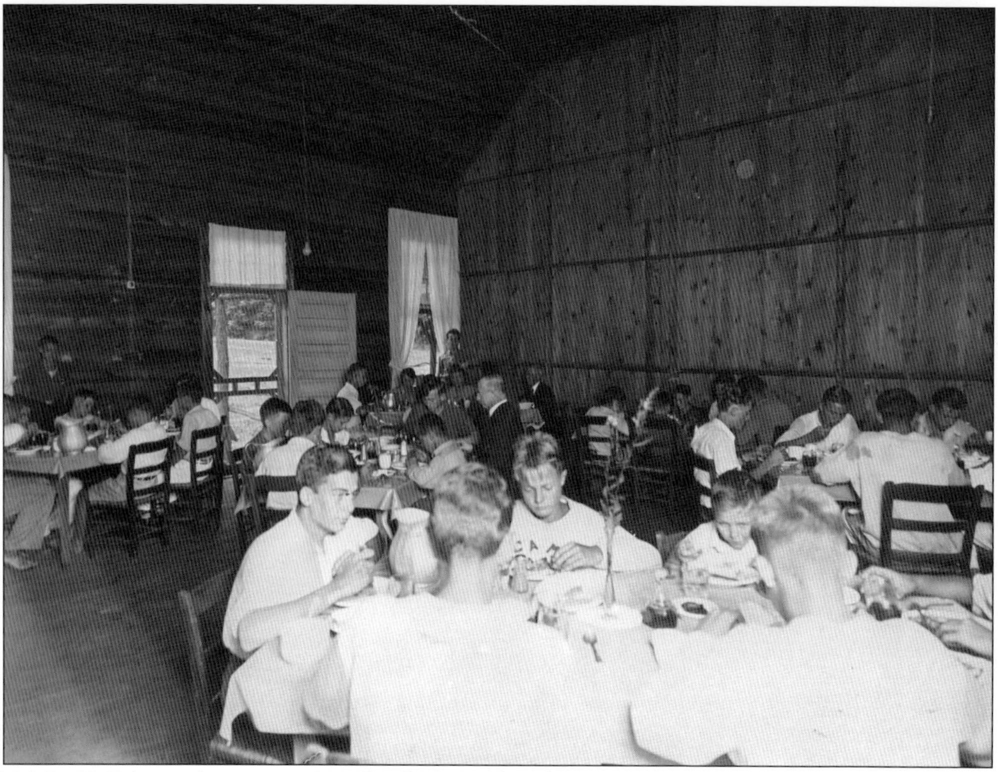

Fidelis Hall, better known as the "Shack," served as the recreation center and dining hall before Spilman Lodge was built in 1942 at Ridgecrest. The Shack hosted staff meetings, indoor games, boxing, wrestling, gymnastics, and Sunday worship services. One end of the hall had a screen to show movies. The Shack was below the present location of the tennis courts. (Courtesy of Camp Ridgecrest.)

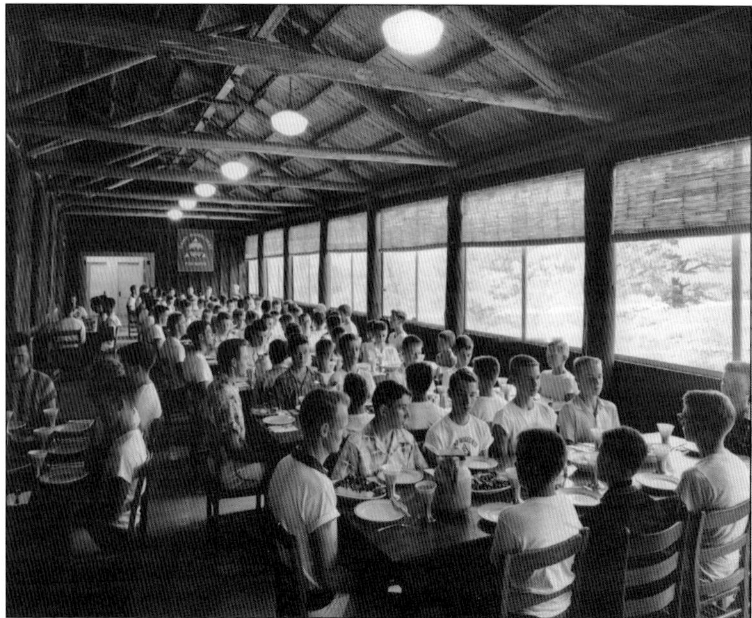

Spilman Lodge, the log building at the center of Camp Ridgecrest, is the largest and oldest vertical log structure east of the Mississippi. Constructed in 1942, it houses the kitchen, dining halls, and gym, and features a fireplace for cool mountain evenings. This 1954 photograph shows well-mannered young men in the dining hall. (Courtesy of Camp Ridgecrest.)

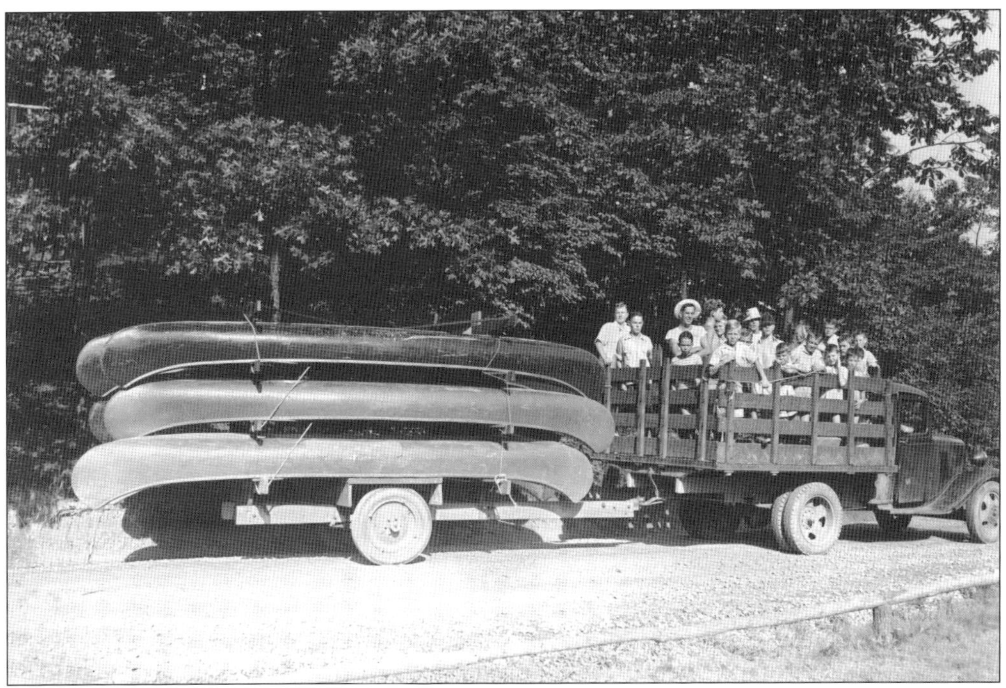

Canoeing is a traditional activity at Camp Ridgecrest. Since the camp's founding, boys have taken overnight canoe trips down the French Broad River past George Vanderbilt's Biltmore Estate. (Courtesy of Camp Ridgecrest.)

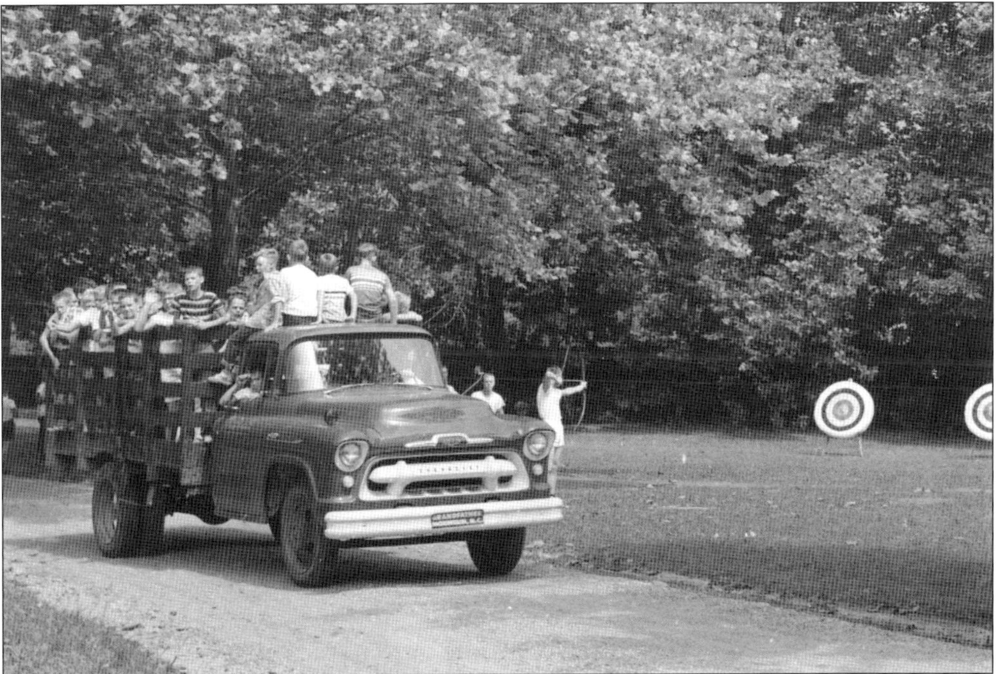

Campers refine their skills at archery as a group of boys riding in back of the camp truck pass by. Many campers recall the thrill of hitting their first bull's-eye after one-on-one instruction from the camp's staff. (Courtesy of Camp Ridgecrest.)

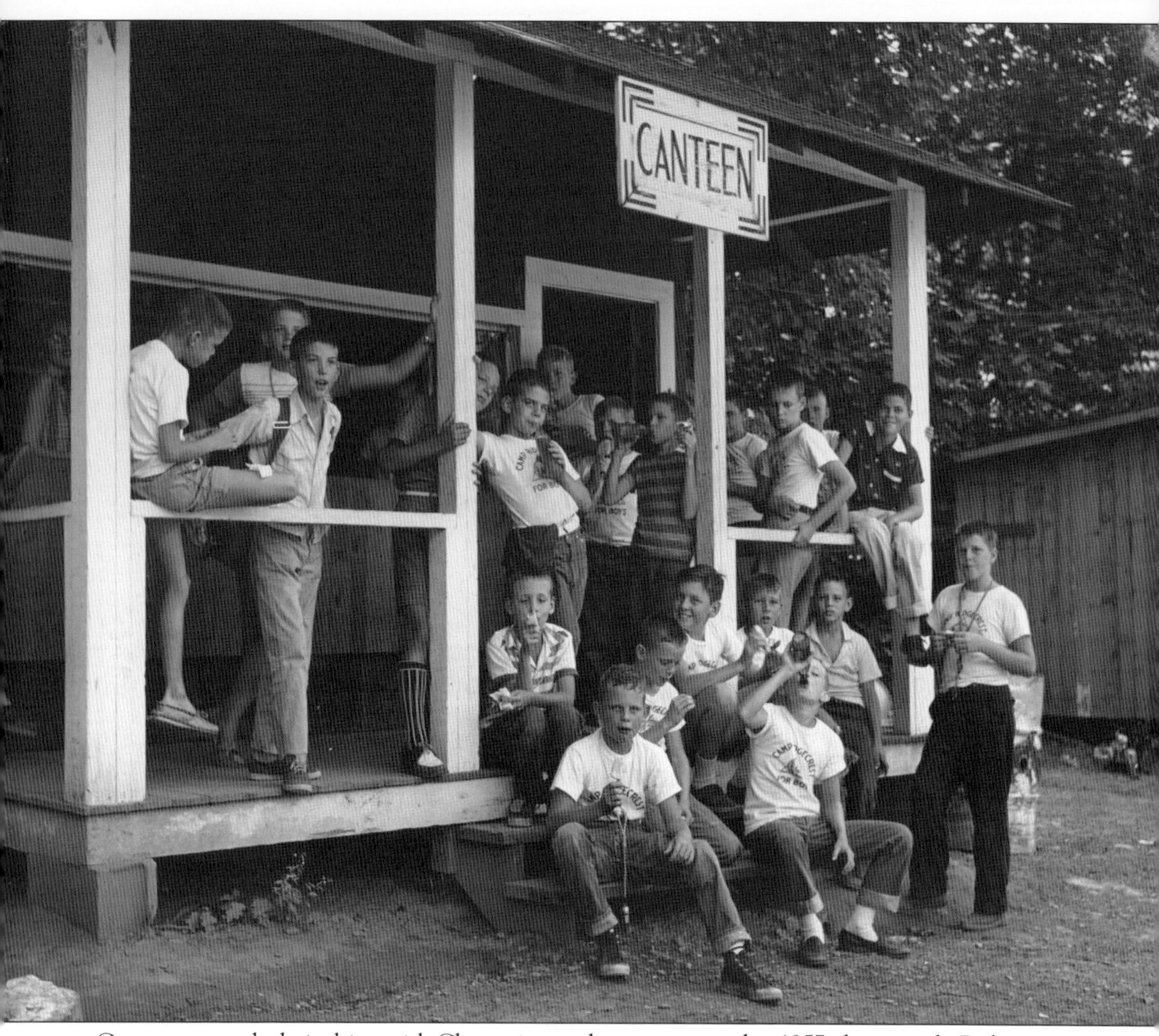

Campers quench their thirst with Cheerwine at the canteen in this 1957 photograph. Ridgecrest's former train depot later replaced this structure. The railroad station was once called Terrell. Spilman chose the name Blue Mont, but the railroad abbreviation proved too similar to nearby Black Mountain. The station was renamed Ridgecrest in 1912. The depot witnessed the arrivals and departures of many campers over the years. (Courtesy of Camp Ridgecrest.)

Camp Ridgecrest stresses discipline along with adventure, as this photograph of a counselor inspecting a camper's cabin from the 1960 camp catalog demonstrates. Prolific photographer Edward DuPuy from nearby Black Mountain took this photograph. (Courtesy of Camp Ridgecrest.)

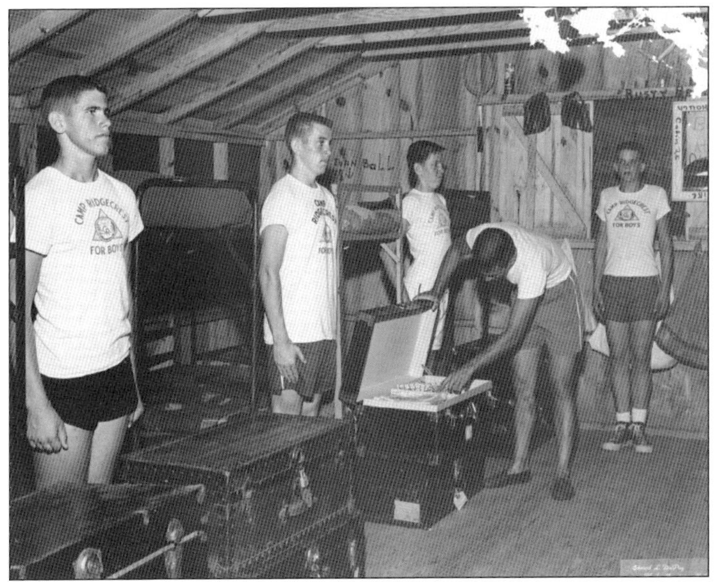

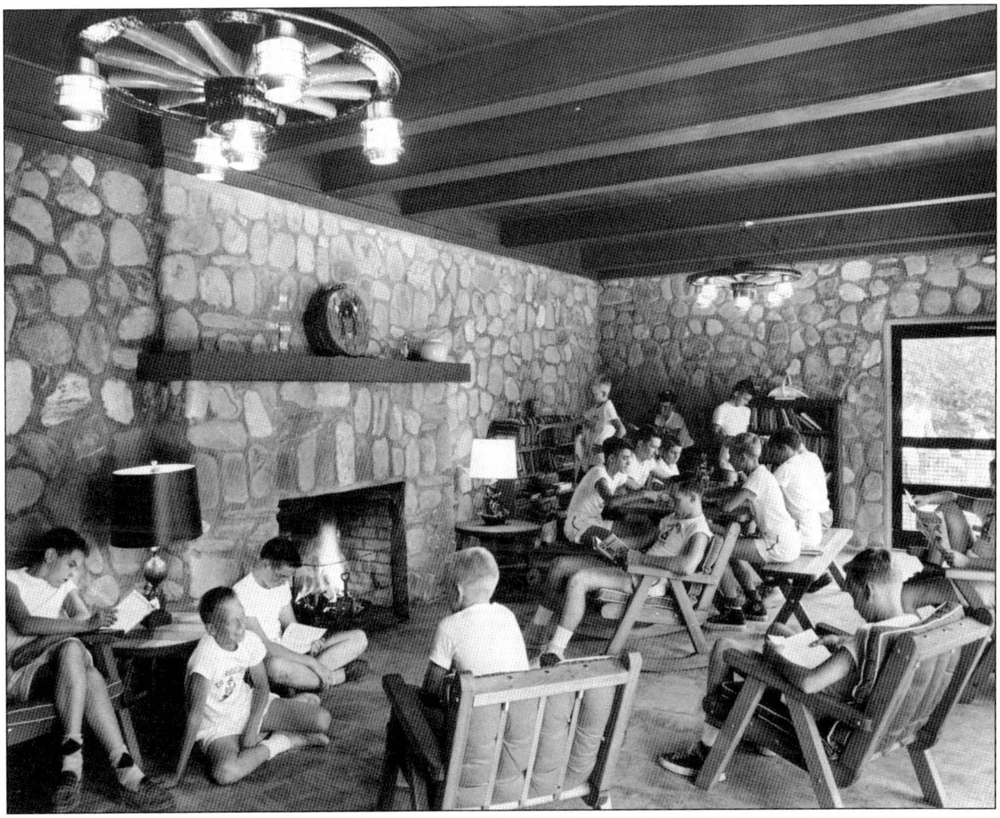

Daily activities at camp were strictly regimented. Reveille was followed by exercises and a morning "dip" before inspection of the huts, then breakfast. Next, the boys took riflery, lifesaving, and swimming lessons. After lunch, campers enjoyed a rest period, as shown here, followed by hikes, sports, supper, evening inspections, inspirational talks, and lastly, taps. (Courtesy of Camp Ridgecrest.)

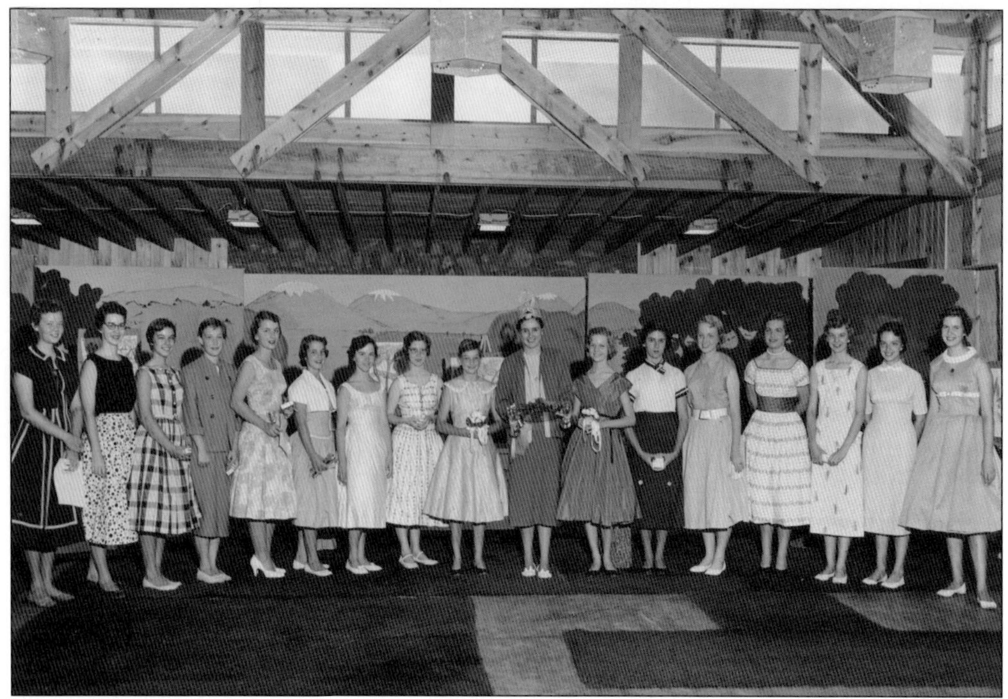

As early as 1926, the Baptist Education Board endeavored to establish a girls' camp similar to Camp Ridgecrest. Camp Star Note operated briefly in 1926 and 1927, but it was not until the 1950s that funds were allocated for a girls' camp. Groundbreaking ceremonies were held in 1954, and Camp Crestridge opened in 1955. This 1956 photograph shows an early Queen Crester, Paula Parks. (Courtesy of Camp Crestridge.)

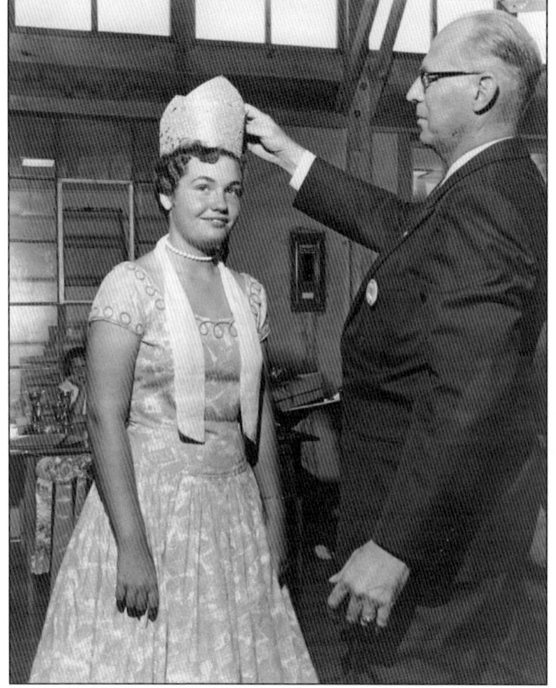

The Council of Progress is a distinctive Crestridge tradition. Campers advance in rank by meeting challenges in four skill set areas. The highest rank is the "Belle." At the end of the session, the belles compete to be Queen Crester. The paper crown of the 1950s was replaced by a jeweled tiara beginning in 1967. Swan Harrell was named the second Queen Crester in 1955. (Courtesy of Camp Crestridge.)

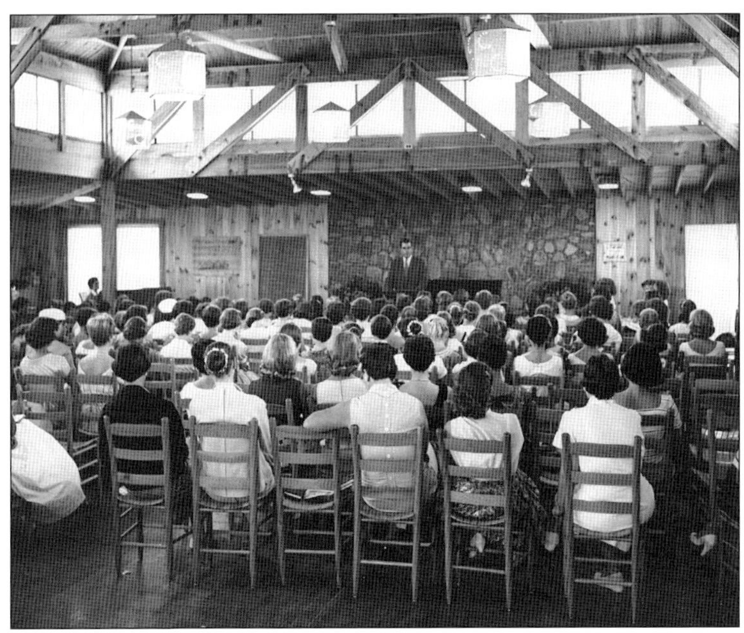

Camp Crestridge offers opportunities for physical enrichment and social interaction rooted in Christian faith. Through all activities, campers are instilled with grace and reverence for God. The camp motto is "With my feet on the ground and my heart attuned, I shall reach for the stars." This photograph shows a Sunday service in 1957. (Courtesy of Camp Crestridge.)

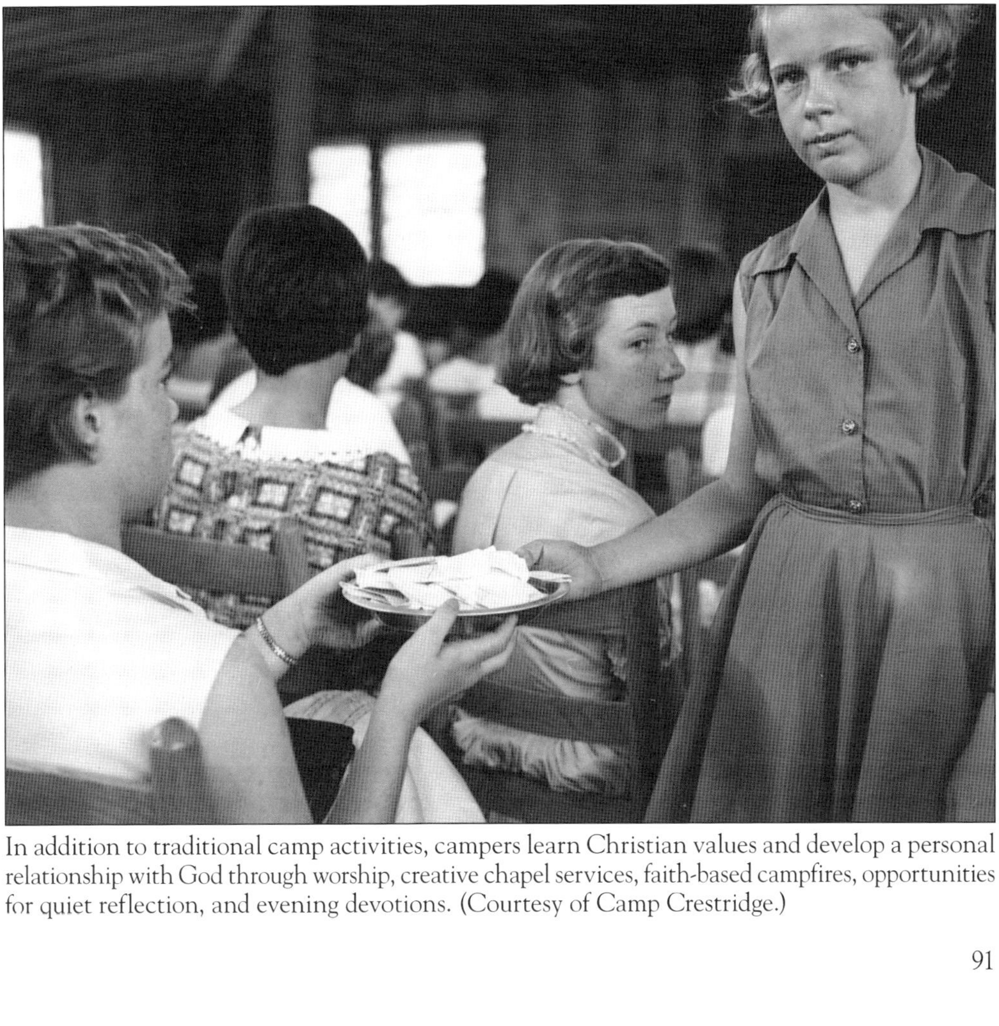

In addition to traditional camp activities, campers learn Christian values and develop a personal relationship with God through worship, creative chapel services, faith-based campfires, opportunities for quiet reflection, and evening devotions. (Courtesy of Camp Crestridge.)

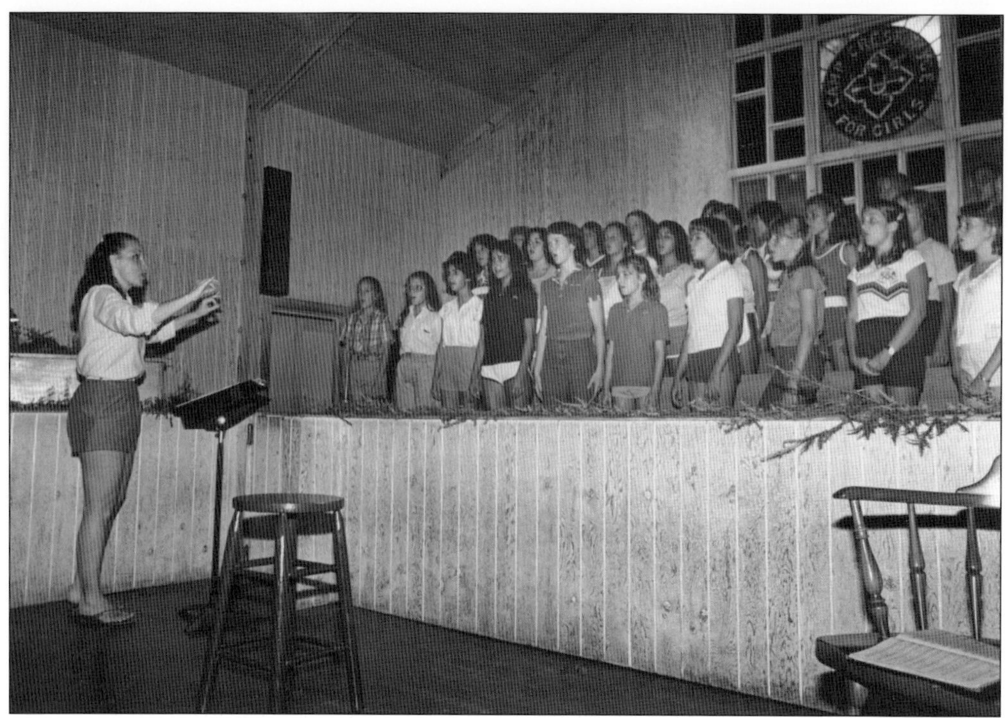

The Crestridge emblem visible in the chapel's stained-glass window behind the choir illustrates the camp's mission. The logo features a horseshoe and arrow, symbolizing the sincere aspiration that each camper finds her purpose in life. The circle represents completion through spiritual, mental, physical, and social growth, as denoted by four points. (Courtesy of Camp Crestridge.)

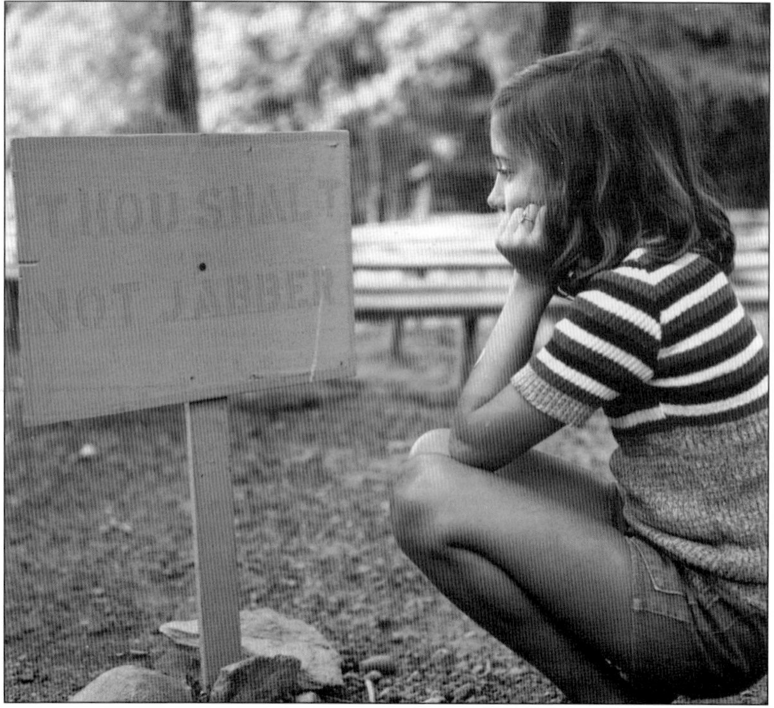

In the camp's early years, campers received lessons in manners and domestic skills, such as how to properly set a table and make a bed. These were called "Lessons in Loveliness." In this 1972 photograph by commercial photographer Edward DuPuy, a camper is instructed that "Thou Shall Not Jabber." (Courtesy of Camp Crestridge.)

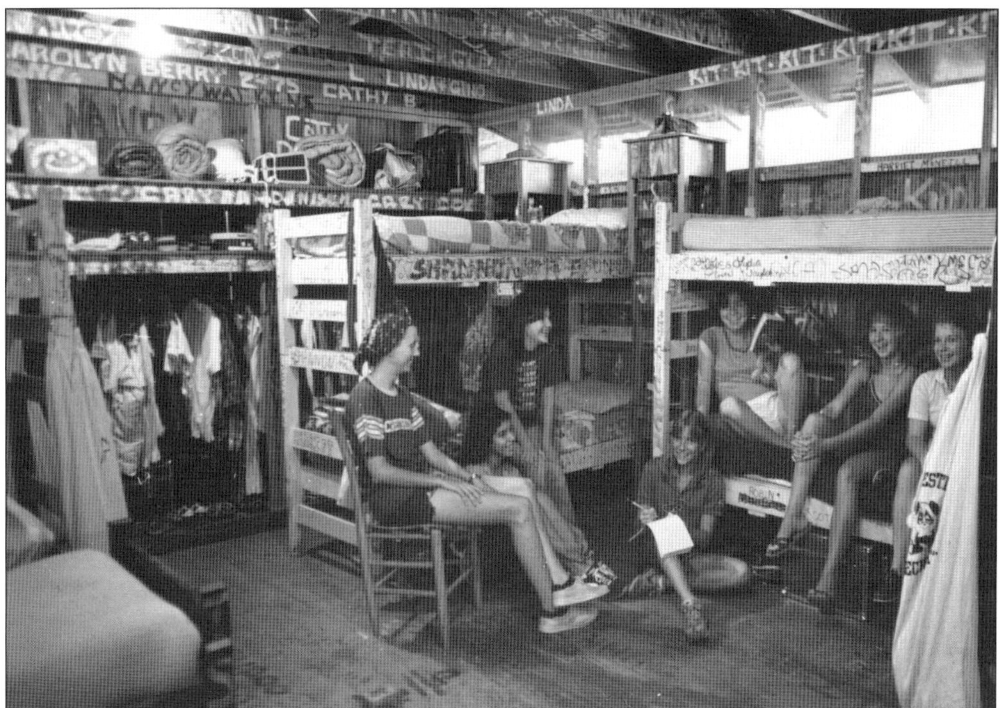

Construction was not complete when Crestridge opened for its first session, and campers and staff spent the first few nights at Ridgecrest Conference Center. Fifty girls attended the first session, and enrollment nearly doubled by the second session. By the 1970s, when this photograph was taken, the cabins showed the imprint of generations of girls. (Courtesy of Camp Crestridge.)

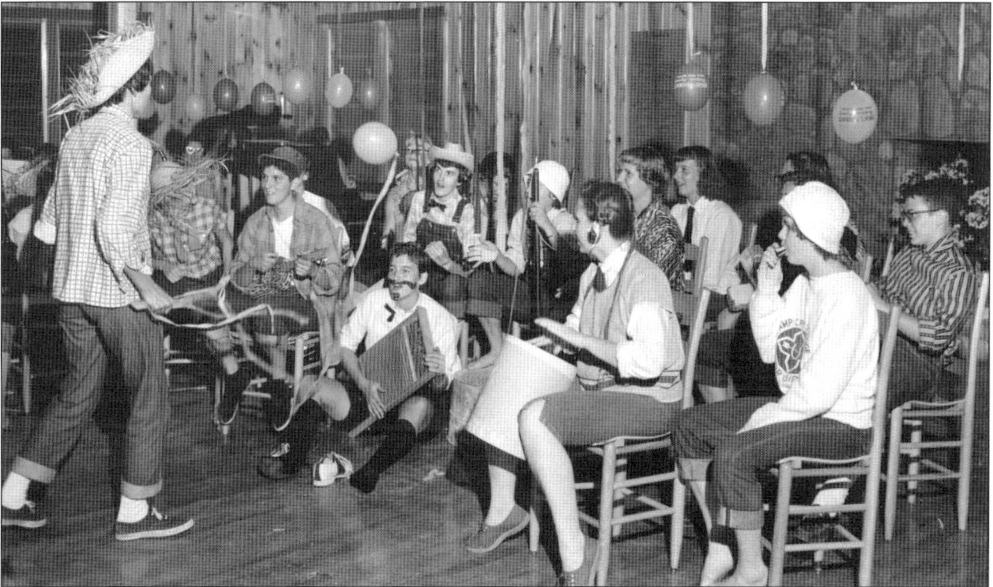

Camp-wide activities allow girls of all ages, grouped into different "villages," to interact. Favorite events include Singspiration, Country Western Nights, movie night, Night of Chaos, Christmas, Sock War, and Carnival. This 1950s photograph shows campers engaged in a musical jamboree. (Courtesy of Camp Crestridge.)

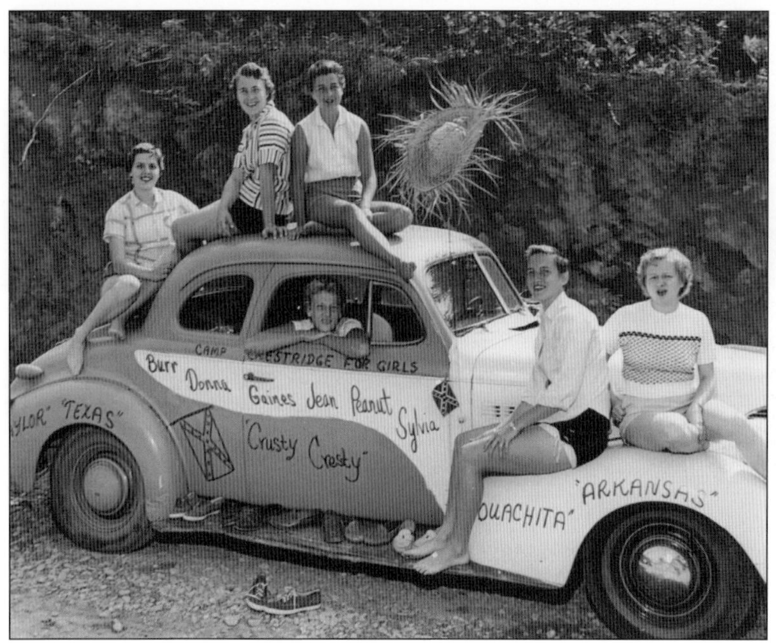

Crestridge attracted campers from across the South. The girls in this 1950s photograph show some state pride. Sylvia Roberts is pictured in the passenger's seat, while Donna Sullivan, Billie Gaines Mann, and Jean Emrich sit on the roof and "Peanut" and Jane Burroughs sit on the hood. (Courtesy of Camp Crestridge.)

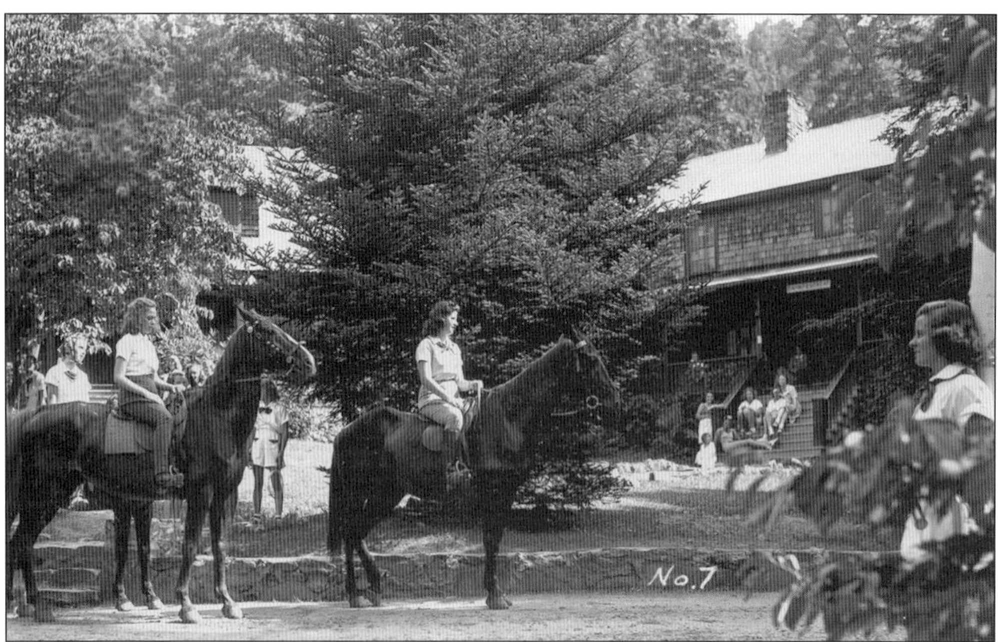

In 1897, a group of interdenominational clergy purchased 4,500 acres on the eastern boundary of the Blue Ridge Mountains near Asheville to found Montreat—a portmanteau of the words "mountain" and "retreat"—for physical and spiritual renewal and Christian study and practice for both adults and youth during the summer. The property includes over 40 miles of hiking trails. (Courtesy of the Swannanoa Valley Museum.)

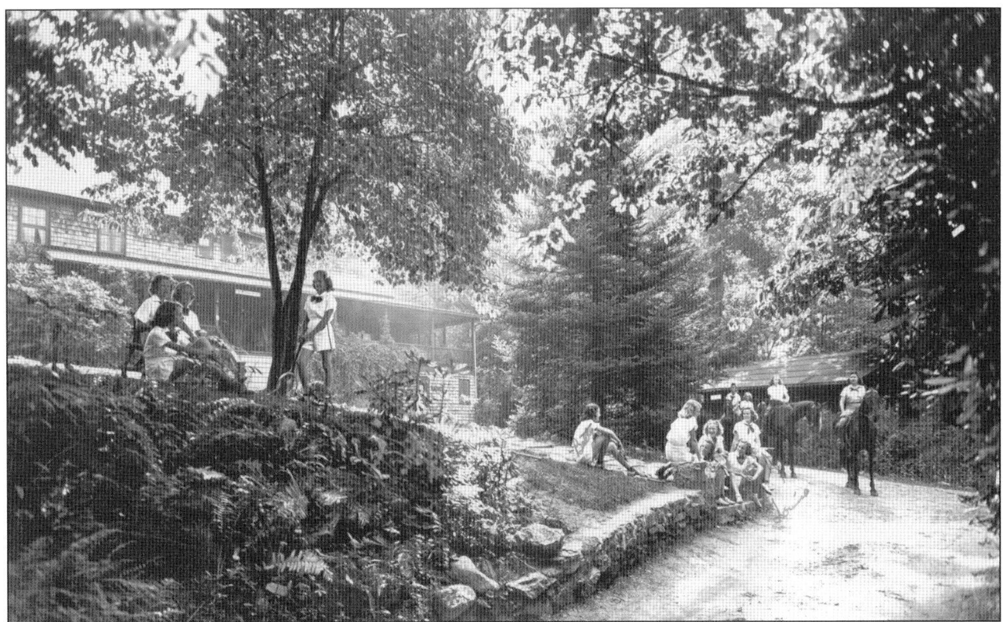

In 1912, Robert Anderson and William Henry Belk purchased 28 acres in the center of Montreat, where they founded Montreat Camp for Girls in 1925. Alice Anderson "Mackey" McBride from French Camp, Mississippi, directed the camp during the 1930s and 1940s. Girls from across the Southeast attended the camp. (Courtesy of the Swannanoa Valley Museum.)

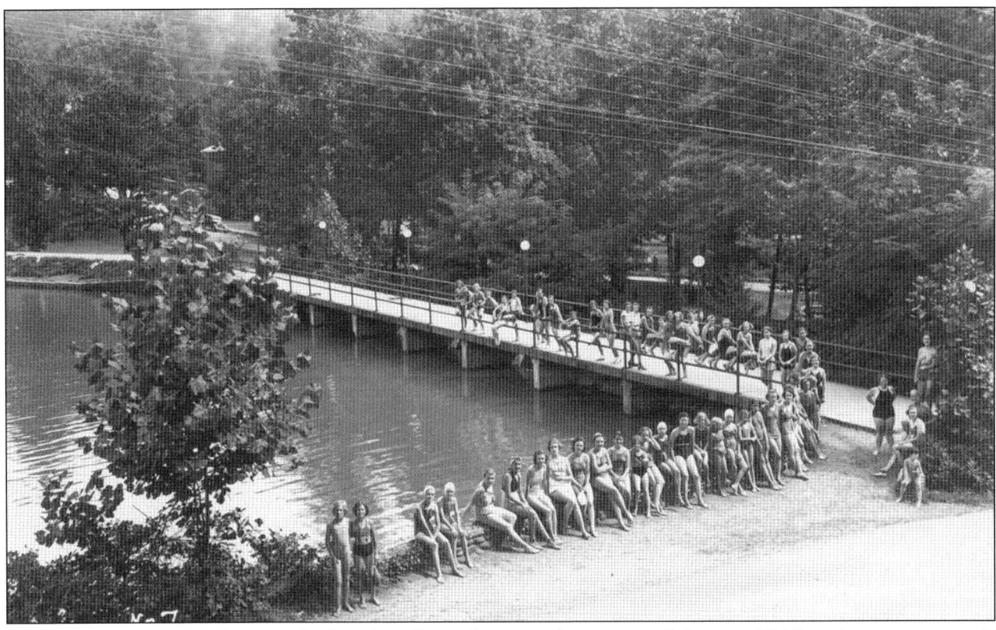

In 1908, Montreat dammed Flat Creek to form a three-acre lake. A 1910 ordinance stated, "Bathing suits must have sleeves extending half way from the shoulder to elbow and pants or skirts extending to the knees." The wooden dam collapsed in the flood of 1916. Susan Graham and her son Allen financed a new dam in 1924. Lake Susan was named in her honor. (Courtesy of the Swannanoa Valley Museum.)

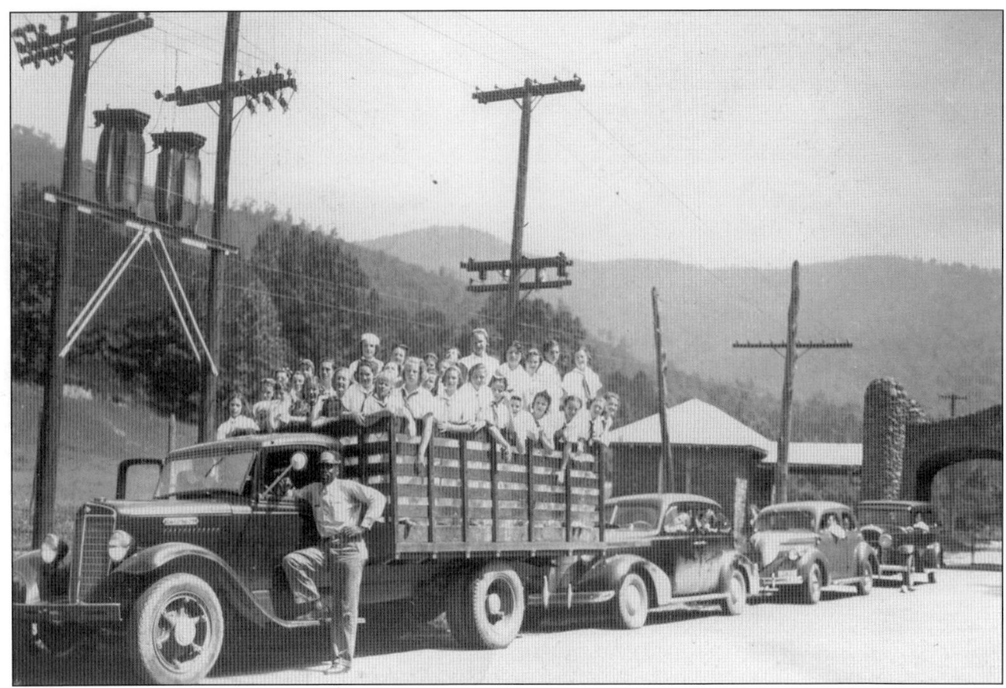

Campers rode through the iconic gate marking the entrance to the Montreat Conference Center, Montreat College, and the town of Montreat. The gate, constructed from local stone, was funded by the Women's Auxiliary of the Presbyterian Church in 1922. The toll for entering the gate in 1910 was 25¢ per day or $5 for the season. (Courtesy of the Swannanoa Valley Museum.)

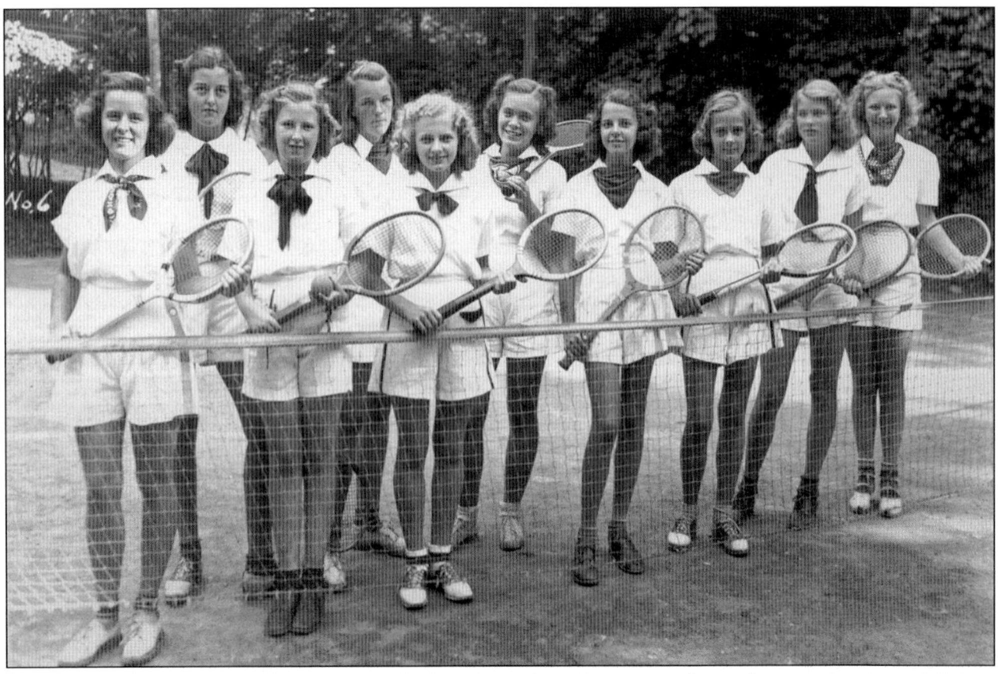

Recreational activities at Montreat include arts and crafts, music, barn dances, boating, fishing, swimming, hiking, and tennis. (Courtesy of the Swannanoa Valley Museum.)

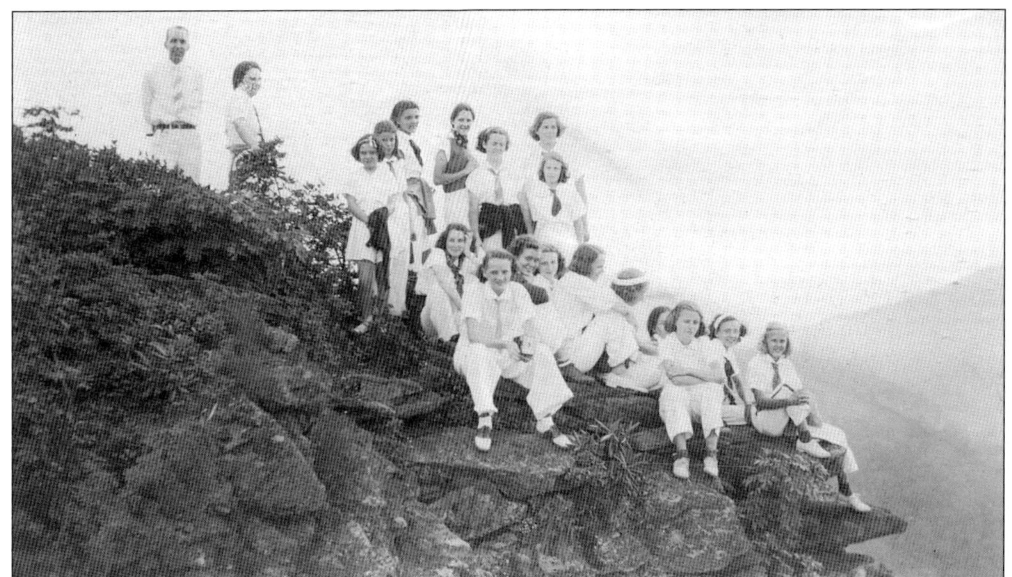

In 1938, after having lunch at Craggy Gardens, Camp Montreat girls embarked on a hike to the summit of Craggy Pinnacle, where this photograph was snapped. A summer thunderstorm rolled in, and the girls were drenched on the way down. Still, a camper wrote in her scrapbook, "How glorious it was!" (Courtesy of the Swannanoa Valley Museum.)

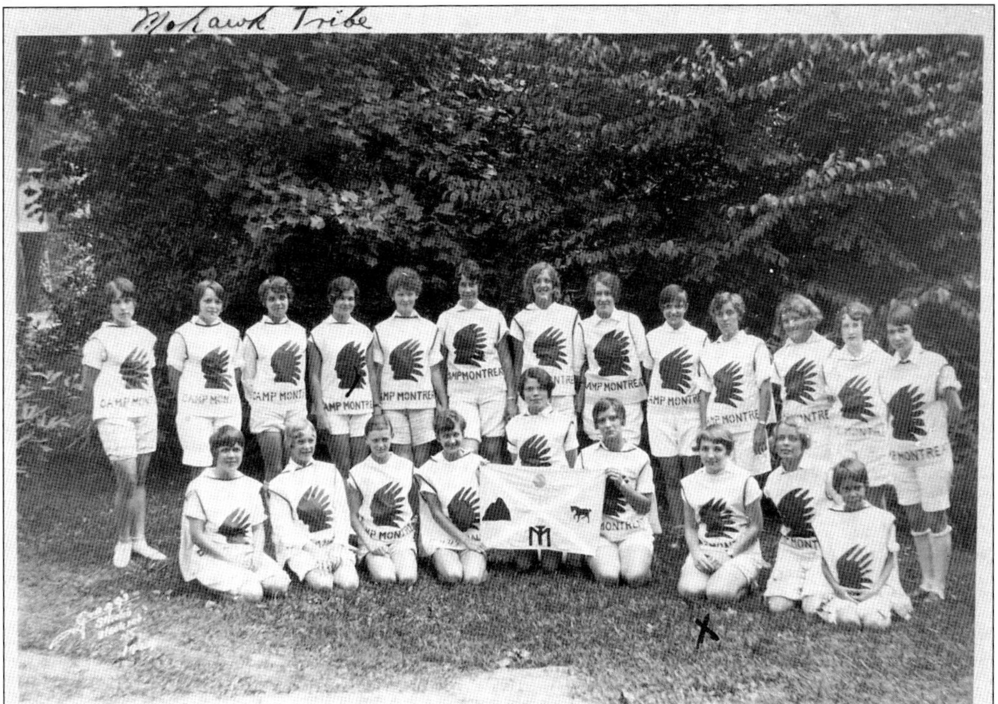

Campers forged lifelong friendships at Camp Montreat. Girls were grouped into tribes, such as the Mohawk tribe pictured here. Director Alice Anderson "Mackey" McBride continued the Native American theme when she opened her own camp in 1945. (Courtesy of the Swannanoa Valley Museum.)

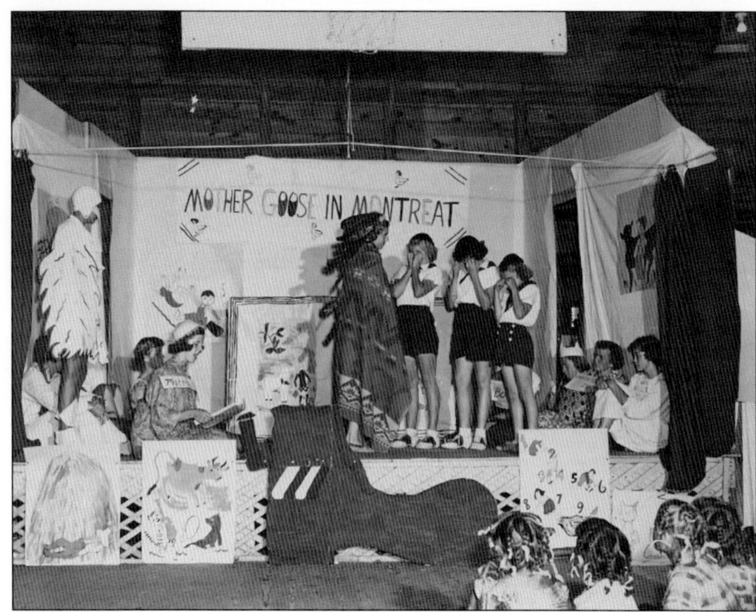

Girls at Camp Montreat perform in a play. Montreat draws thousands of families each summer and continues to offer recreation and fellowship opportunities for the children of conferees and summer residents through youth programs and day camps. (Courtesy of the Swannanoa Valley Museum.)

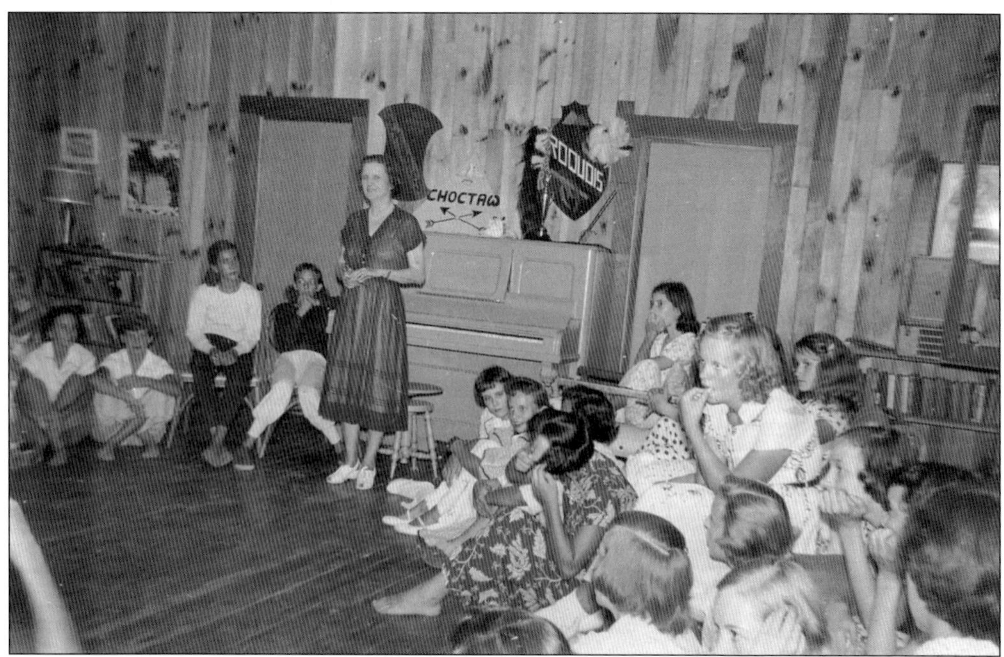

In 1945, Camp Montreat's director, Alice Anderson "Mackey" McBride, pictured standing in front of a piano, founded Camp Bridewood with Doris Tucker. It was a Christian camp for girls set at an elevation of 2,400 feet on Black Mountain in Bridewood Acres. They changed the name to Merri-Mac in 1950. (Courtesy of Camp Merri-Mac.)

In the camp's first decades, parents were instructed to purchase railway tickets for campers to the Black Mountain station. McBride personally arranged chaperones to escort girls from Miami, Florida; Washington, DC; Shreveport, Louisiana; and Jackson, Mississippi. (Courtesy of Camp Merri-Mac.)

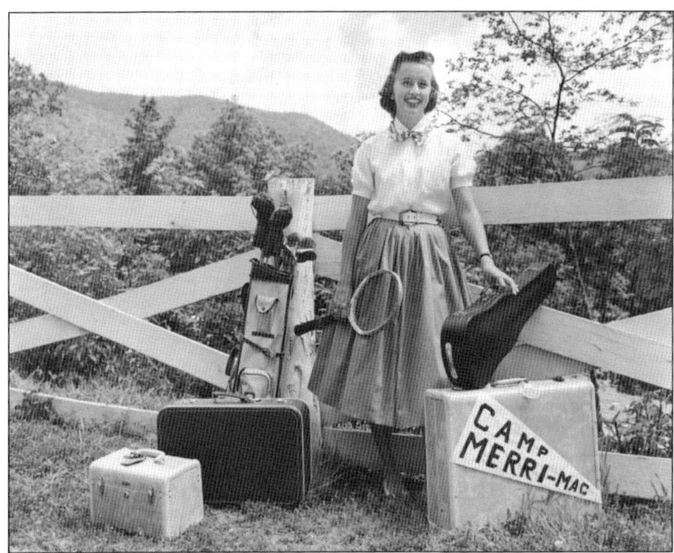

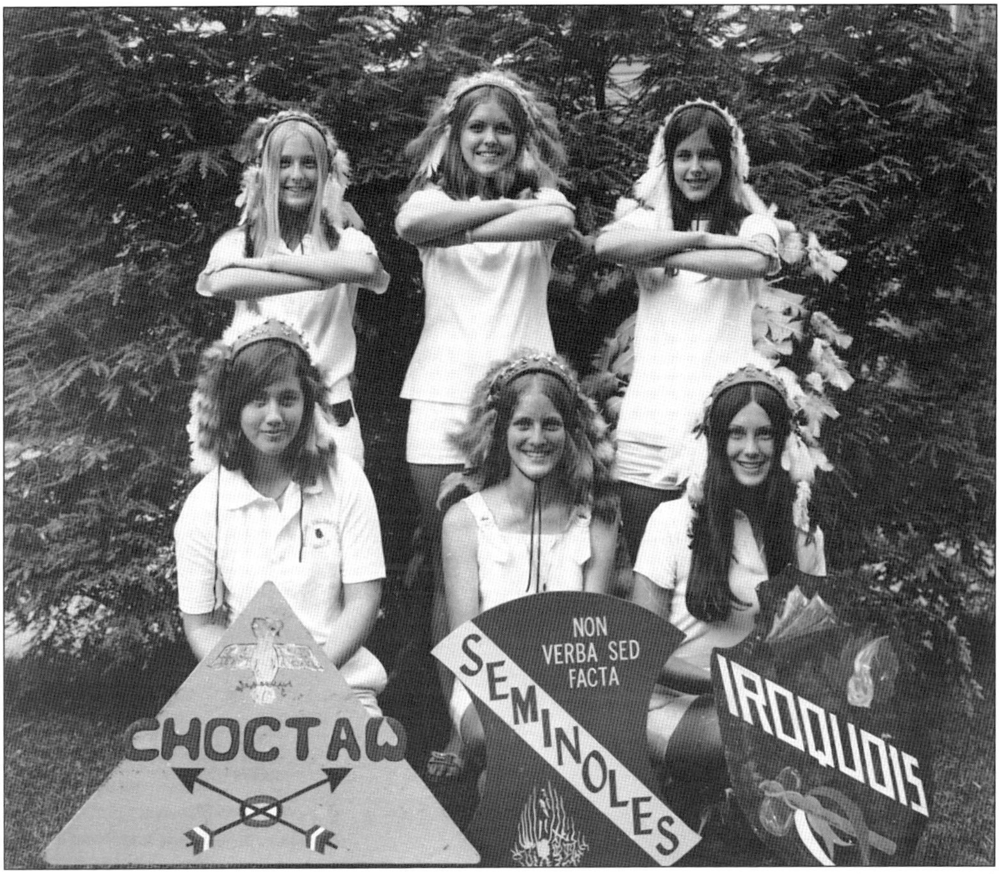

Like Montreat, Merri-Mac campers are divided into tribes, such as Iroquois, Choctaws, and Seminoles. Many of the traditions inaugurated by the founders like princess parties, tribal competitions, camp songs, and morning chapels endure today. (Courtesy of the Swannanoa Valley Museum.)

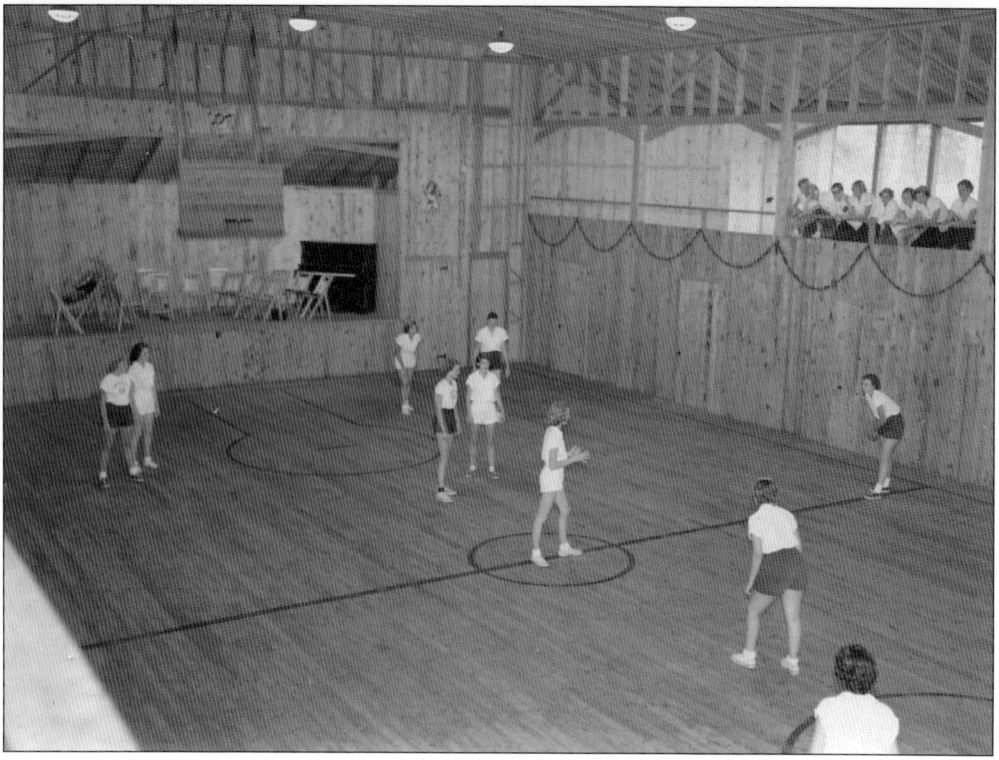

Upon arrival at camp, campers and counselors joined an Indian tribe and forged lifelong bonds with fellow group members. Each evening featured a competition between tribes, such as the basketball game shown here. At the end of the session, the tribe that achieved the most victories won the Merri-Mac banner. (Courtesy of Camp Merri-Mac.)

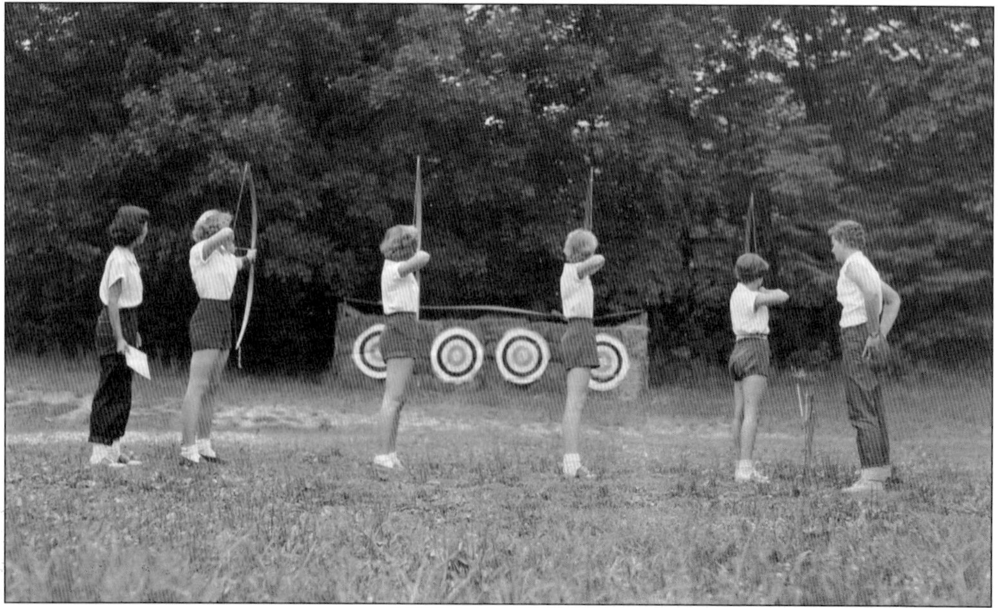

In addition to tribal competitions, Merri-Mac offers a range of traditional camp activities like archery, which develops poise, good posture, and steady nerves. (Courtesy of Camp Merri-Mac.)

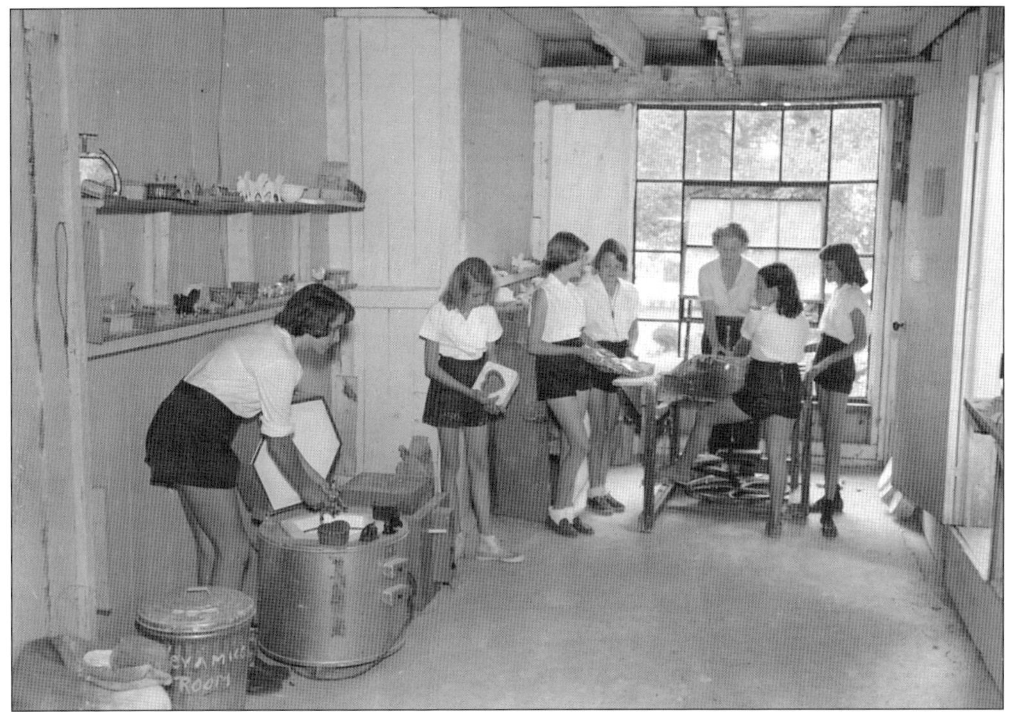

The ceramics room and craft shop were popular camp locales. Merri-Mac offered arts and crafts instruction, teaching girls to make bowls, vases, lanyards, belts, and jewelry. (Courtesy of Camp Merri-Mac.)

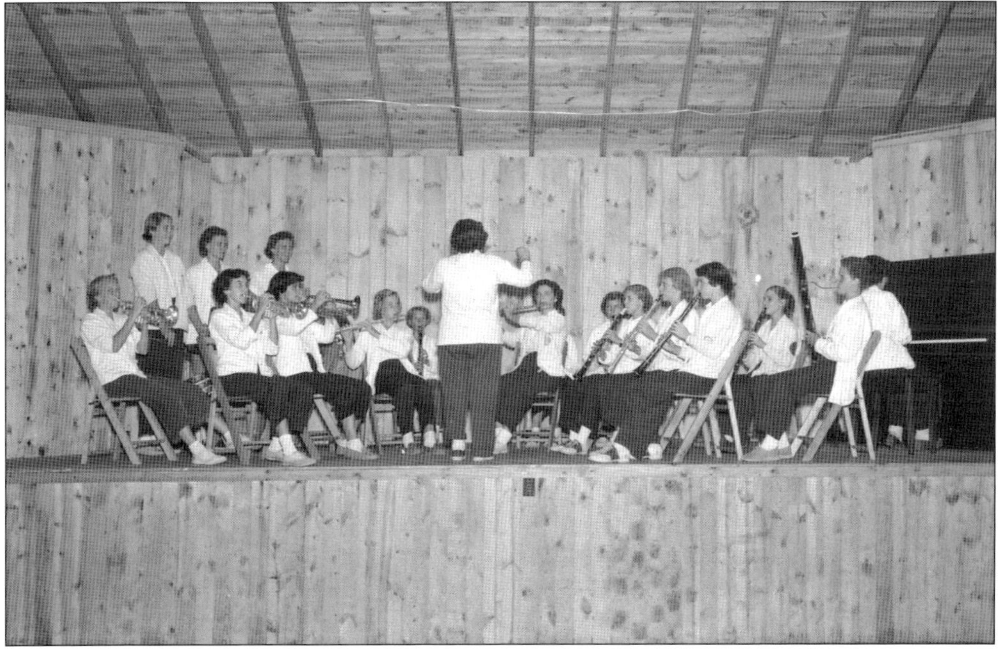

Merri-Mac's alma mater, published in the 1953 catalog, lauded, "Tell me why the stars do shine. Tell me why the ivy twine. Tell me why the sky so blue. Tell me Merri-Mac just why I love you." (Courtesy of Camp Merri-Mac.)

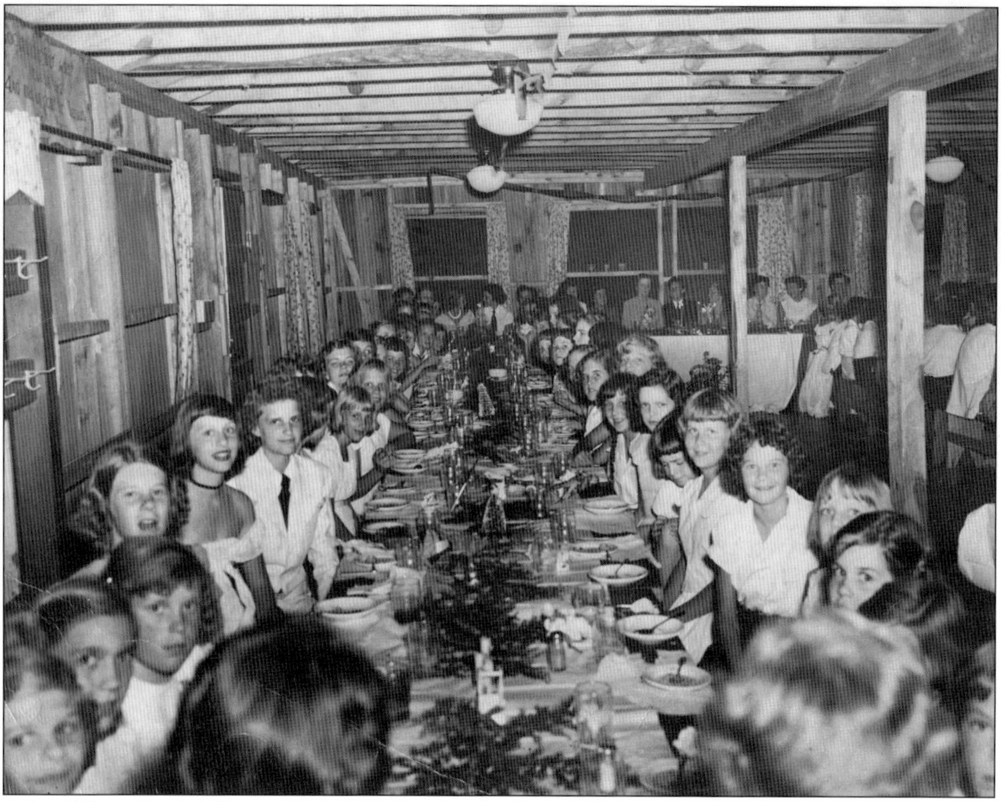

After a day chock-full of activity, Merri-Mac campers and staff gathered around a massive table in the dining hall to partake in this meal of wholesome food. (Courtesy of Camp Merri-Mac.)

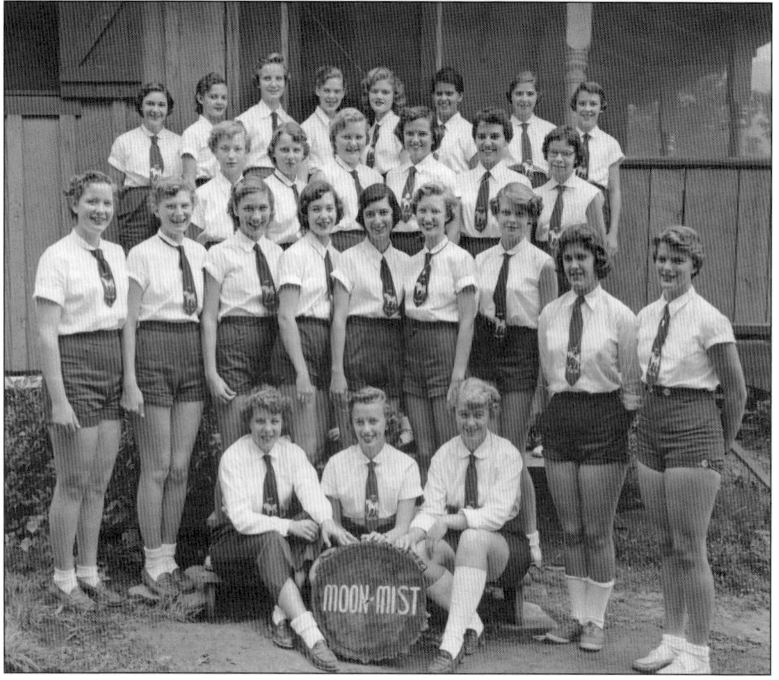

Campers pose in front of Moon Mist cabin wearing ties, standard to the Merri-Mac uniform in the 1950s. (Courtesy of Camp Merri-Mac.)

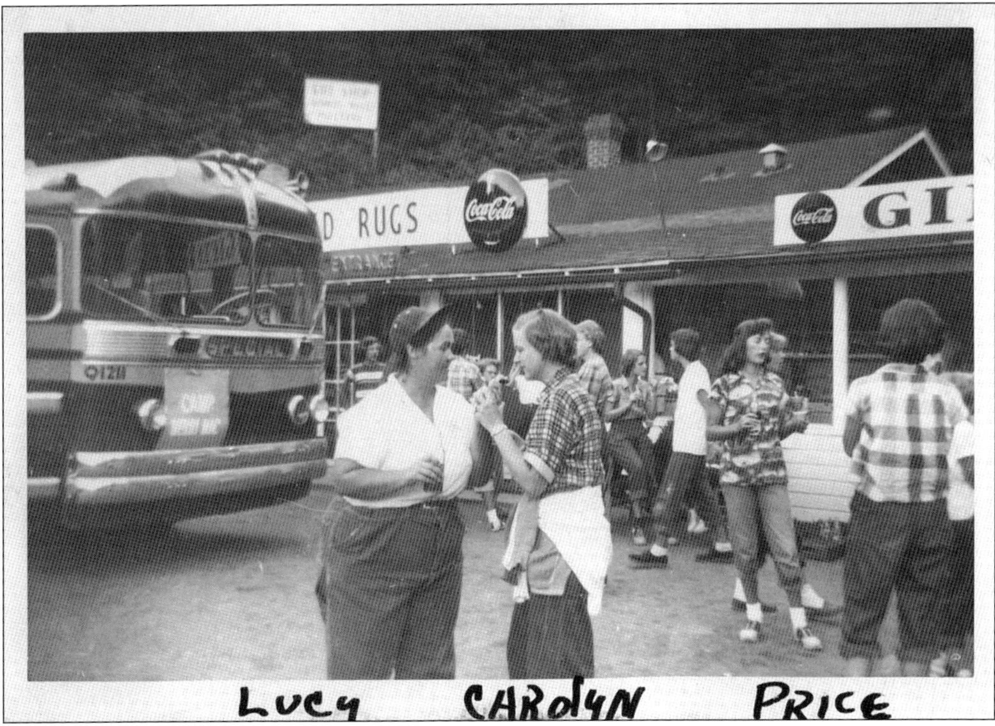

In 1952, Merri-Mac chartered a Trailways bus to take campers to nearby Mount Mitchell, the highest peak in eastern America, for an overnight camping trip. The campers and staff stopped at a tourist stand for "sin drinks," also known as Coca-Cola, and hot dogs. The campers slept at the summit and watched the sunrise the next morning. Campers took excursions to Biltmore Estate and Chimney Rock. (Courtesy of Camp Merri-Mac.)

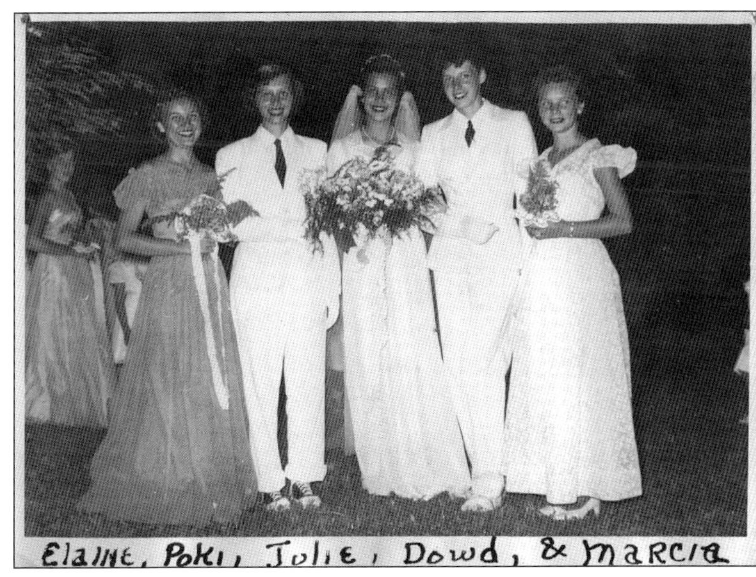

Camp Merri-Mac had many unique traditions, including an annual Independence Day picnic, Christmas held on July 25, and weddings staged between costumed campers, as shown here. The symbolic camp wedding was meant to bring campers, old and new, together in love, loyalty, and friendship. (Courtesy of Camp Merri-Mac.)

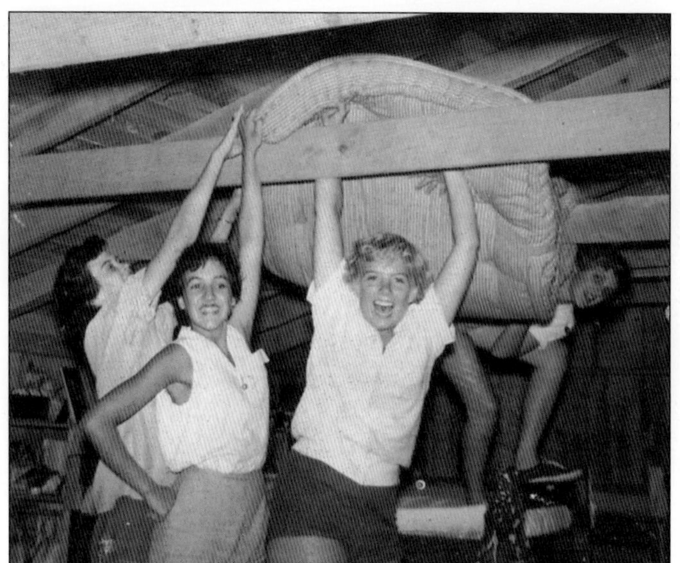

While Alice Anderson "Mackey" McBride hoped that the stability, peace, and power of the Blue Ridge Mountains would inspire campers to be lovely, pure, and true, camp still allowed plenty of opportunities for horseplay. (Courtesy of Camp Merri-Mac.)

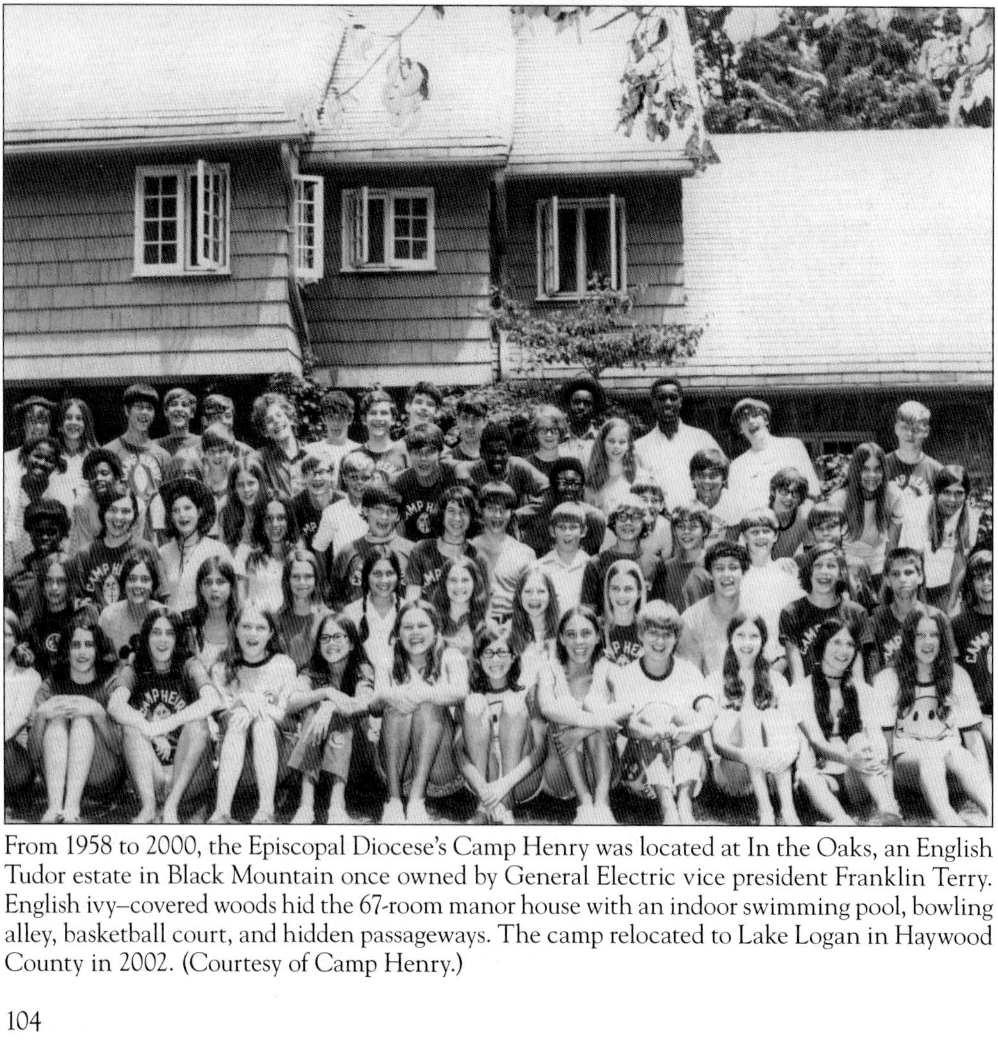

From 1958 to 2000, the Episcopal Diocese's Camp Henry was located at In the Oaks, an English Tudor estate in Black Mountain once owned by General Electric vice president Franklin Terry. English ivy–covered woods hid the 67-room manor house with an indoor swimming pool, bowling alley, basketball court, and hidden passageways. The camp relocated to Lake Logan in Haywood County in 2002. (Courtesy of Camp Henry.)

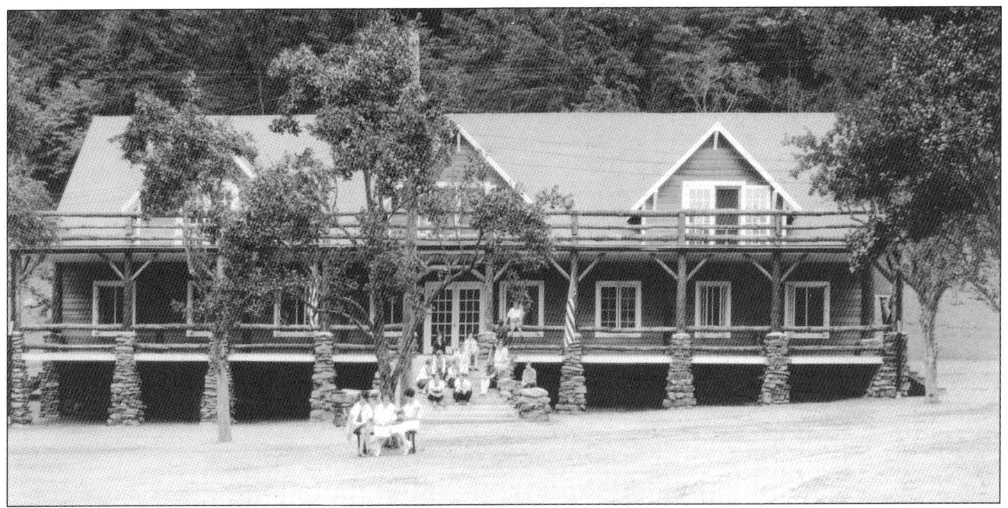

E.W. Grove, of Asheville's Grove Park Inn, developed Lake Eden near Black Mountain as a camp for girls and a summer resort between 1923 and 1924. This 1920s photograph, embossed with the Plateau Studios imprint, the studio of George Masa, shows the dormitory. Black Mountain College purchased the property in 1937, and today, Camp Rockmont operates on the site. (Courtesy of North Carolina Collection, Pack Memorial Public Library.)

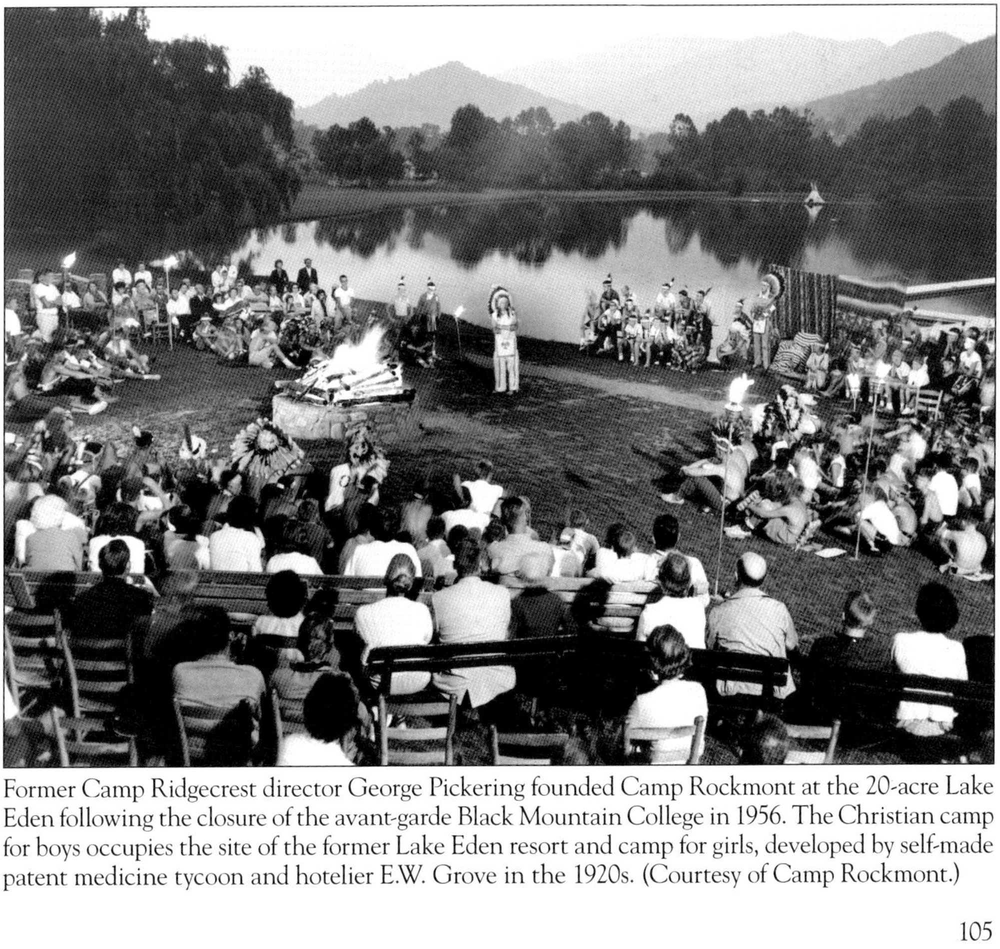

Former Camp Ridgecrest director George Pickering founded Camp Rockmont at the 20-acre Lake Eden following the closure of the avant-garde Black Mountain College in 1956. The Christian camp for boys occupies the site of the former Lake Eden resort and camp for girls, developed by self-made patent medicine tycoon and hotelier E.W. Grove in the 1920s. (Courtesy of Camp Rockmont.)

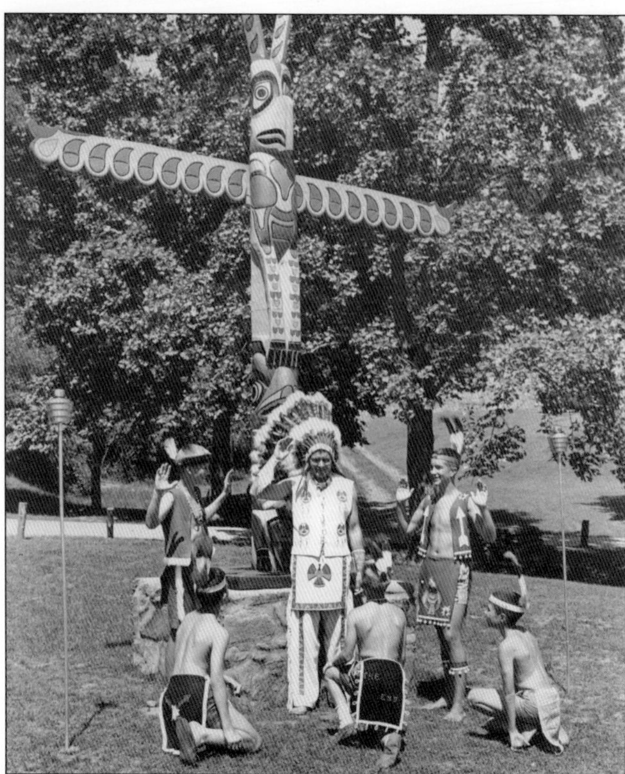

Camp Rockmont incorporated Native American iconography until the millennium. Totem poles, teepees, headdresses, and loincloths were commonplace. (Courtesy of Camp Rockmont.)

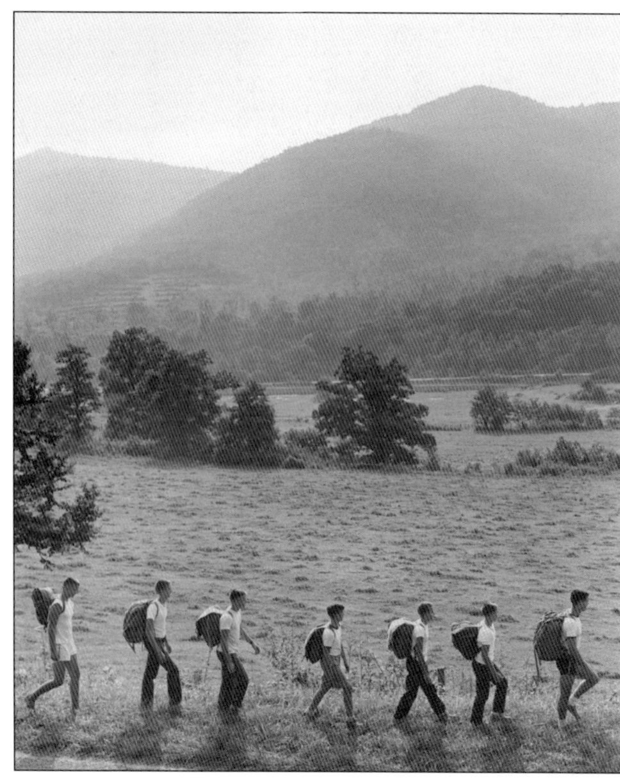

Camp Rockmont sits on 550 private acres in the shadow of the Black Mountains surrounded by thousands of acres of national forest wilderness, the ideal setting for challenging outdoor adventures. (Courtesy of Camp Rockmont.)

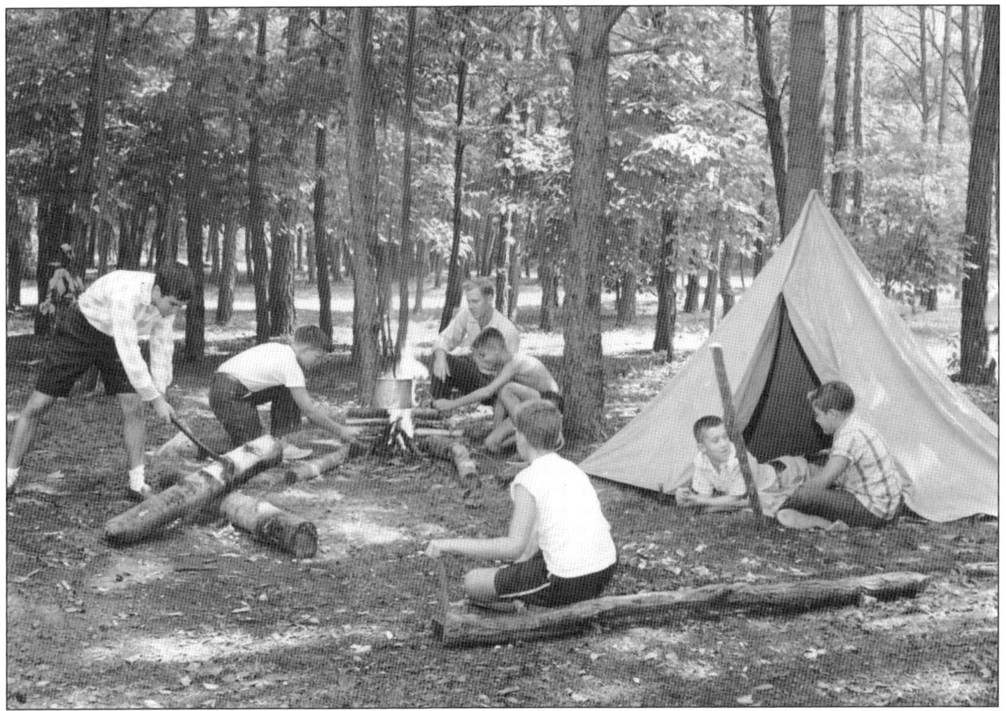

Campouts taught boys wilderness skills, self-reliance, and respect for the environment. (Courtesy of Camp Rockmont.)

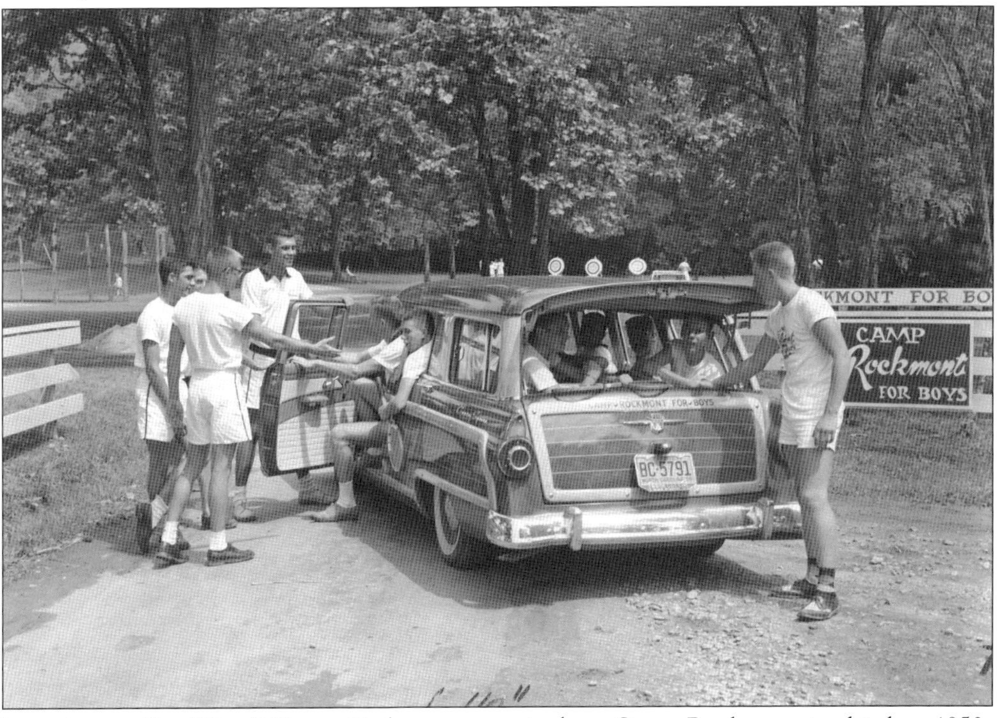

Longtime staffer "King" Henry Taylor greets arrivals at Camp Rockmont in this late 1950s photograph. (Courtesy of Camp Rockmont.)

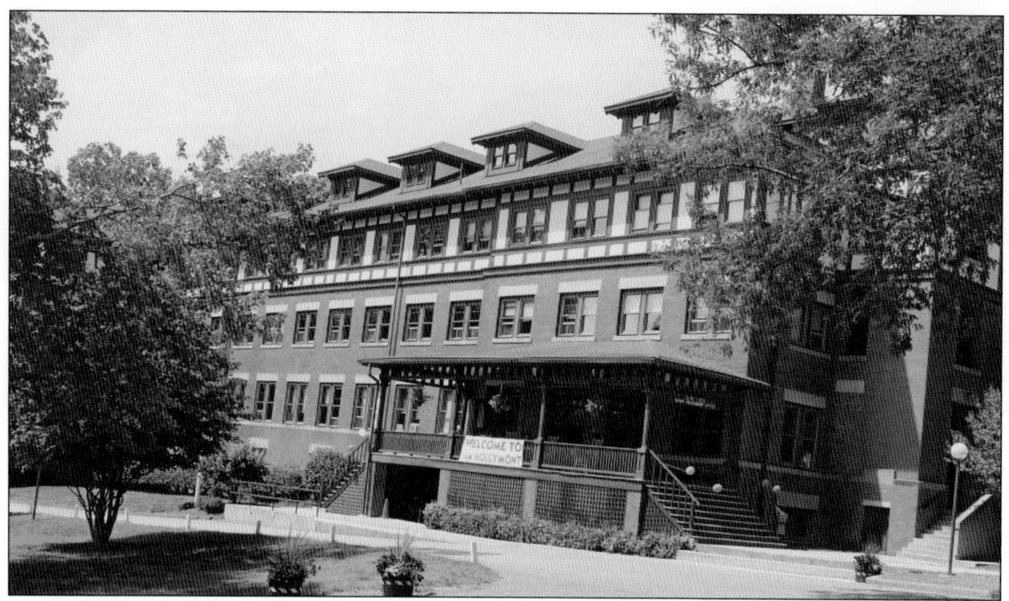

Camp Rockmont's founder George Pickering established Camp Hollymont, a Christian camp for girls at the Asheville School, a private coeducational boarding school, featuring Tudor-style architecture and listed in the National Register of Historic Places. (Courtesy of Camp Hollymont.)

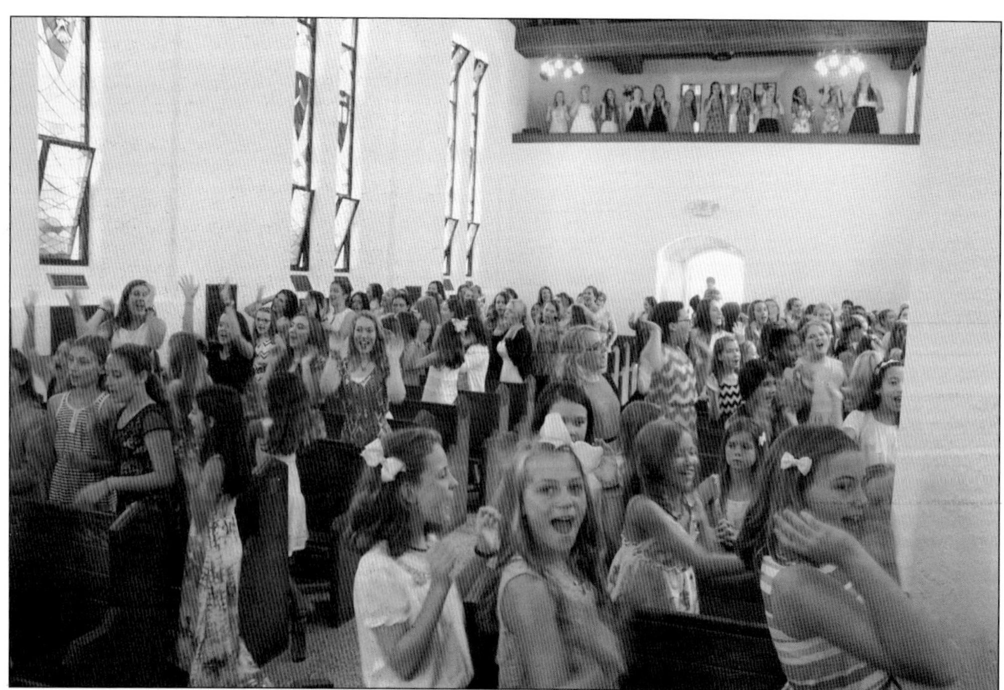
Camping traditions span generations at Asheville-area camps. Missy McKibbens attended her first session of Camp Hollymont in 1983. In 1992, her family purchased the camp, and she became the director. In 2013, her daughter became a camper. (Courtesy of Camp Hollymont.)

Four

Be Prepared

Scout, YMCA, and 4-H Camps

Linking muscular Christianity and social reform, American branches of the international Young Men's Christian Association arose starting in 1851. The YMCA founded the nation's first and longest continually operating summer camp, New York's Camp Dudley, in 1885. The Asheville branch of the YMCA was formed in 1889 to allay social anxieties about juvenile delinquency since the city lacked parks or playgrounds for children. For over a century, the YMCA's Blue Ridge Assembly has galvanized generations of young leaders, including summer campers. The Young Women's Christian Association of Asheville was founded in 1906 as a boardinghouse for "transient, self-supporting women of good character" to support their spiritual, mental, moral, and physical well-being. The YWCA operated Camp Kenjocketee, a summer camp for girls, near Candler from 1924 until the early 1930s. The YMCA continues to offer day camps for area children each summer.

As America became increasingly more urban, public schools in the county organized agricultural science and technology clubs for young people around the turn of the 20th century. Administered by the Cooperative Extension Service since 1914, these clubs adopted the name 4-H in 1924. The state's oldest 4-H summer camp opened in Swannanoa in the 1920s and closed in 2013.

Inspired by Ernest Thompson Seton's Woodcraft Indians, Sir Robert Baden-Powell's Boy Scout Association and Girl Guides, and the Camp Fire Girls, Boy Scout and Girl Scout troops formed across the United States in the 1910s. Asheville's first Girl Scout troop met in 1918. Endeavoring to provide girls outdoor recreation in addition to traditional domestic skills, local Girl Scouts set up overnight camps at established summer camps around the area before Camp Pisgah opened in 1956. In 1920, a decade after the Boy Scouts of America's founding, members of the Asheville Rotary Club established the Daniel Boone Council. The Scouts camped at various sites across the region before Camp Daniel Boone, located in Haywood County approximately 14 miles south of Canton, welcomed its first Scouts in the summer of 1941. As a 1930s *Scout-o-gram* professed, "Scouting is camping. Camping enables a scout to better care for himself, helps to prepare him to meet the requirements of life, and gives him a week or more of outdoor life that he will remember for a long, long time both because of the instruction received and the fun had during his stay at camp." The primeval forests and crystal-clear lakes of western North Carolina provided an optimal environment for children with these organizations to participate in canoeing, swimming, hiking, and campcraft while growing into good citizens.

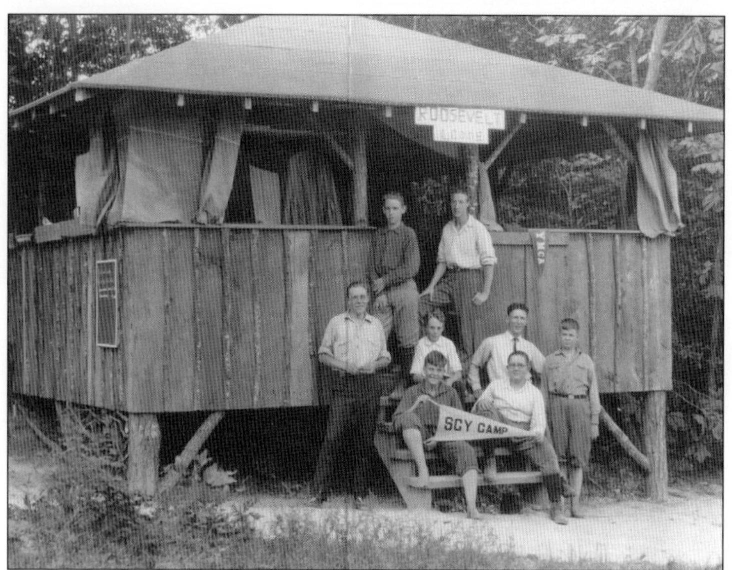

The Blue Ridge Assembly operated SCY Camp for boys at Roosevelt Lodge during the late 1920s. According to a 1929 article in NC State College of Agriculture and Engineering's *The Technician*, the camp was "not interested in turning out 'stars' or 'champions,' but boys who can live, play, and enjoy a variety of activities correctly and happily, getting and giving the best all the time." (Courtesy of the Swannanoa Valley Museum.)

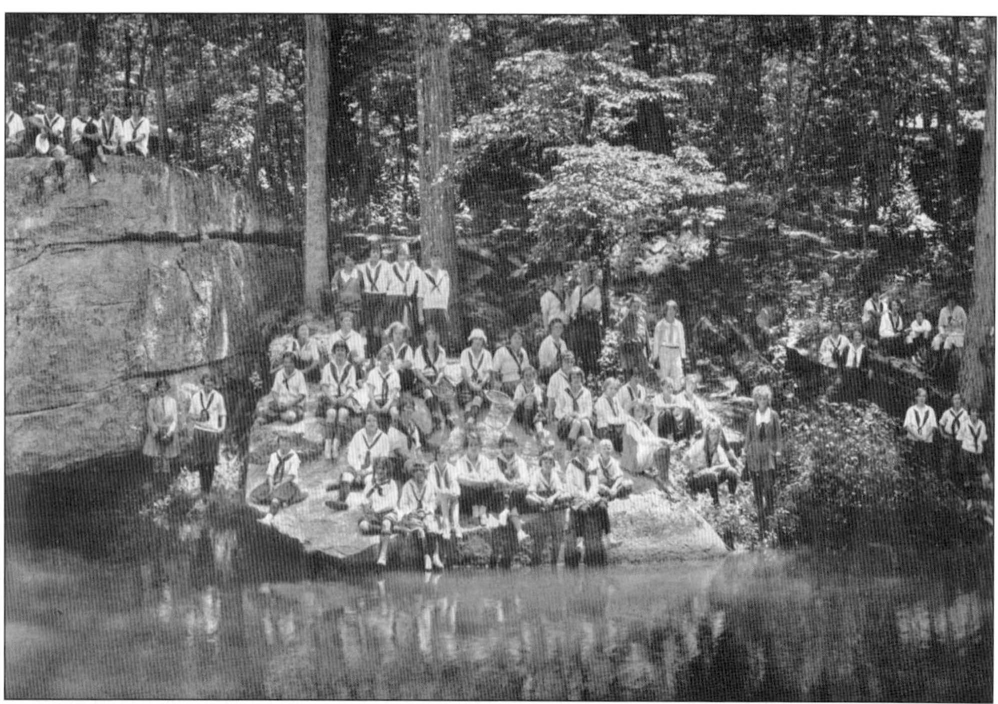

Louise L'Engle started the first Girl Scout troop in Asheville in 1918. One of the girls in her troop was Katharine Bynum Shepard, who later played a pivotal role in the growth of Girl Scouts locally. She is seen seated with crossed legs on the middle left side of the rock in this 1923 photograph taken at Camp Rockbrook near Brevard. (Courtesy of Girl Scouts Carolinas Peaks to Piedmont.)

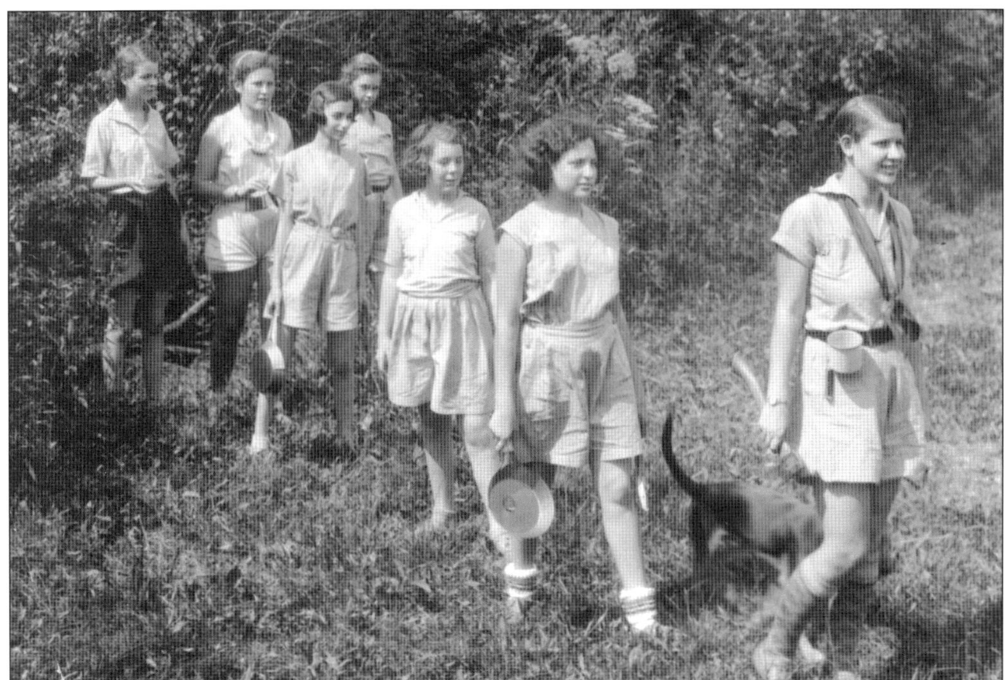

As the first director of the Asheville Girl Scout Council, Katharine Bynum Shepard arranged the first organized overnight camp for Girl Scouts in Buncombe County in 1934. Camp Katharine, named for Shepard, was located in Pisgah National Forest near Mills River. (Courtesy of Girl Scouts Carolinas Peaks to Piedmont.)

From 1932 to 1935, the Girl Scouts camped overnight at Camp Elliott near Old Fort. Acclaimed writer Wilma Dykeman, whose fiction and nonfiction chronicle the people and environment of Appalachia, is pictured second from the left. (Courtesy of Girl Scouts Carolinas Peaks to Piedmont.)

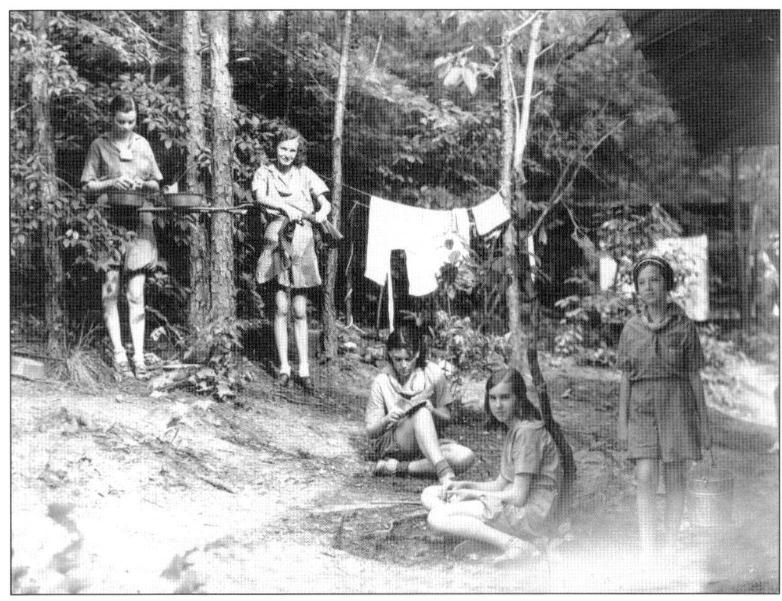

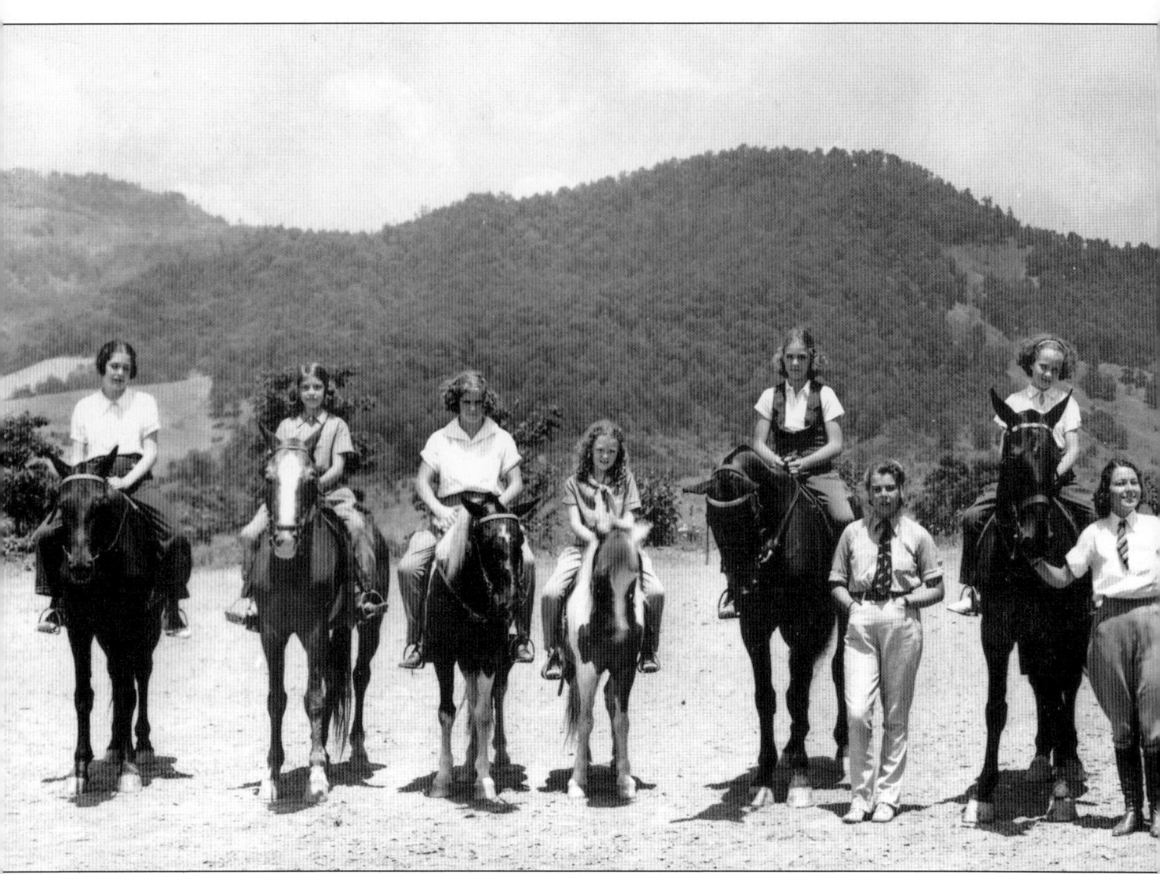

Throughout the 1930s, the Girl Scouts camped at various established camps across the region. In 1936, the Scouts camped at Camp Mondamin in Tuxedo. The list of items to bring included "serviceable underwear." In 1937, the girls camped at Lake Junaluska, nestled in the Great

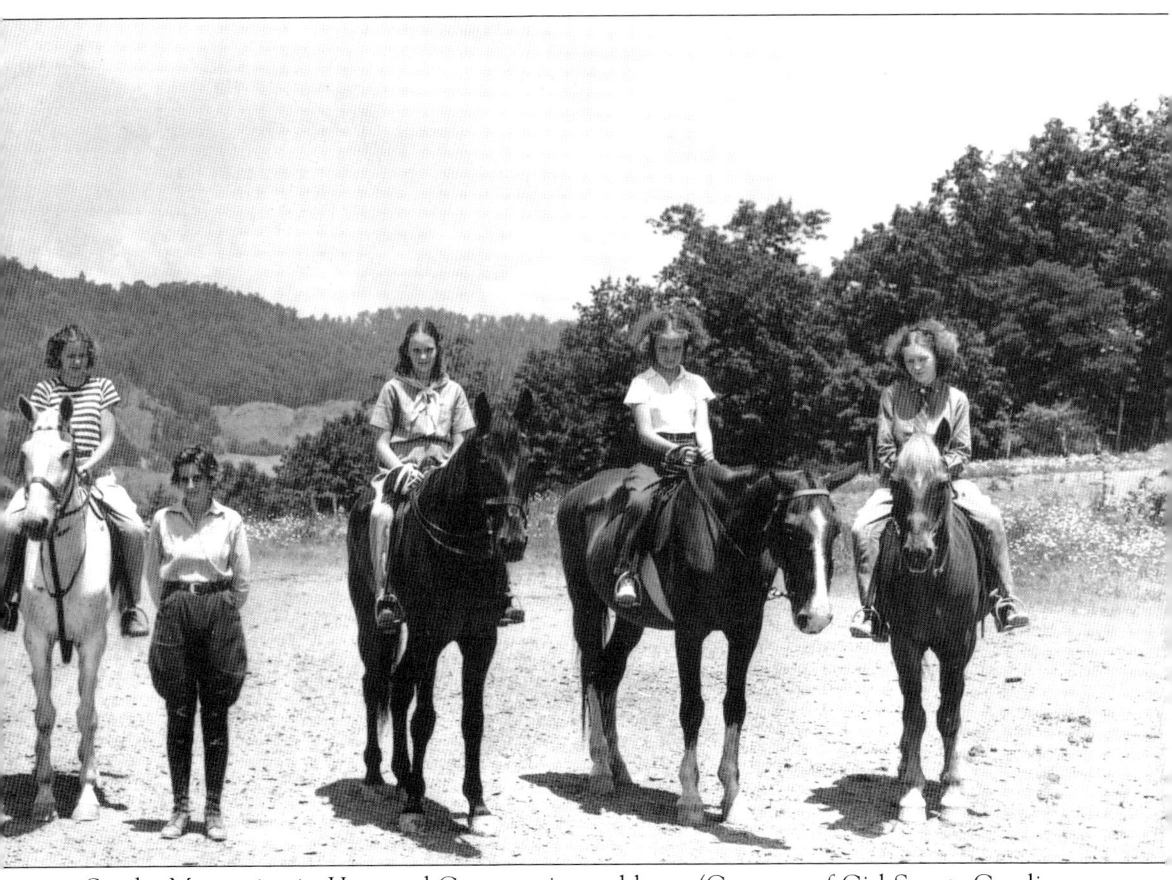

Smoky Mountains in Haywood County, pictured here. (Courtesy of Girl Scouts Carolinas Peaks to Piedmont.)

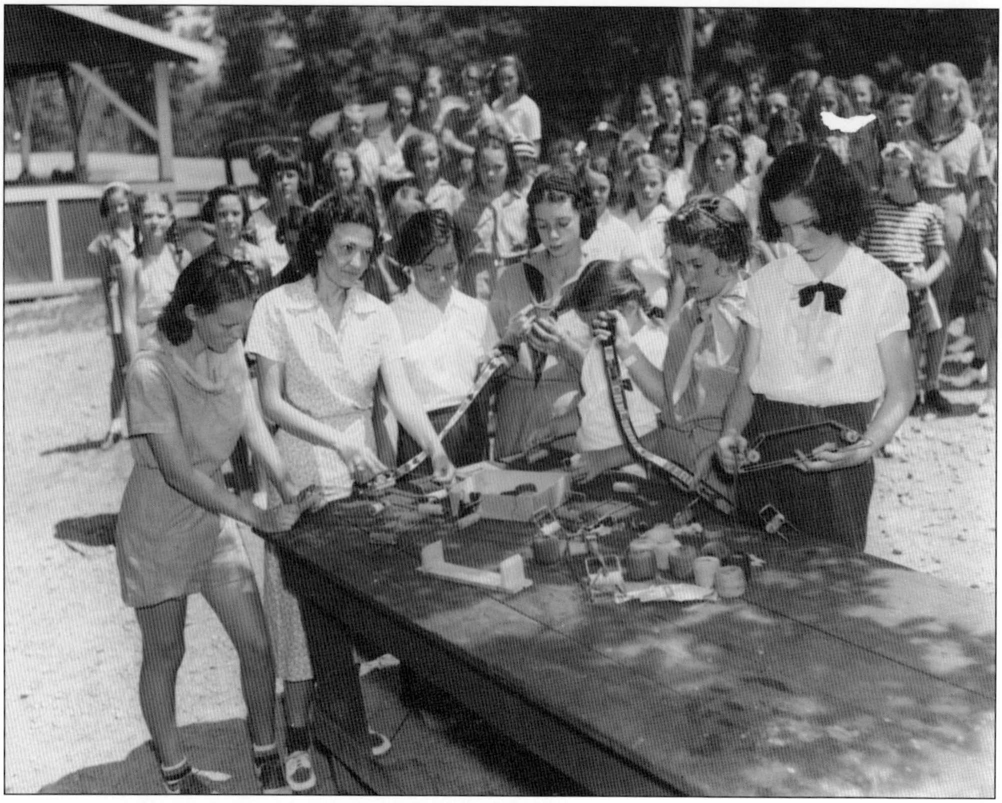

The Girl Scouts also held day camps in the summer during the 1930s. This 1937 photograph shows campers beading on a loom at the Recreational Park Day Camp in Asheville. (Courtesy of Girl Scouts Carolinas Peaks to Piedmont.)

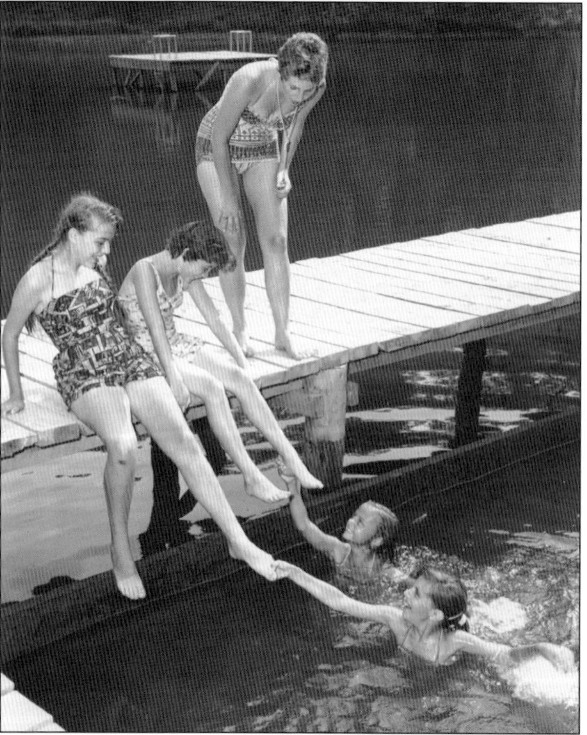

In 1952, the Pisgah Girl Scout Council formed to oversee troops in seven local counties. In 1953, with cookie sale profits, the council purchased 133 acres in the East Fork area of Transylvania County from A.S. MacFarlane for $4,300 for a camp. Camp Pisgah was fondly called the "Camp Built from Cookies." (Courtesy of Girl Scouts Carolinas Peaks to Piedmont.)

The property included a three-acre lake, and the waterfront was one of the first areas developed. Although primitive camping commenced as early as 1954, the first organized camping program was held in the summer of 1956. The camp was dedicated in 1958 and has hosted Girl Scouts every summer since. This 1960s photograph shows campers practicing synchronized diving into the lake. (Courtesy of Girl Scouts Carolinas Peaks to Piedmont.)

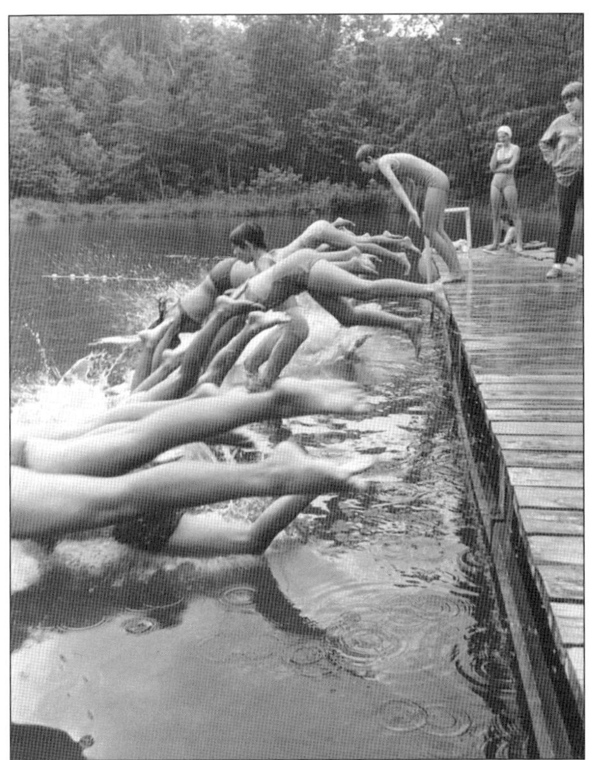

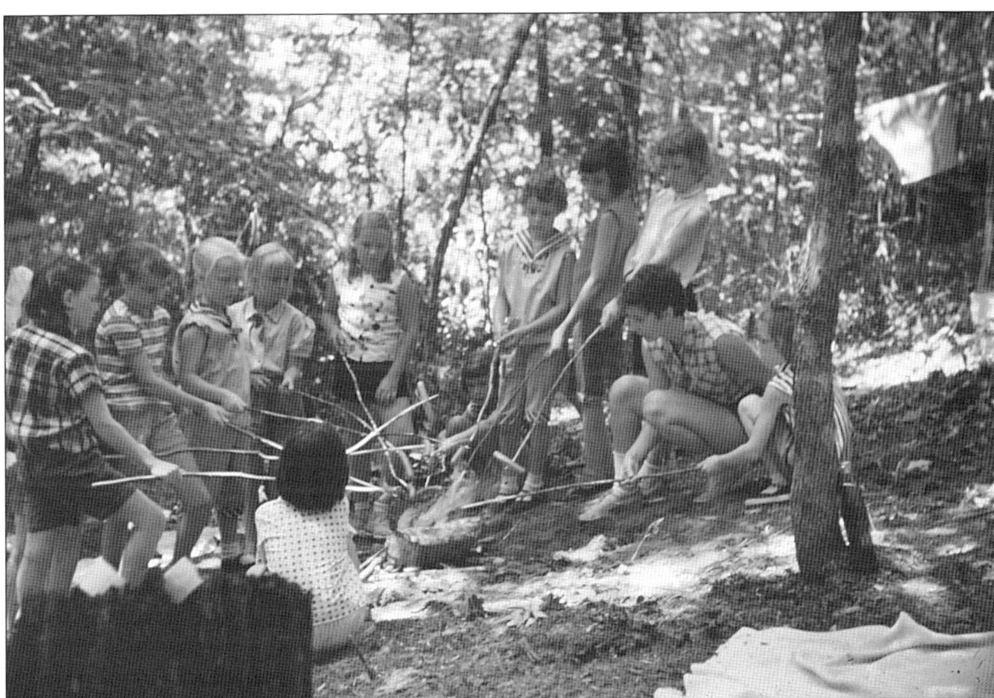

The Girl Scouts also held day and overnight camps in Brevard at Camps Sapphire, Illahee, Transylvania, and Deerwoode. This 1957 photograph shows a cookout during a summer day camp. (Courtesy of Girl Scouts Carolinas Peaks to Piedmont.)

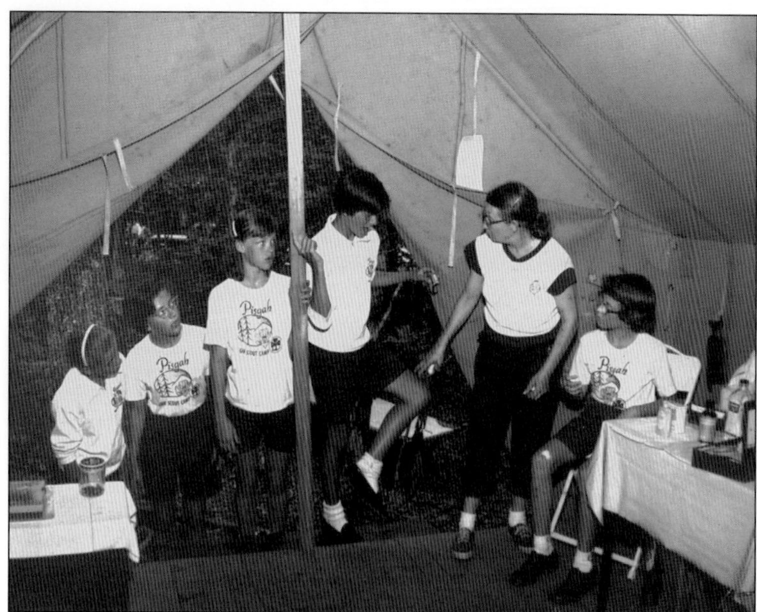

By 1957, Camp Pisgah had a designated infirmary tent. (Courtesy of Girl Scouts Carolinas Peaks to Piedmont.)

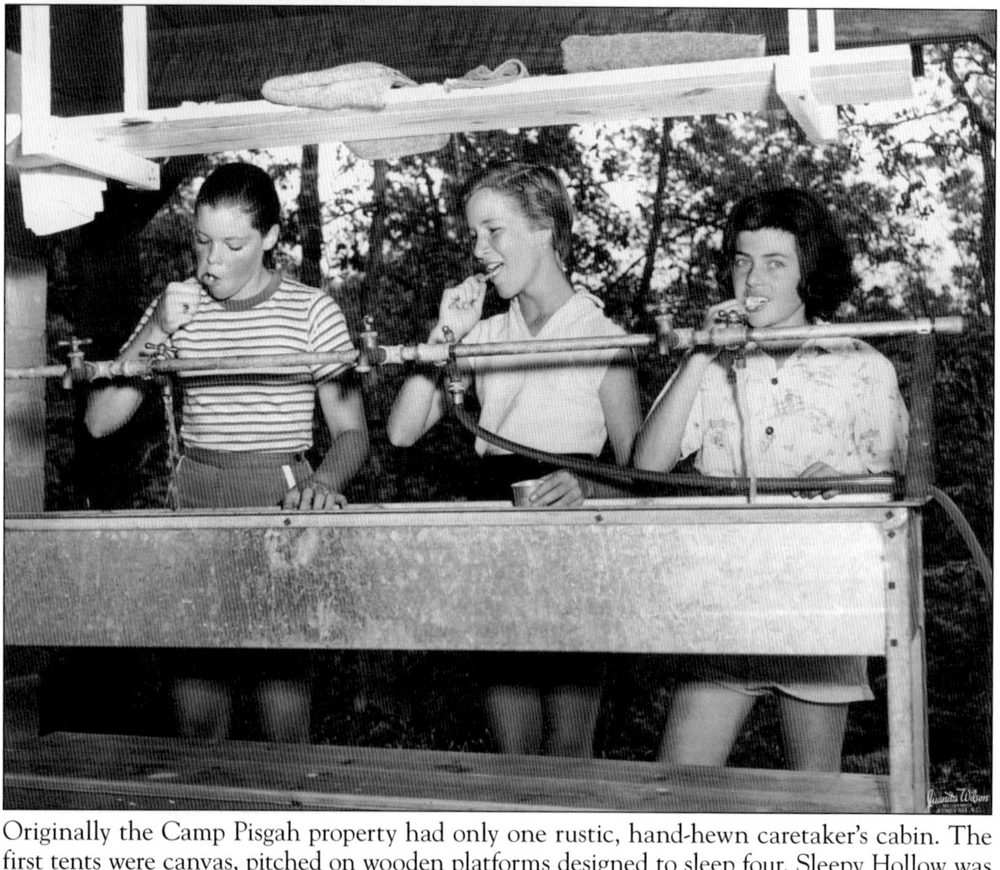

Originally the Camp Pisgah property had only one rustic, hand-hewn caretaker's cabin. The first tents were canvas, pitched on wooden platforms designed to sleep four. Sleepy Hollow was constructed in 1957, and High Top was built in 1958. The High Top units were replaced with yurts in 2007. (Courtesy of Girl Scouts Carolinas Peaks to Piedmont.)

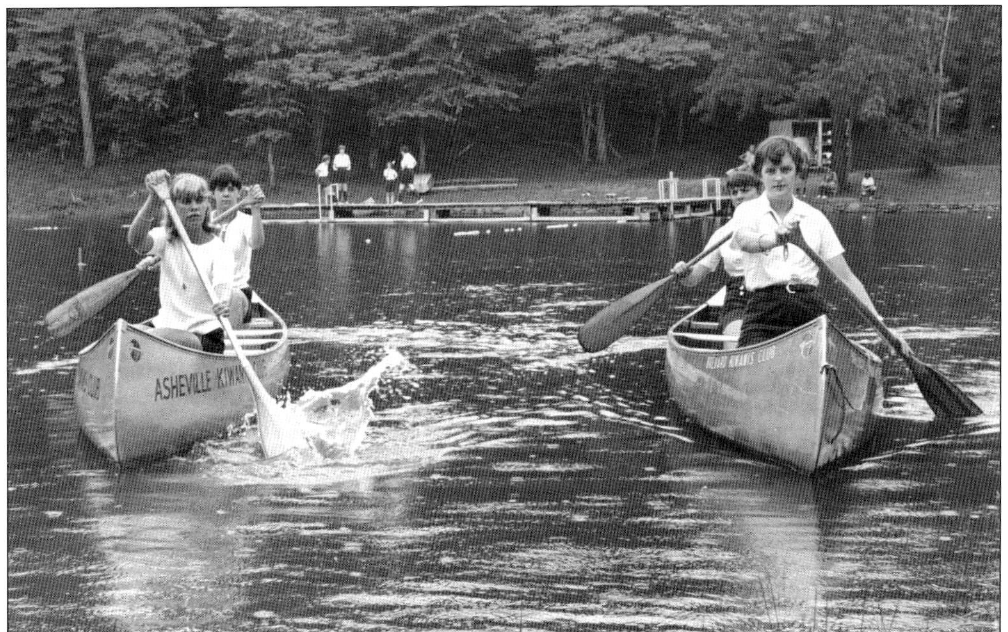

The Asheville and Brevard Kiwanis Clubs donated canoes to upgrade Camp Pisgah's boating program in the 1960s. (Courtesy of Girl Scouts Carolinas Peaks to Piedmont.)

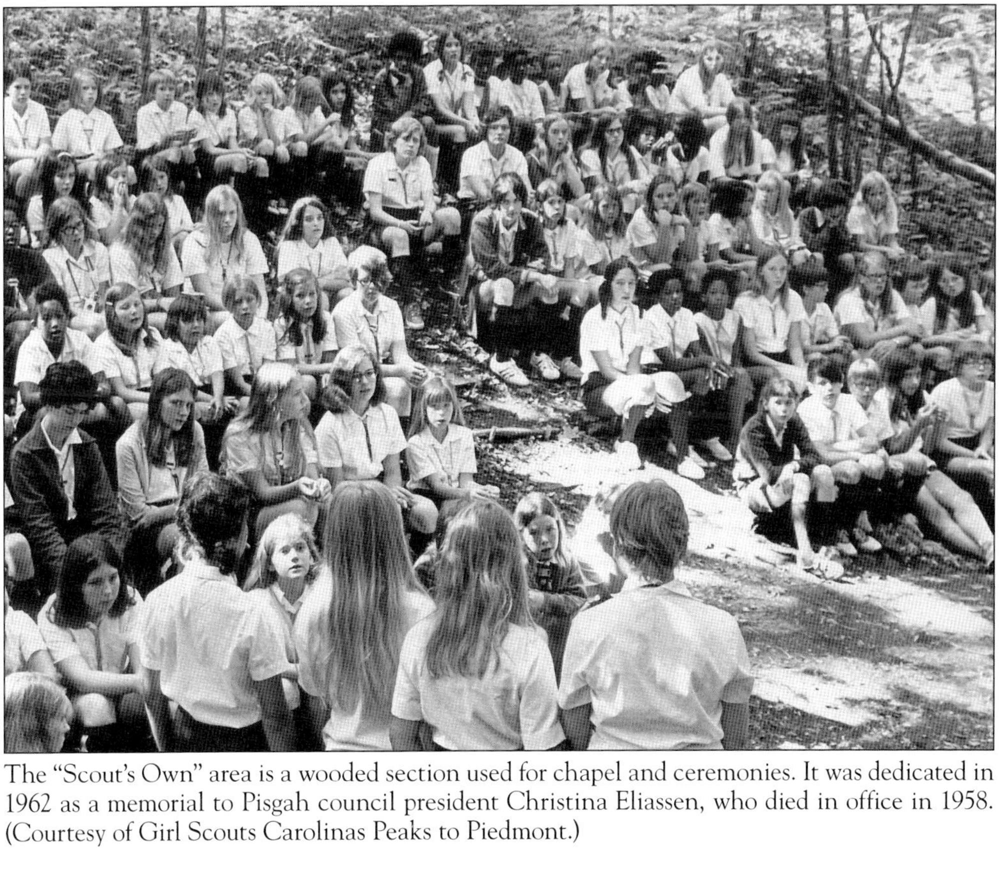

The "Scout's Own" area is a wooded section used for chapel and ceremonies. It was dedicated in 1962 as a memorial to Pisgah council president Christina Eliassen, who died in office in 1958. (Courtesy of Girl Scouts Carolinas Peaks to Piedmont.)

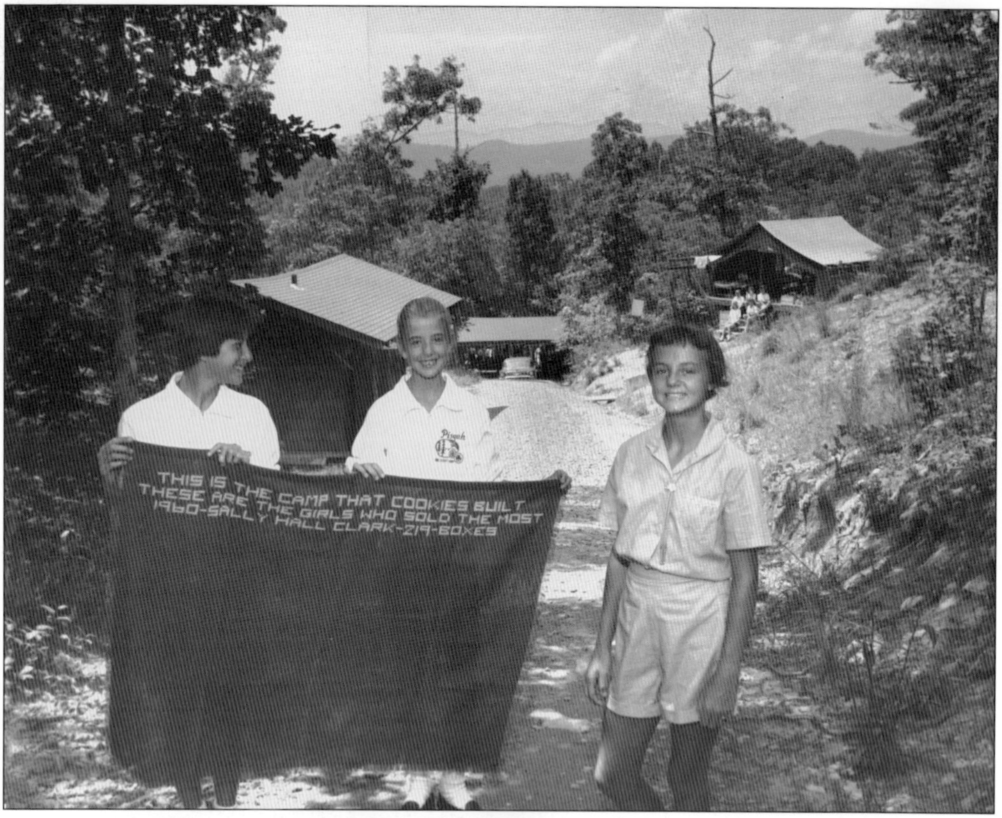

Sally Hall Clark, pictured with other Scouts in front of High Top overlooking Pisgah National Forest, sold the most cookies in 1961. (Courtesy of Girl Scouts Carolinas Peaks to Piedmont.)

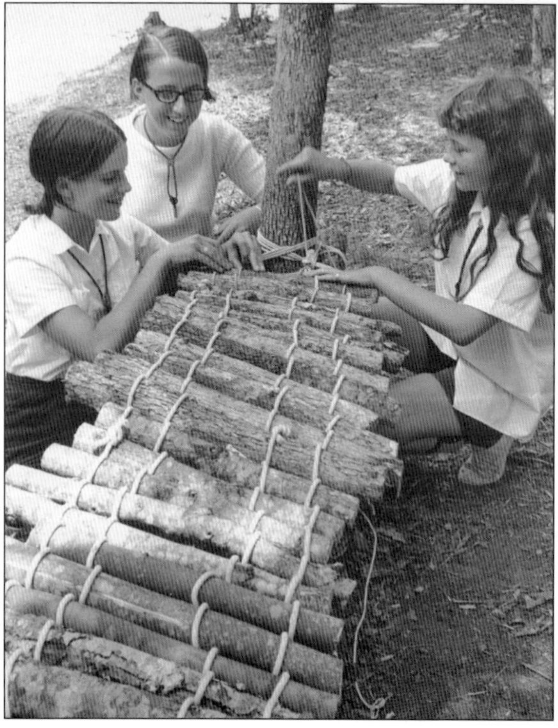

Girls learned lashing skills to build a table for their campsite, as shown in this 1960 photograph. Scouts also learned Cherokee weaving and received first aid training. (Courtesy of Girl Scouts Carolinas Peaks to Piedmont.)

In 1964, Camp Pisgah added Pioneer Ridge. Brevard High School students, with the help of a local outdoor equipment purveyor, Diamond Brand, designed custom-made covered wagons to sleep four girls. The camp replaced the wagons with cabins in 1994. (Courtesy of Girl Scouts Carolinas Peaks to Piedmont.)

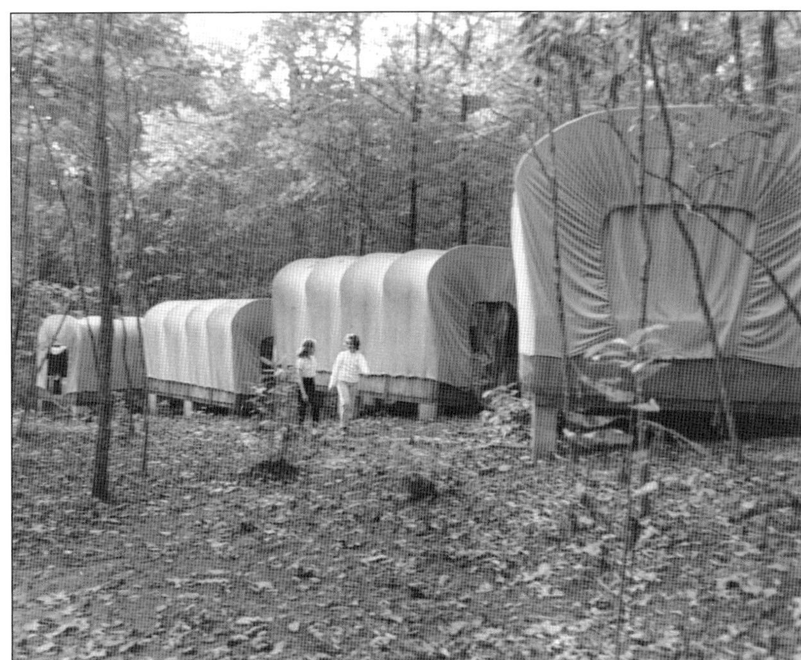

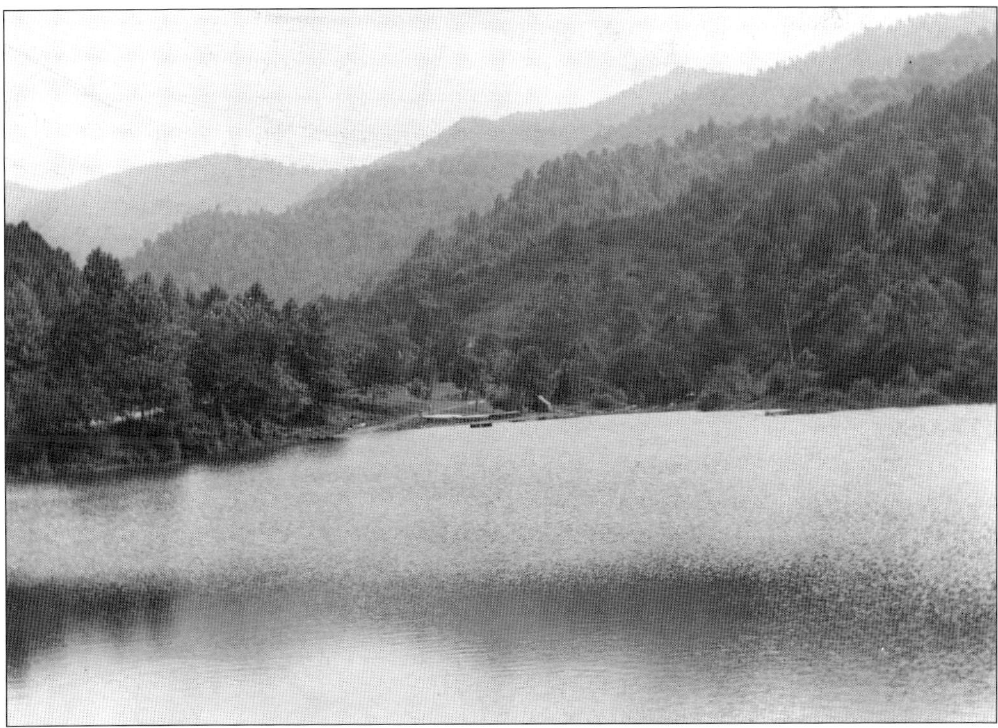

The Asheville Rotary Club organized the Daniel Boone Council of the Boys Scouts of America in the summer of 1920 to oversee troops in 14 counties in western North Carolina. The council purchased the Lee Ellis Boy Scout Reservation in Haywood County and established Camp Daniel Boone in 1941. In addition to a summer session, the camp hosted patrol camporees, hikes, camping trips, and weekend camping. (Courtesy of the Daniel Boone Council.)

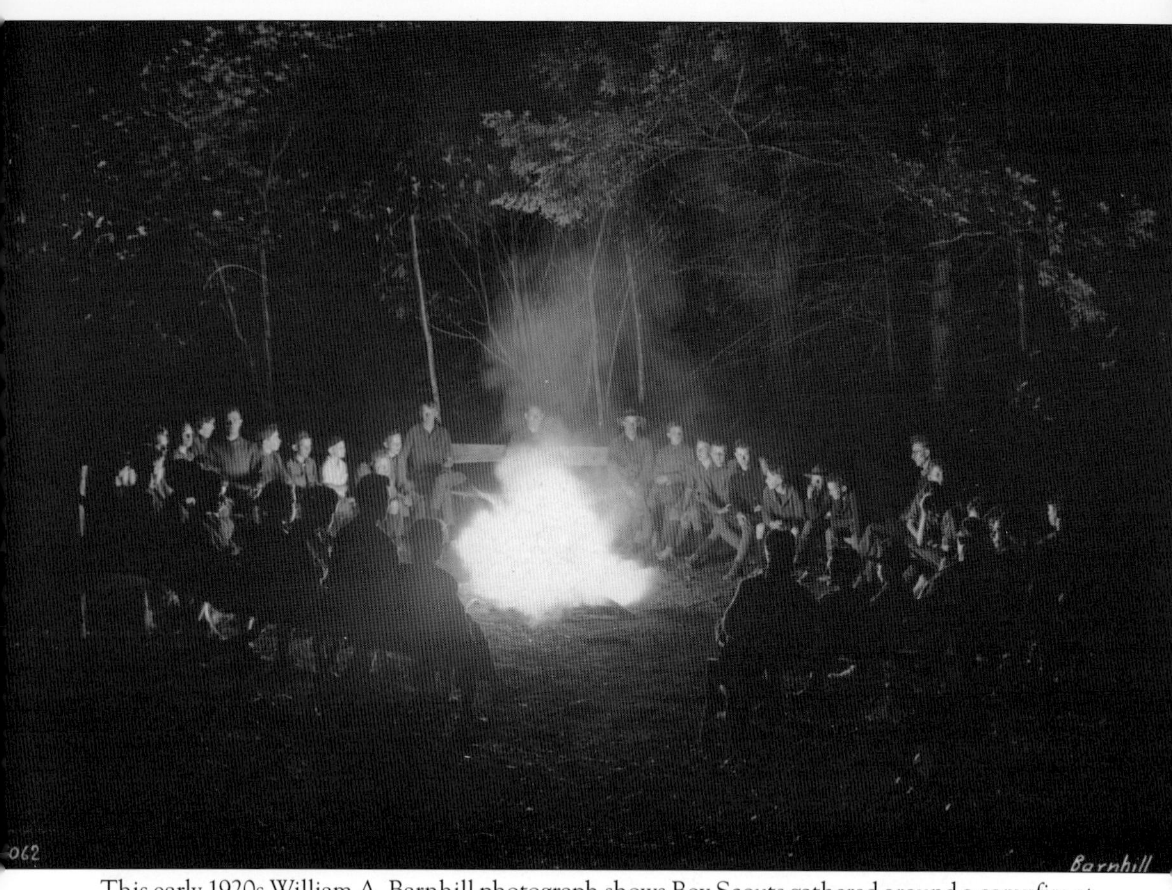

This early 1920s William A. Barnhill photograph shows Boy Scouts gathered around a campfire at the base of Mount Pisgah. The acclaimed photographer documented the Appalachian Mountains in the first half of the 20th century and established a commercial studio in Asheville after World War I. His work appeared in *Life* magazine and the *New York Times*. (Courtesy of North Carolina Collection, Pack Memorial Public Library.)

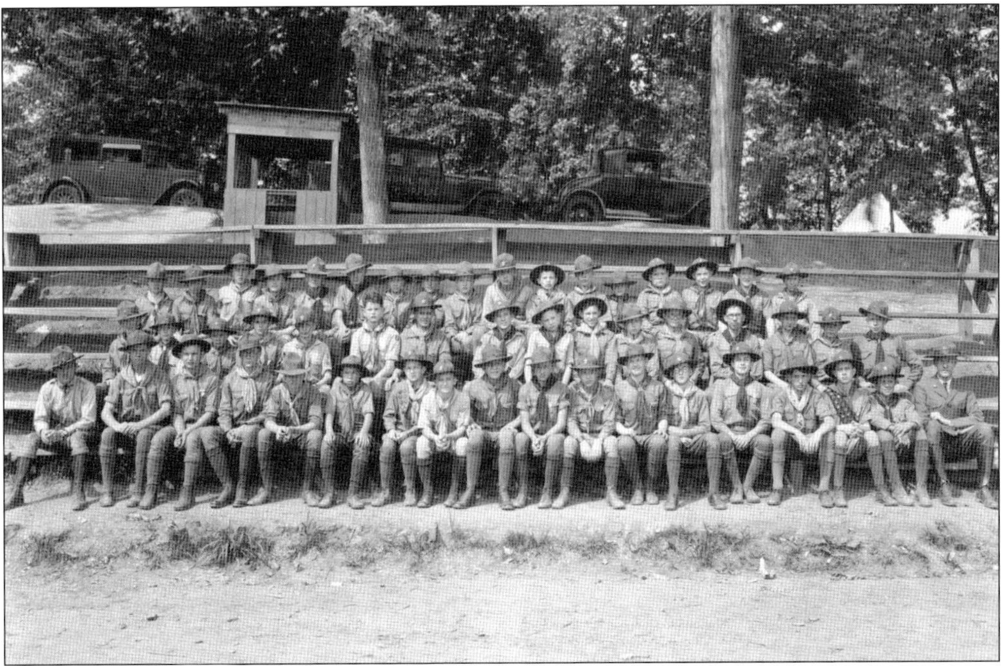

Worn with pride, the Scout uniform signaled respect, even at camp. The uniform was expected to be clean and neat, and above all, complete. Partial or mixed uniforms were considered worse than no uniform at all. Parents were instructed to place campers' names in all articles of clothing. Scouts also packed wool underwear, army boots, neckerchiefs, and ponchos. (Courtesy of the Daniel Boone Council.)

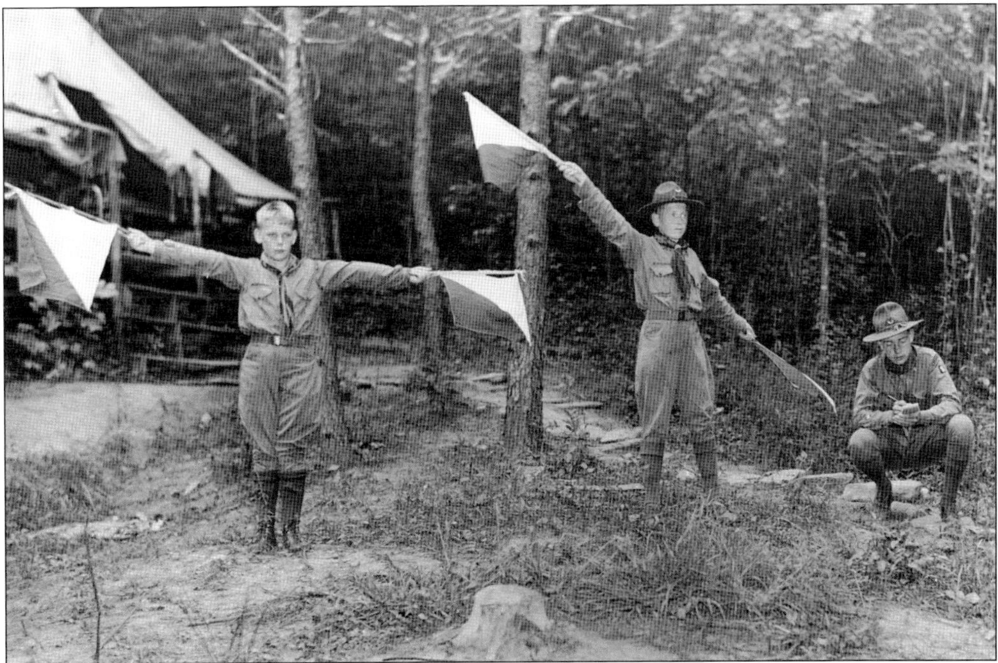

Scouts practiced semaphore signaling at camp. The diagonally divided flags represented different letters of the alphabet, depending on their position. (Courtesy of the Daniel Boone Council.)

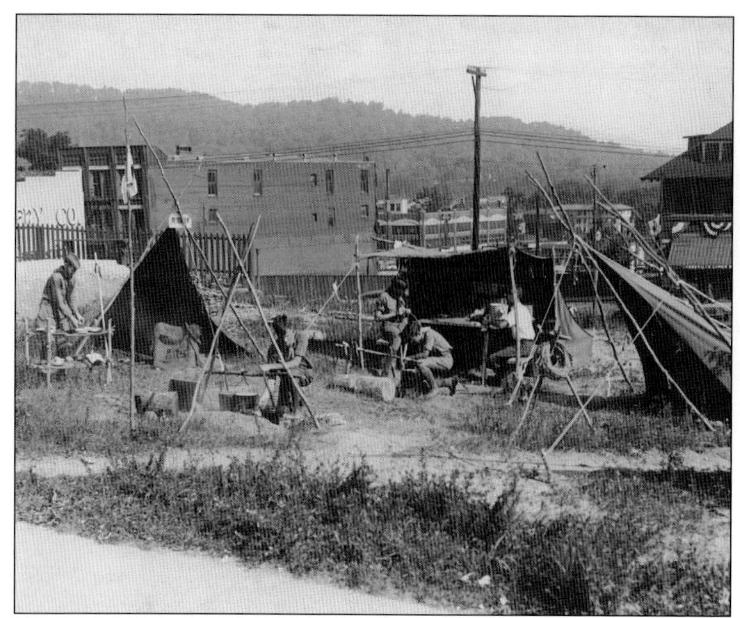

Scouts set up camp on Patton Avenue in Asheville. Scouts camped in pup tents and "Appalachian tents" made of balloon silk, which offered more headroom and were large enough to accommodate two people. The M.V. Moore department store at 45 Patton Avenue was the official Boy Scout outfitter, supplying the boys with tents, packs, hatchets, and first aid kits. (Courtesy of the Daniel Boone Council.)

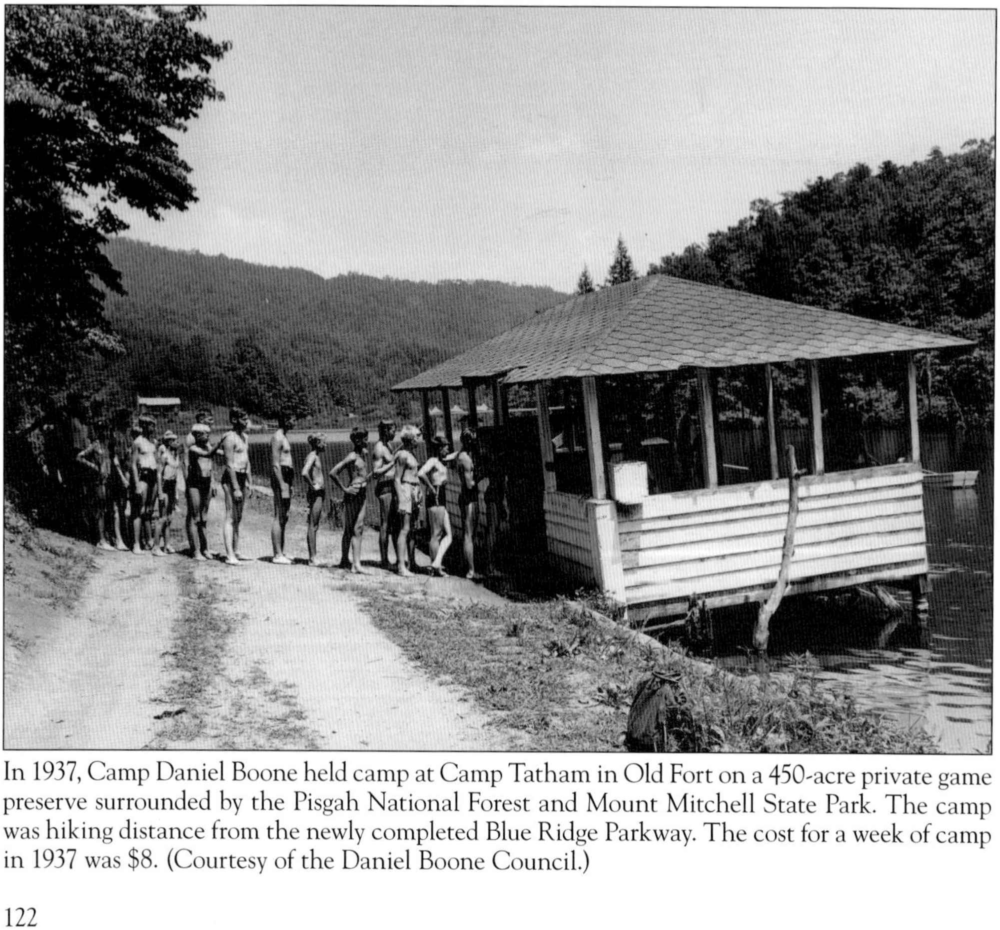

In 1937, Camp Daniel Boone held camp at Camp Tatham in Old Fort on a 450-acre private game preserve surrounded by the Pisgah National Forest and Mount Mitchell State Park. The camp was hiking distance from the newly completed Blue Ridge Parkway. The cost for a week of camp in 1937 was $8. (Courtesy of the Daniel Boone Council.)

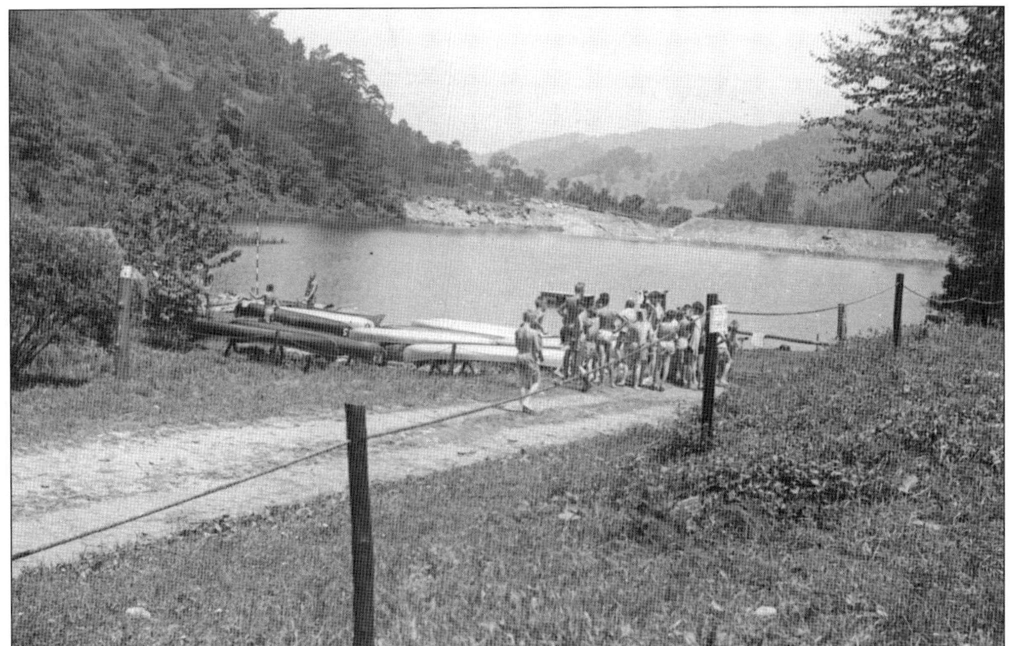

In 1948, the local civic clubs from nearby Asheville and Canton pitched in to provide the Scouts with new canoes. Unfortunately, the polio epidemic curtailed camp sessions in 1948. Fears of polio outbreaks led to the designation of specific visiting times for parents, rather than allowing parents to drop by at will. (Courtesy of the Daniel Boone Council.)

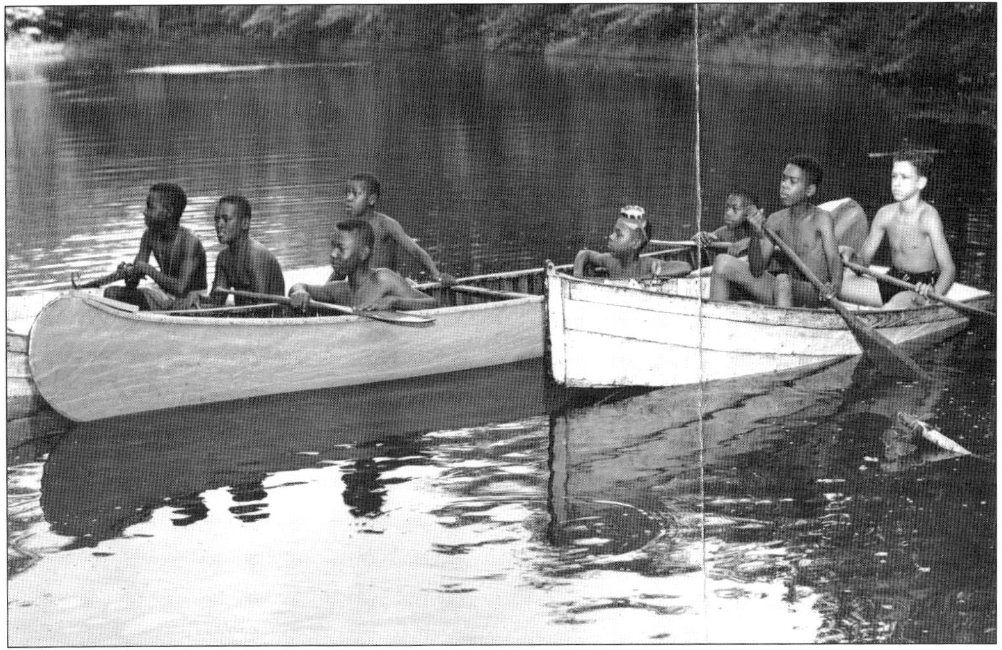

Asheville's first African American Boy Scout troop was formed in 1938. That year, the troop attended a camp in East Flat Rock. In 1942, the Daniel Boone Council established a permanent camp, named Camp Clark Kennedy, for African American Scouts at Sandy Bottoms, along the French Broad River in Pisgah National Forest. (Courtesy of the Daniel Boone Council.)

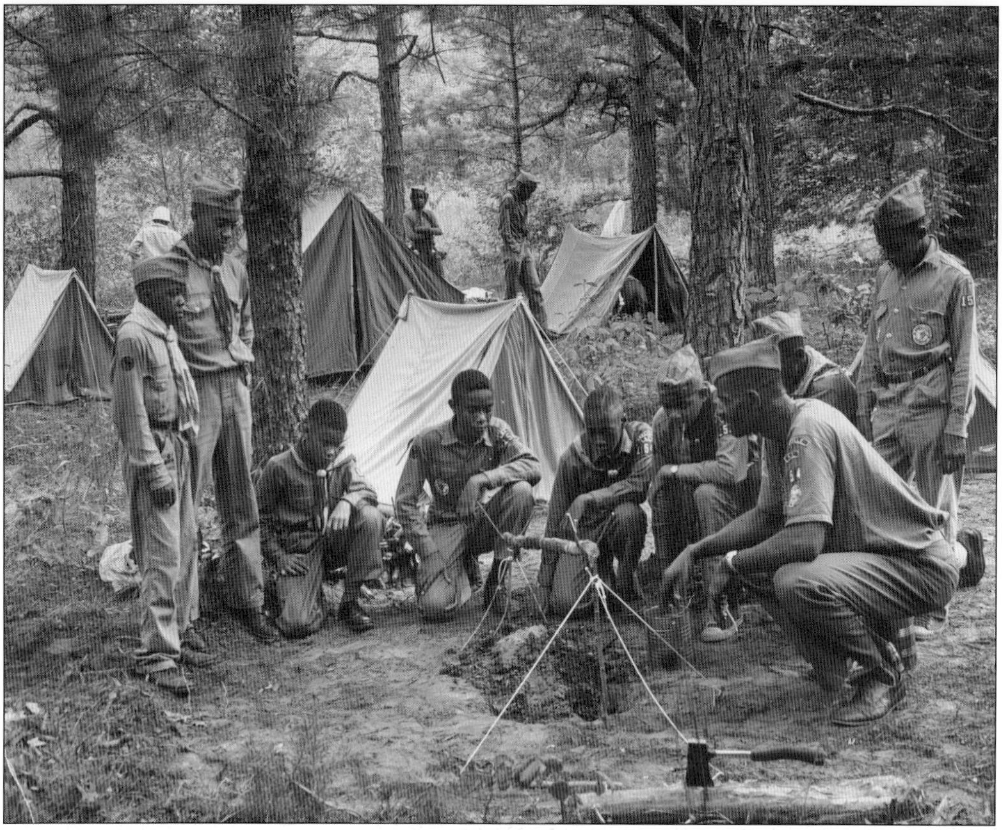

Walter Mapp was a Boy Scout for 29 years and served as the program director of Camp Clark Kennedy for 19 years. He also served as president of Stephens-Lee High School. In 1959, he received the Silver Beaver distinguished service award for his impact on youth. (Courtesy of the Heritage of Black Highlanders Collection, D.H. Ramsey Library Special Collections, University of North Carolina Asheville.)

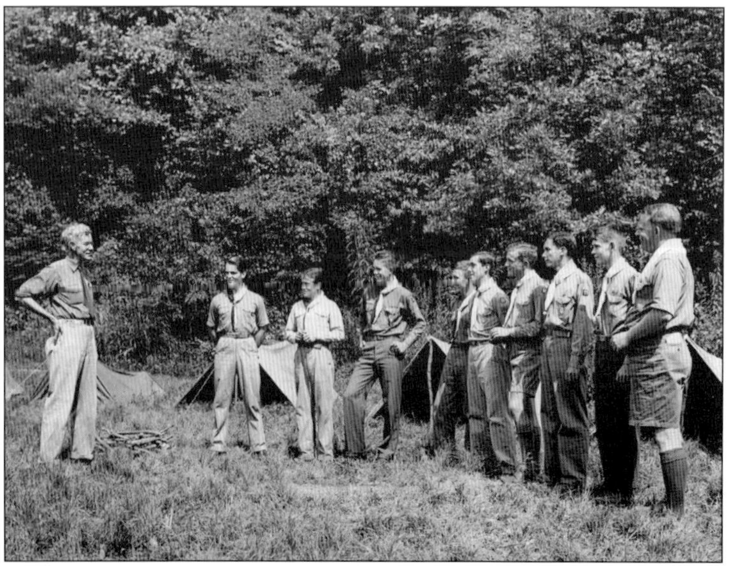

First World War veteran Alfred Williamson Allen, pictured at far left, served as chief executive of the Daniel Boone Council from 1920 until 1956. Camp Daniel Boone's Lake Allen was named in his honor. (Courtesy of the Daniel Boone Council.)

Camp Daniel Boone offered a real camping experience for Scouts. As the 1935 brochure affirmed, "There will be no city hotel stuff in Camp Daniel Boone." Camp activities included "a lot of things that you can't do in your own back yard" just like Indians and pioneers. Campers slept in large eight-man Army surplus tents, with metal cots and straw tick mattresses. (Courtesy of the Daniel Boone Council.)

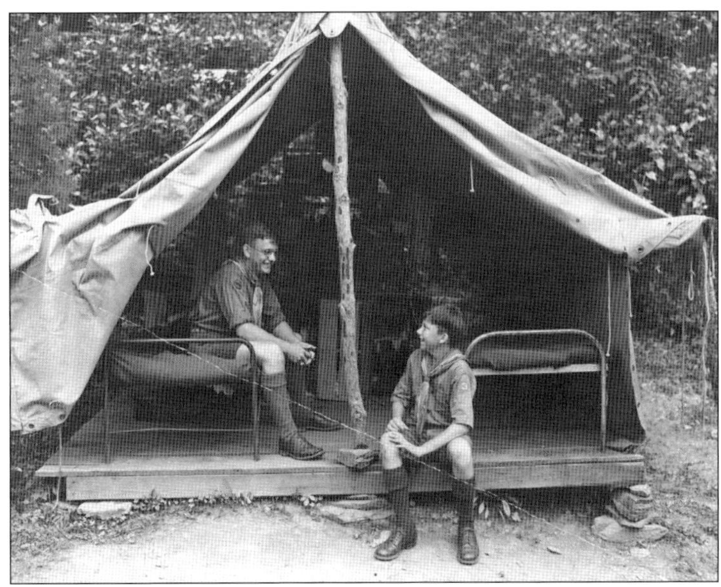

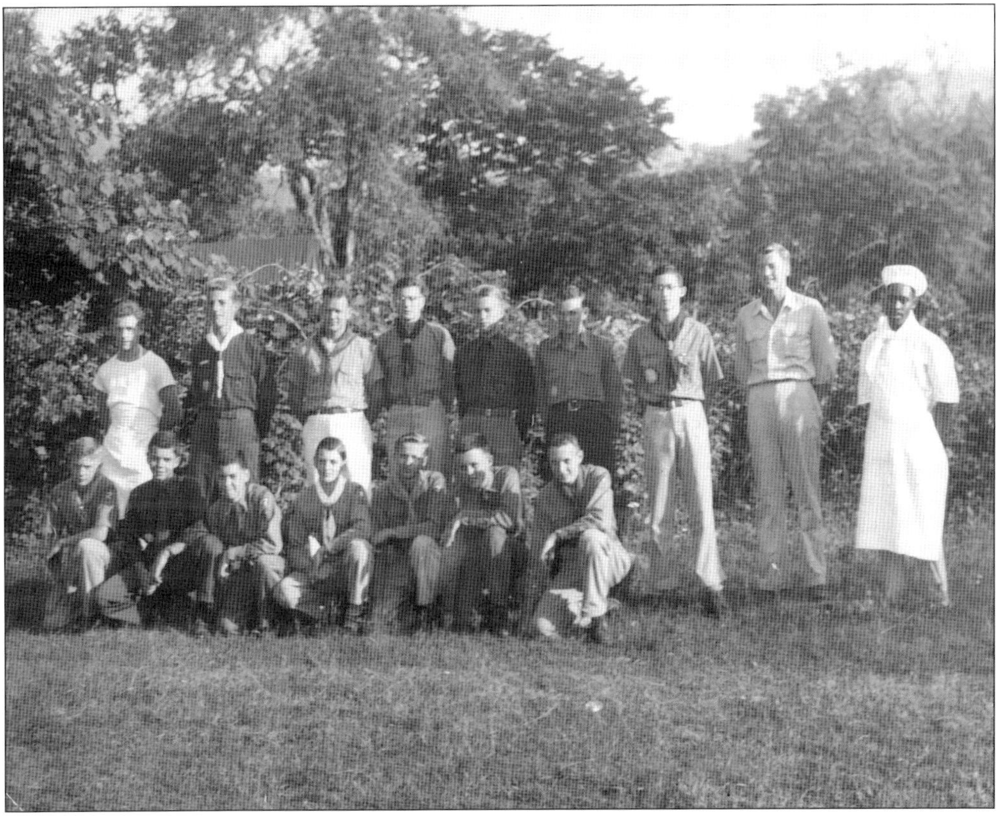

Camp Daniel Boone held its first summer session at its Canton site in 1941. The staff arrived a week prior to the campers to stake the tents, weed, dig latrines, and cut wood for the kitchen. Staff worked without a day off the entire summer for a wage of $5. Each evening after taps, staff gathered in the kitchen for hot chocolate. (Courtesy of the Daniel Boone Council.)

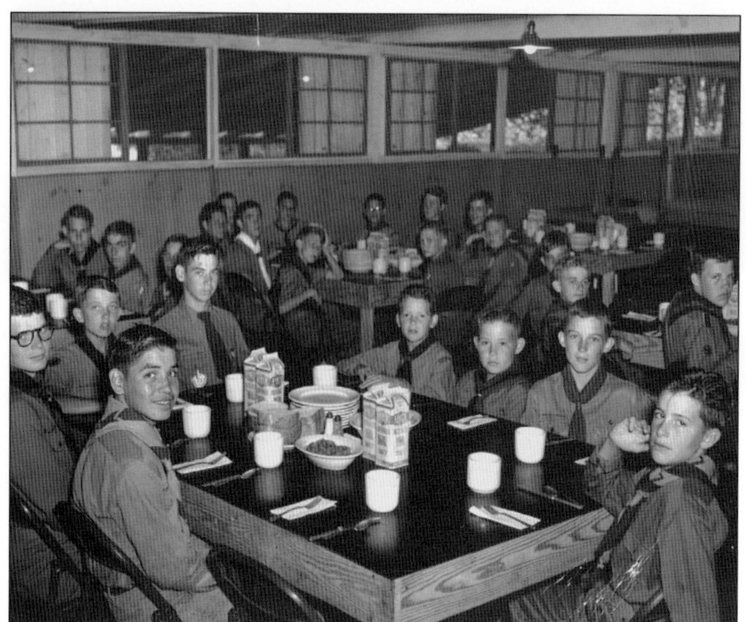

In 1942, the camp reconstructed a Civilian Conservation Corps building as the dining hall. By the early 1950s, the hall seated over 100 Scouts and had a walk-in electric refrigerator, electric cooking range, hot water heater, and covered porch for washing dishes. The building was enlarged over the years, until it was torn down in 2000 for the construction of Ledbetter Lodge. (Courtesy of the Daniel Boone Council.)

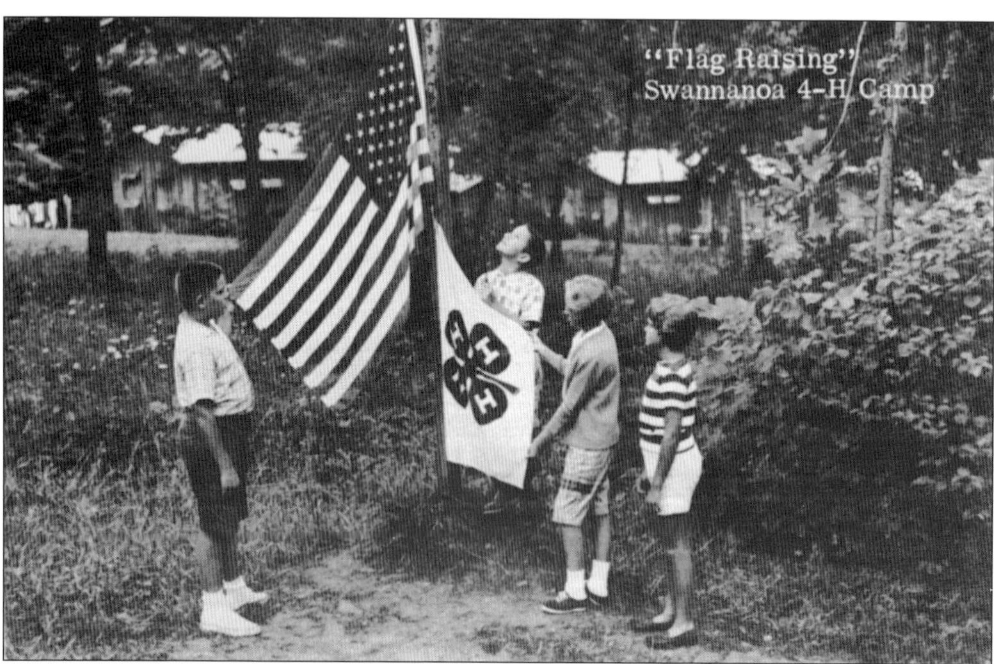

Nestled in the foothills of the Great Craggy Mountains east of Asheville, Swannanoa 4-H Camp operated from 1929 until 2013, when state budget cuts forced its closure. The rustic 90-acre camp was the first 4-H camp in North Carolina. The residential camp aimed to offer summer camp opportunities for children at reasonable rates and served as a conference and retreat center during the remainder of the year.

Bibliography

Eells, Eleanor. *Eleanor Eells' History of Organized Camping: The First 100 Years*. Martinsville, IN: American Camping Association, 1986.

Fint, Courtney. "The American Summer Youth Camp as a Cultural Landscape." *Cultural Landscapes: Balancing Nature and Heritage in Preservation Practice*, edited by Richard Longstreth, 73–90. Minneapolis, MN: University of Minnesota Press, 2008.

Kahn, Laurie. *Sleepaway: The Girls of Summer and Camps They Love*. New York, NY: Workman Publishing, 2003.

Maynard, W. Barksdale. "An Ideal Life in the Woods for Boys: Architecture and Culture in the Earliest Summer Camps." *Winterthur Portfolio* 34, no. 1 (1999): 3–29.

Paris, Leslie. *Children's Nature: The Rise of the American Summer Camp*. New York, NY: New York University Press, 2010.

Popkin, Herman. *Once Upon a Summer: Blue Star Camps, Fifty Years of Memories*. Fort Lauderdale, FL: Venture Press, 1997.

Van Slyck, Abigail A. *A Manufactured Wilderness: Summer Camps and the Shaping of American Youth, 1890–1960*. Minneapolis, MN: University of Minnesota Press, 2010.